Understanding World Jury Systems Through Social Psychological Research

Understanding World Jury Systems Through Social Psychological Research

Edited by
Martin F. Kaplan and Ana M. Martín

Routledge
Taylor & Francis Group
LONDON AND NEW YORK

First Published in 2006 by Psychology Press

Published 2019 by Routledge
2 Park Square, Milton Park, Abingdon, Oxon OX14 4RN
52 Vanderbilt Avenue, New York, NY 10017

First issued in paperback 2013

Routledge is an imprint of the Taylor & Francis Group, an informa business

Typeset by Macmillan India Ltd, Bangalore, India

Cover design by Design Deluxe

Library of Congress Cataloging in Publication Data

Understanding world juries through social psychological research/edited by Martin F. Kaplan, Ana M. Martín.
p. cm.
Includes bibliographical references and index.
ISBN-13: 978-1-84169-421-4 (hardback : alk. paper)
ISBN-10: 1-84169-421-5 (hardback : alk. paper) 1. Jury—Social aspects. 2. Jury—Psychological aspects. I. Kaplan, Martin F. II. Martín, Ana M.
K2292.U53 2006
347.'.0752—dc22
2006005415

ISBN 13: 978-0-415-65297-1 (pbk)

Contents

About the Editors

Martin F. Kaplan received his Ph.D. at the University of Iowa (1965). He is Distinguished Research Professor Emeritus at Northern Illinois University, where he founded the Ph.D. program in social psychology. Visiting professorships were spent at the University of California, San Diego; the University of North Carolina; Melbourne University; and Leiden University. He is Director of the Osher Institute at California State University Channel Islands. He has published on social judgment, small group processes, and jury decision making. He is a fellow of the American Psychology-Law Society and the American Psychological Association, and a member of the Society of Experimental Social Psychology and the European Association of Experimental Social Psychology.

Ana M. Martín received her Ph.D. from the University of La Laguna (Spain) in 1986, where she is now Professor of Social Psychology. She has been a Fulbright Research Fellow at Northern Illinois University and a Research Visitor at California State University Channel Islands. She is a member of the European Association of Psychology and Law, the European Association of Experimental Social Psychology, and the American Psychology-Law Society. She has published widely on psychology and law, on topics such as decision making by mixed juries, psychosocial features of Spanish juries, evaluation of programs for offenders, and social perception of ordinary and environmental offences.

Contributors

Thomas Bliesener
Institute of Psychology
University of Kiel
Kiel, Germany

John C. Brigham
Department of Psychology
Florida State University
Tallahassee, FL, USA

Patrizia Catellani
Department of Psychology
Catholic University of Milan
Milan, Italy

Magali Ginet
Laboratoire de Psychologie Sociale de la Cognition
Université Blaise Pascal
France

Jane Goodman-Delahunty
School of Psychology
University of New South Wales
Sydney, NSW, Australia

Catherine Greffeuille
Laboratoire de Psychologie Sociale de la Cognition
Université Blaise Pascal
France

Serge Guimond
Laboratoire de Psychologie Sociale de la Cognition
Université Blaise Pascal
France

Jordan M. Henkel
Department of Psychology
North Dakota State University
Fargo, ND, USA

Janine Hertel
Department of Psychology
Chemnitz University of Technology
Germany

Verlin B. Hinsz
Department of Psychology
North Dakota State University
Fargo, ND, USA

Lorraine Hope
Department of Psychology
University of Portsmouth
Hampshire, UK

Martin F. Kaplan
Osher Institute
California State University Channel Islands
Camarillo, CA, USA, and
Department of Psychology
Northern Illinois University
DeKalb, IL, USA

Ana M. Martín
Departamento de Psicología Social
Facultad de Psicología
Universidad de La Laguna
Spain

Amina Memon
School of Psychology
University of Aberdeen
Aberdeen, Scotland

Patrizia Milesi
Department of Psychology
Catholic University of Milan
Milan, Italy

Yohsuke Ohtsubo
Department of Psychology
Faculty of Sociology
Nara University
Misasagi-cho, Nara-City, Japan

Danuta Parlak
Graduate School for Social Research
Institute of Philosophy and Sociology
Polish Academy of Sciences
Warsaw, Poland

David Tait
Court of the Future Network, Law School
University of Canberra
ACT, Australia

R. Scott Tindale
Department of Psychology
Loyola University Chicago
Chicago, IL, USA

Preface

This volume has been gestating for an extended period of time. At the outset there was only the conviction that some specific jury features required innovative research and that traditional research on juries was not enough to understand the dynamics of existing jury systems outside North America. Note that the vast majority of research is centered on North American lay juries.

Supported by a Fulbright grant, Ana M. Martín visited Martin F. Kaplan at Northern Illinois University in 1987–1988. Then they started to use social psychological research to study the influence processes in mixed juries—composed of laypersons and professional judges—and to compare these juries with traditional lay juries. Having the contentious discussion on the nature of the proposed jury in Spain at that time as a framework, two empirical studies were run and results were presented in international forums and were later published. Eventually the Spanish government decided to institute a lay jury, but the results of the applied research were relevant to the mixed juries found in many other nations. At that point, the authors realized that their interest was shared by other social psychologists in North America, Europe, and Asia, and decided to organize symposia at several international conferences outside North America: the Society of Australasian Social Psychologists in Melbourne, Australia (July 2001), the European Association of Experimental Social Psychologists in San Sebastian, Spain (July 2002), and the European Association of Psychology and Law and American Psychology and Law Society Joint Meeting in Edinburgh, Scotland (July 2003). Several of the chapters of this book have their origin in these symposia, whereas others were solicited independently to enhance coverage and to answer questions arising in previous symposia. In all cases, contributors were chosen because they were social or cognitive psychologists interested in the interface between psychology and law, residents of the countries whose jury systems were targeted, and involved in experimental research in the field. The result is a kaleidoscopic look at existing jury systems, united by the conceptual models and methods most supported in core social psychology. Each chapter describes the central features of the national jury system exhaustively, raises issues and potential consequences that bear investigation, presents existing research on these issues both within and outside that particular jury system, and suggests future research programs within the targeted system. It is our hope that the volume goes beyond presenting a state-of-the-art description of research and theory relevant to world juries, to providing a template for further research.

1

Introduction and Overview

MARTIN F. KAPLAN and ANA M. MARTÍN

Psychology has contributed to the understanding of court trials for nearly a century (Munsterberg, 1908). Beyond the obvious point that trials involve a broad range of human behavioral events including judgment, cognition, affect, memory, attitudes and values, norms, and so forth, social psychology has a fundamental role in providing insight into trial processes. On a general level, social psychology and law are inextricably bound. Law, after all, is a codification of rules to enable people to get along with one another. Jury systems adjudicate problems in social relations, and within trials, rules and norms govern the behavior of trial participants in order to facilitate and organize adjudication. Social psychology is a systematic means of *discovering* the *de facto* rules governing social relations, and as such, is a critical tool in assessing the intended or unintended consequences of legal practices, and, at least as important, discovering the processes and dynamics unleashed by those practices.

On a more focused level, jury trials put legal decision making into the hands of small groups, with certain procedures and safeguards imposed by law to lead to desired consequences in both jury process and outcomes. In jury trials, social psychology is again bound with law. From its inception, social psychology has studied group structure and process, social decision-making, conflict between group factions, attitudes and values, biases and prejudice, information credibility, and persuasive argumentation—all the ingredients of a jury trial!

Just as social relations vary among nations and cultures, administration of their legal counterparts—that is, rules governing social relations and forms of trials for departures from these rules—will also vary. There is every reason to expect that trial procedures will vary among different nations and cultures (see, e.g., Vidmar (2000) for a description of the wide variations among national jury systems). In turn, these variations invoke different interactive processes in juries, and thus different social psychological principles.

The remainder of this volume describes variations among national jury systems and the (primarily) social psychological research and principles that apply to these diverse systems. A wealth of research has been conducted and reported since Munsterberg opened the door in 1908, but the vast majority has been on North American juries, which, as we shall see, are not the only forms of juries in the world. In Europe, Asia, Australia, and New Zealand, trial by jury has been flourishing (or, in some cases, existing, and in yet others, just starting) but in forms different from those in the US and Canada. Psychological study of these systems has been meager, and empirical work, until very recently, even more rare. Application of empirical findings from North American jury research leaves large gaps because of differences in cultural norms and trial procedures. This volume hopes to bring attention to systems outside North America, display their defining features, and offer insight into the consequences of these features by applying social psychological principles and reviewing recent and ongoing research within the systems. Most importantly, we hope to provide an impetus and guide for future research conducted in the context of the issues raised by jury practices in the targeted nations, issues that to date have been addressed only in fundamental social psychological research.

Each of the following chapters examines jury procedures in one (or more) nation, and then offers insight into the psychological processes and potential outcomes generated by the salient features of that system. By design, Chapter 2 deals with American juries, as a comparison for the jury systems that follow. This chapter underlines the similarities and differences between national jury systems. Each system has to grapple with the same fundamental question: Can laypersons be trusted to competently and fairly administer justice at trial? The theme of this volume is that different systems handle this issue differently. One major dichotomy grows from this difference: Some nations have *pure* juries composed entirely of laypersons, while others have *mixed* juries composed of laypersons and professional judges. Within the former, different formal means are used to enhance the quality of lay juries, ranging from having strong rules of evidence and procedure to govern lay jury trials (USA), to extensive and exclusionary steps to empanel jurors (USA again), and to requiring jurors to answer questions about elements of the decision and to justify the verdict (Russia, Spain). The first set of the following chapters addresses various issues in nations employing pure juries, and the second set of chapters demonstrates the variations (and similarities) in nations with mixed juries. Each chapter concentrates on a different facet of that nation's jury system and therefore appeals to a different set of social psychological mechanisms (see the chapter preview below). Across chapters, we get an exhaustive view of the issues emerging in pure and mixed world juries and their corresponding psychological mechanisms, but at the same time there is sufficient overlap in coverage between chapters to permit comparisons across nations.

OVERVIEW OF CHAPTERS

Part I: Nations with Pure Juries

In Chapter 2, John Brigham first presents a concise but thorough historical foundation of the American jury. It is clear from this discourse that the jury was (and is) intended as a check on the powers of the government (but see the founding of the English jury in the *Magna Carta*). This historical purpose produced something unique to American juries—the common-law power to nullify laws perceived as unpopular or unfair, that is to provide a verdict based on social rather than legal issues. Unlike some other pure jury systems (see Russia and Spain, this volume), verdicts do not require formal justification. Thus, jurors concern themselves as much with fairness (according to social norms, or the "conscience of the community") as with legal requirements.

Though not a constitutional right, the discretionary power of lay jurors has produced a practice unique to US jurors, and a lucrative cottage industry for enterprising social scientists—the intricate stage of jury selection. There is neither the check of having professional judges deliberate with jurors, nor of requiring justification of their verdicts, so great care is exercised by courts and opposing counsels in determining who sits on juries. Brigham discusses at length the examination and selection of jurors and the assumptions made by attorneys. The ethicality and validity of selection procedures are reviewed, and the potential for bias in deciding the death penalty (itself a fairly unique feature of the US legal system) is offered as a case study of jury selection issues.

In Chapter 3, Hope and Memon compare the key features of the neighboring systems in England and Scotland. Though both systems and the US jury are historically related, there are marked differences between the three lay juries. Unlike the US jury, there is little opportunity for opposing counsels to affect jury composition in either UK jurisdiction. The three systems differ with regard to imposed decision rule, and therefore the implications of the rules for jury processes and verdicts. One unique aspect of decision rules is the Scottish "not proven" verdict, which is an acquittal on the basis that the defendant's guilt was not adequately proven, in distinction to a "not guilty" verdict, which is a clear statement of proven innocence. The implications of this third verdict option for both process and outcome are meticulously explored.

Jury process is given full attention. The authors discuss implications of the decision rules and of formation of verdict minority and majority factions for deliberations centering on understanding the evidence vs. defending certain verdict preferences. This analysis of deliberation style is echoed in several other chapters in this volume as a function of a variety of determinants other than decision rule.

Finally, the authors describe the rather convoluted (our phrase) forms that indictments and jury instructions take in the Scottish system. Consequences for memory and evidence processing are discussed, and it is concluded that the potential for biased thought and decisions is heightened by current practice. In the same vein, the authors address empirical studies of the effect of pretrial publicity on English juries. Analyses of instructions and pretrial publicity effects are undertaken through the lens of social cognition. They conclude that, aside from improving the semantics of the indictment and juror instructions in Scotland, and continued restraints on pretrial publicity in England, the functioning of lay juries can be improved by adopting the requirement of verdict justification by providing critical questions to jurors. The reader is urged to compare this suggestion to the issues raised in the chapter on Spain and Russia, nations where lay jurors must justify verdicts and answer formal sets of questions about case elements.

In the third entry on Anglo-American lay juries (Chapter 4), Goodman-Delahunty and Tait examine three major issues in Australia and New Zealand. First is the implications of legal reforms in Australia intended to facilitate communication with jurors. This topic is also addressed in several other venues in the volume. Second is the effects of several sources of juror bias on jury dynamics and verdicts, an issue explored in other nations in this volume as well. It is instructive to see how these problems emerge, and are treated differently in other jurisdictions. Third, the authors examine questions about juror competence to render legally appropriate decisions, especially in complex cases.

These three issues are currently receiving a great deal of attention in Australia and New Zealand. The analyses undertaken in this chapter are critical in the light of calls in Australia to curtail the use of lay juries, or to eliminate them entirely. The authors suggest both systemic and systematic innovations to improve juror processing to offset actual and perceived misuse of evidence. Their analyses and recommendations accord with the concerns addressed in the chapter on England and Scotland. As in that chapter, the authors call for more study of juror experiences via mock studies and real juror surveys. Note that in the chapter on England and Scotland, Hope and Memon go a step further and call for direct intervention by instituting verdict justification requirements.

The lay juries of Spain and Russia (Chapter 5) are fairly new institutions following decades of absence in totalitarian regimes. Re-establishment of juries in both instances was not without social and political controversy; hence there is a lingering distrust of pure lay juries and an institution of safeguards in their discretion. Review of perceptions of lay jurors in the legal and lay community provides a chilling picture of distrust and disrespect (see also the chapter on Poland, which gives a similarly jaundiced view). To ease negative expectations of lay jury competence, and to provide a basis for appellate review, both nations require formal verdict justification. In both instances, this takes the form of requiring responses to a list of questions about the case. The questions pose propositions about case elements, which must be decided before reaching an overall decision. Moreover, juries in Spain must decide on aggravating and mitigating circumstances as posed by the presiding judge.

Martín and Kaplan discuss the psychological consequences of asking for detailed responses to specific questions in justifying decisions. Does this requirement enhance the probability of lay jurors attending more to the facts of a case, or does it lead to use of simpler strategies and biases in the face of cognitive overload? The possibilities are examined in terms of whether the requirement enhances verdict- vs. evidence-driven deliberation styles, that is, whether deliberation will focus on using evidence and argumentation to support verdict preference as opposed to using a broader range of evidence to construct a complete story of the case. Similarly, the authors ask what sorts of influence will be used by jury members given extensive question lists, that is, normative influence, in which one relies on social support to further one's point of view, or informational influence, in which argumentation for a particular verdict relies on relevant factual evidence. Finally, dual-process theory is applied, asking whether the unique characteristics of the two systems will foster information processing based on superficial, simplistic strategies (*heuristic reasoning*), or on deeper, more effortful processing employing a broader range of relevant information (*systematic reasoning*).

Chapter 6, on the American military courts-martial, is indeed unique to compendia on jury systems. Hinsz, Henkel, and Tindale report a system based in principle on a jury of peers, but in a context quite different than that normally associated with national juries. The jurisdiction is limited to the military, and the governing laws (both statutory and procedural) are restricted to infractions under the military code, and trial within the military. As seen in the chapter, the procedural rules for trial are unique. Yet, the psychological issues raised by the procedures are amenable to psychological analysis, hence the inclusion of this venue in this volume. It is timely and instructive to observe the procedures of military tribunals, and how they differ from civil courts, given the controversy as this volume is written over trying civilians (that is, persons who are not members of the military) under military law. We refer here to the proposed trials of persons apprehended in the invasion of Afghanistan by the US military.

To enumerate here all the differences between military and civilian courts would be redundant with the exhaustive account in Chapter 6. We will note, however, two important features: Jury members must be equal to or senior to the accused in rank, and they may ask questions of witnesses. The chapter examines questions raised by these and other departures from civilian juries by reference to research on social influence in small groups, paying equal attention to procedural consequences for jury dynamics and verdict outcomes. Similar to mixed juries, courts martial often contain mixtures of military ranks, evoking the same questions about status effects as addressed in the chapters on mixed juries. In courts martial, in fact, status differences between jury members should be very palpable in the context of military structure.

Part II: Nations with Mixed Juries

Whereas each of the chapters on individual European national jury systems focuses on a subset of the distinguishing features of that nation's juries, Chapter 7 offers a broad overview and comparison of European juries. Kaplan, Martín, and Hertel identify three central features that characterize European juries, and distinguish between practices in the different national systems within these dimensions. The features are lay juror selection, jury composition, and verdict justification.

Juror selection varies in how the initial jury pool is selected, whether citizens can volunteer for service, and length of service. The consequences of these variations are considered in terms of attitudinal differences, effects on social identification processes, and the ability to resist influence by professional members of the jury.

Jury composition largely refers to whether juries are composed purely of laypersons or are mixed—lay and professional jurors. However, where service requirements are lengthy, even pure juries may be heterogeneous in experience and expertise. Effects of composition on jury dynamics and verdict outcomes are explored in the context of small group behavior research, invoking research and principles pertaining to role differentiation and status, effects of minority dissent, and influence and processing styles. Naturally existing jury factions, such as professional vs. lay jurors, or experienced vs. novice lay jurors, have implications for level of reasoning (heuristic/systematic), type of influence (normative/informational), and deliberation style (verdict-/evidence-driven).

Finally, European lay juries vary in whether they must *justify verdicts* by responding to questions about case elements and voting on propositions that support a given overall verdict. Question lists can sometimes be extremely detailed. The consequences of the justification requirement for group dynamics are explored by reference to the same social-psychological tools used for jury composition issues: depth of reasoning, type of influence, and deliberation style. While some research is available on the effects of the cited practices in both North American and European juries, it is obvious that the many questions that are raised in this chapter call for an extensive program of research in the European context.

In Chapter 8, Catellani and Milesi concentrate on the asymmetries in reasoning between professionals and laypersons in Italian mixed juries. The main tool used in analyzing reasoning during deliberation is the mechanism of *counterfactuals*, whereby case events are compared with "what ifs"—what if the defendant had acted differently, what if the victim had been in another place, and so on. Interestingly, the Italian jury code explicitly recommends that juries explore counterfactuals, that is, that they compare given actions with expected norms. A major point in the chapter is that different results will occur as counterfactuals are used in an uncontrolled way, for example, if employed more for the accused vs. the victim. In addition, people are more likely to use as counterfactuals those events that are consistent with norms. Norms, in turn, open the door to bias since norms can be based on stereotype, ideology, and culture. Thus, extensive use of counterfactuals—which involve a comparison between actions and norms—can affect verdicts and penalties, and an asymmetrical use of counterfactuals can bias the outcome. Implicitly, there is a concern that lay jurors will be more prone to counterfactual reasoning, and to applying it asymmetrically.

As in several other chapters, reference is made to dual-process theory in understanding effects of counterfactual reasoning. The authors conclude by offering suggestions for training lay jurors so that reference to extra-legal norms is reduced, and relevant, realistic, and balanced counterfactuals are generated. Such counterfactuals are constructive and facilitate in jurors a systematic, unbiased analysis of alternative information in constructing a story of the case.

Ginet, Guimond, and Greffeuille (Chapter 9) emphasize the importance of oral testimony in French courts, hence the importance of understanding and improving such testimony. The behavior of the eyewitness is embedded in the fabric of French society via *social dominance theory* (SDT), which treats intergroup relations, stereotyping, and prejudice. The authors extend SDT to show its relevance to the justice system. They then apply the individual difference dimension, *social dominance orientation* (SDO) to eyewitnesses, concluding that one's level of SDO will affect judgment of stigmatized groups, and consequently, eyewitness reconstructions of events.

The chapter applies research on eyewitness identification and the cognitive interview though the lens of SDT to improve both eyewitness communication (to juries) and accuracy. The cognitive interview, whose use the authors advocate to insure improved testimony, is based on a well-accepted model of memory.

In Poland, there are strong and explicit expectations set by jury law for the effectiveness and competence of lay members of mixed juries. Parlak describes in Chapter 10 the lengths to which the court and supporting laws go to insure that lay jurors will have their share of influence in verdicts. But are they successful? The author marshals considerable evidence to suggest that they are not successful. First, there is ample evidence that perceptions of lay jurors by professional judges are very negative (this is true as well in data cited in the chapters dealing with Russia and Spain, and Germany). Next, Parlak shows how these perceptions translate to obstacles in lay and professional judge collaboration. Despite formalized procedures to equalize the power of the lay and professional jury faction, deliberation and decision-making is dominated by the latter. Particularly troublesome in Parlak's view is the difficulty the factions have in adopting a point of view different from one's own reference group, as described by the mechanism of *Sociocentrism*.

Suggestions are offered that would change the perceptions of lay jurors (and thereby change their own self-perceptions), removing this source of Sociocentrism. The author also applies a *social power* analysis to understand and modify both the relative power and type of power wielded by factions.

The central question addressed by Bliesener in Chapter 11 is whether lay judges in German mixed courts are achieving the systemic goals that are set for them. Do they represent the attitudes and values of the citizenry? Do they have a firm sense of right and wrong? Are they motivated out of duty to serve? Are they competent judges of actions related to the law, and can they contribute on an equal plane with professional judges?

The author tracks these questions alongside an analysis of the recruiting and empanelling of lay jurors, and their service at trials. He identifies flaws in the process that interfere with achieving the desired goals. Not the least critical is the low esteem in which lay jurors are held by the legal community at each step. According to professional judges, the wrong jurors volunteer or are selected for service; once in court they are unmotivated or incompetent, and in deliberation they are sheep to be led. The chapter concludes by suggesting ways to better train and inform lay jurors in order to improve motivation, competence, and ability to advance their opinions.

The chapter by Ohtsubo appears last in the section on mixed juries by design; unlike the other juries surveyed, the Japanese jury has not yet been instituted, and therefore the issues raised in preceding treatments of existing juries can be applied by the reader to Japan. The enabling laws have been passed, and the Japanese mixed jury will be instituted in 2009 after a preparation period. In the enabling law, many details are left open. This chapter has particular urgency since research on mixed juries will be instrumental in determining procedural details. The author examines a number of issues that will be critical in implementing the jury in 2009, illustrating nicely the potential for social psychology to affect emerging policy in addition to assessing existing practices.

After examining the parameters of the enabling law, which is in large part general and ambiguous, the author addresses perceptions of lay juror competence vis-à-vis cultural norms, and steps that should be taken to improve perceptions of laypersons in the system. Stereotypes about lay jurors are discussed in other chapters, but here we see that cultural norms have particular consequences for beliefs about lay jurors that are specific to Japan.

Next, Ohtsubo treats predeliberation biases that can lead to false acquittals or convictions. Using statistical and probability models, he predicts verdicts based on distributions of predeliberation verdict preferences, that is, leniency or conviction biases. Thus, it is possible to predict the likelihood of false convictions or acquittals by knowing the number and distribution (among factions) of pre-existing biases, the strength of the evidence, and the prescribed decision rule. But as important as the prescribed rule (e.g., majority, unanimity, two-thirds) is the implicit *social decision scheme* (SDS) adopted by the jury. Much attention is given to the likely SDSs that will emerge in mixed juries in order to aggregate verdict preferences to meet the explicit decision rule.

Finally, the chapter examines, as do some of the previous chapters, deliberation styles in mixed juries. This is done by reference to verdict- vs. evidence-driven deliberation, and happily, the author can report empirical research on mock Japanese mixed juries to flesh out his analysis of deliberation style. Note that deliberation style is also treated in the context of the pure juries of Spain and Russia, but in those instances, style is studied as a consequence of response requirements (verdict justification) rather than jury composition (mixed). This emergence of a common social-psychological phenomenon (i.e., deliberation style) to enhance the understanding of different jury factors (in this instance, jury requirements and jury composition) in different systems (lay juries in Spain and Russia, and mixed juries in Japan) is a recurrent theme in this volume.

World juries present an array of distinctive features, which in turn invoke many interesting questions about consequent psychological processes. These questions can be addressed by a common set of social-psychological conceptual and methodological tools. The remaining chapters give evidence of research that has been, and importantly, *should be* conducted on relatively neglected jury characteristics found outside North America.

REFERENCES

Munsterberg, H. (1908). *On the witness stand*. New York: Doubleday, Page.
Vidmar, N. J. (Ed.). (2000). *World jury systems*. Oxford, UK: Oxford University Press.

Part I

Pure (Lay) Juries

2

The Jury System in the United States of America

JOHN C. BRIGHAM

THE HISTORICAL ROLE OF THE JURY IN AMERICAN SOCIETY

The Jury as a Counterweight to Abuses of Government

The trial jury holds a revered status in the American legal system. Juries became a lightning rod of controversy in the American colonies during the eighteenth century. The colonists became increasingly dissatisfied with the British legal system as it operated in the American colonies, and the right to a jury trial was seen as a vital aspect of citizens' rights. Indeed, the right to a jury trial was the only factor common to the constitutions of all 13 American colonies.

During this period, juries and grand juries served as symbols of the power of ordinary citizens to resist perceived abuses of government, and American juries sometimes exonerated those who had resisted English colonial policy. In part because of such actions by colonial juries, the British began to try controversial cases in the British Admiralty Courts, which did not have juries, rather than in Common Pleas courts with juries. In cases involving treason, the defendant was shipped to Britain and tried there (Starr & McCormick, 1993).

Even when cases were tried in Admiralty Court, the results were not always unfavorable for the colonists. In one case, for example, an accused smuggler whose ship was seized agreed in Admiralty (nonjury) Court to pay 500 pounds to get his ship back. After regaining his ship, he went to civil court and filed suit for civil trespass against the colonial customs official who had seized his ship. The jury awarded him 600 pounds, 100 pounds more than the amount he had paid to get the ship back! When this verdict was overturned, a second jury also awarded damages to him (Alschuler & Deiss, 1994).

Seen in the social and political context in which it originated, namely the widespread distrust of central government in America at the time of the revolution, the

American jury system developed during a period of low confidence in the judiciary, and was influenced by a desire for open procedures, a sensitivity to the struggles to overcome racial and ethnic injustice, and a commitment to the adversarial adjudication process (King, 2000).

The Jury as a Means of Resisting Unpopular Laws: Jury Nullification

As generally defined, the role of the jury is to arrive at the facts of a case given the particular testimony and evidence presented at trial, and to render a decision by applying the law, as administered by the judge, based upon their interpretation of the facts. In contrast, juries occasionally appear to disregard the law, instead following their personal sentiments, a process known as *jury nullification*. An early example of this process was the 1734 libel trial of John Peter Zenger in New York. Zenger, a printer, had mocked New York's Royal Governor, writing that the governor had interfered with the citizens' right to a trial by jury (Alexander, 1963). Zenger was accused of seditious libel, but three separate grand juries refused to indict him. When he was finally brought to trial, his attorney told the jurors that they "had the right beyond all dispute to determine both the law and the facts" (Wrightsman, Greene, Nietzel, & Fortune, 2002, p. 375). Further, the attorney stated, "It is not the cause of a poor printer, nor of New York alone, which you are now trying. No! It may in its consequence affect every freeman that lives under British government in the main of America. It is the best cause. It is the cause of liberty" (Levy, 1985, p. 44). The jury acquitted Zenger.

Instances of jury nullification illustrate the jury's implicit power to arrive at a verdict based upon issues outside of the law, such as political or moral concerns, or even prejudice (Elwork & Sales, 1985; Finkel, 1995). Juries have this power because a verdict does not require explanation as to the jury's rationale (*United States v. Thomas*, 1997, but see chapters in this volume on several European national systems that require justification). Depending on one's viewpoint, this process allows juries to confront issues of fairness and to act as the "conscience" of the community, or to behave as irresponsible "runaway juries" (Weinstein, 1998). In the mid-1800s, some juries acquitted people who were accused of aiding slaves to escape from the South, in violation of the fugitive slave law (Finkel, 2000). In retaliation, many juries in the South refused to convict slave owners under laws that prohibited the mistreatment of slaves. Indeed, until the mid-1800s, it was commonplace for judges to instruct the jury of its right to disregard the court's view of the law (Clark, 2000).

The US Supreme Court has not supported jury nullification. In 1895, the Court ruled that juries in criminal cases were obligated to apply the law as set out by the judge, and had no right to deviate from the law (*Sparf and Hansen v. United States*, 1895; see also *United States v. Dougherty*, 1972). Despite this 1895 decision, the ensuing century saw a number of jury decisions that were at variance with the law and seemed to fit with the concept of jury nullification. These most often involved minor drug offenses, liquor violations (i.e., during the Prohibition era), drunk driving, prostitution, insanity defenses, anti-abortion activities, and instances of euthanasia. There was a resurgence of jury nullification in the 1960s and 1970s, owing largely to cases stemming from the civil rights movement and from protests against American involvement in the Vietnam War (Clark, 2000). A new set of high-visibility cases appeared in the 1990s. These included the 1992 trial of four White Los Angeles police officers, who were found innocent of the beating of a Black man, Rodney King, even though the beating had been videotaped and King suffered a fractured skull and a broken leg. In the 1995 murder trial of former football star O.J. Simpson, his defense attorney exhorted the jury to "send a message [that] ...you are the conscience of the community, and you set the standards. You tell us what is right and what is wrong" (quoted in Gormlie, 1996, p. 49). An attorney for physician Jack Kevorkian, who was tried several times for his role in "assisted suicides," told the media that he would urge the jury to disregard the law in these instances (Slovenko, 1994).

Jury nullification remains controversial. Some argue that jurors should be made aware of their right to disregard the letter of the law, so that they can act in fairness as the "conscience of the community" (Clark, 2000). A report by an American Bar Association committee concluded, "...the law and ethical rules do not clearly prohibit lawyers from arguing for jury nullification" (Committee on Professional Responsibility, 1999, p. 203). A second avenue would be via judges' instructions prior to deliberation. Currently, three states (Maryland, Georgia, and Indiana) permit the trial judge to tell the jury that they can rely on their "conscience" when deciding the case (Duane, 1996). Research on mock juries has shown that such "nullification instructions" can significantly affect the verdict that is reached (Horowitz, 1988; Meissner, Brigham, & Pfeifer, 2003; Pfeifer, Brigham, & Robinson, 1996).

FEATURES OF THE AMERICAN JURY SYSTEM

In a typical jury trial in the United States, 6 or 12 persons are selected, after questioning by attorneys from both sides, from a pool of jury-eligible citizens. After viewing the trial, they attempt to deliberate to a unanimous verdict. However, each of the central characteristics of a jury has been, and often remains, a source of controversy within the legal system and within American society as a whole, as will be reviewed below. To begin, I will consider the range of situations in which a citizen is considered to have the right to a trial by jury, after which I will address issues surrounding the size of the jury, and the decision rule that is applied. I will then focus on the use of peremptory challenges in jury selection, jury composition, and "scientific jury selection."

Scope: Who has the Right to a Jury Trial?

Although the Sixth Amendment describes the general right to a jury trial, the courts were not quick to grant that right to everyone. In fact, it was not until 1968 that the US Supreme Court declared that the right to a jury trial, granted by the Sixth Amendment, was an element of due process that was guaranteed to *all* citizens by the 14th Amendment. The Court's opinion in *Duncan v. Louisiana* (1968, pp. 155–156) stated that, "The deep commitment of the nation to the right of jury trial in serious criminal cases is a defense against arbitrary law enforcement and qualifies for protection under the due process clause of the 14th Amendment, and must therefore be respected by the states." For less serious offenses, that is, cases carrying possible penalties of no more than 6 months' incarceration, a jury trial may not be required (*Cheff v. Schnackenberg*, 1966). In cases where the penalty is a fine alone, the defendant may be entitled to a jury trial only if the fine is huge.

Jury Size: Must it Always be 12?

The principle that a jury should contain 12 members was passed on to the Anglo-Saxons by the Vikings and became a central part of English common law (Lind, 1995). The standard was upheld in *Patton v. United States* (1930), wherein the Court stated that two "essential features" of the jury was that it "should consist of 12 men [sic], neither more nor less," and that the verdict should be unanimous (an issue also addressed below).

The question of the most desirable jury size involves basic social psychological principles of group process. Researchers who have compared 12-person mock juries with smaller juries have generally found that there are advantages to the larger juries. As reviewed by Saks (1977), researchers found that 12-person juries, compared with smaller juries, spend more time deliberating, engage in more communication, and show better recall of testimony. In addition, minority groups in the general population are more likely to be represented in 12-person juries than in smaller juries. There are costs, too. Larger juries deliberate longer and are more likely to end up as hung juries. Saks (1977) also argued that only in 12-person juries, with their longer deliberation time and better communication, can the minority effectively alter the course set by the majority.

The question of juries with fewer than 12 members was addressed by the Supreme Court in 1970 when, in *Williams v. Florida*, it upheld a Florida statute that called for six-person juries in serious criminal cases. The decision acknowledged the research findings cited by the American Psychological Association (APA) in an *amicus* brief, but the Court apparently misread the data, and declared that the difference in effects between 6- and 12-member juries was "negligible." The apparent "naivete and ignorance of the Court" (Bersoff, 1986, p. 155) stimulated social scientists to conduct more research on the effects of jury size, especially on possible differences between 6- and 12-person juries.

The Court looked at jury size again in *Ballew v. Georgia* (1978). An *amicus* brief summarizing the data from 18 empirical studies, mostly concerned with possible differences between 6- and 12-member juries, was submitted by APA. The Court referred to these studies in its decision, but ignored the differences found between 6- and 12-person juries, focusing its attention on five-member juries (which had *not* been studied in the research) and finding them unconstitutional. Part of the majority's decision derided the research as "numerology derived from statistical studies" (p. 246). As Loh (1981, p. 340) summed it up, "The data were apparently used to ornament a decision reached on other legal and policy grounds. ...The opinion used social science the way a drunk uses a lamp post, for support rather than illumination." At present, juries of less than 12 members are still relatively uncommon, as all but four states require that 12 jurors be seated initially in noncapital felony cases, though attrition is permitted in some states (King, 2000).

The Decision Rule: Must a Verdict Be Unanimous?

One legacy of English common law is the standard that jury verdicts should be unanimous. The requirement for unanimity was established in England in the fourteenth century and was envisioned by the writers of the US Constitution as well. In *Patton v. United States* (1930) unanimity was enumerated as an "essential feature" of the American jury system. However, subsequent decisions ruled that nonunanimous verdicts in noncapital felony cases were acceptable (*Johnson v. Louisiana*, 1972). In *Apodaca, Cooper, and Madden v. Oregon* (1972, p. 191), the majority wrote that the jury's essential feature is that it involves "the commonsense judgment of a group of laymen" and that the requirement of unanimity "does not materially contribute to the exercise of this commonsense judgment." A later decision ruled that verdicts reached by six-person juries must be unanimous (*Burch v. Louisiana*, 1979). At present, only Louisiana and Oregon allow nonunanimous verdicts in felony cases (King, 2000).

Researchers and legal observers have argued that the requirement of unanimity is critically important because it empowers each and every juror. Requiring a unanimous vote forces jurors to resolve disagreements and reach a conclusion that (in theory, at least) is acceptable to every jury member (Hastie, Penrod, & Pennington, 1983). In addition, research has shown that mock juries deliberate longer when the unanimity rule is in force, and this longer deliberation period may allow minority views to get serious consideration. In turn, this may sometimes eventuate in a verdict that is opposite to the one that would have resulted from a quicker majority decision.

THE SELECTION OF JURORS

Juror Eligibility: The Venire

The Sixth Amendment says that a jury should be "impartial" and drawn from the proper district, but does not provide further guidance on who is eligible to serve on a jury. The jury in 1791 was democratic by the standards of the times, but elitist by modern standards. Women could not serve in any state, and in every state except Vermont, only men who owned property or were taxpayers could be jurors. One state, Maryland, disqualified atheists (McKinley, 1905). Three states specifically excluded African-Americans—Georgia, South Carolina, and Virginia.

In response to a long history of exclusion of African-Americans, a series of Supreme Court decisions in the 1930s and 1940s overturned convictions because of intentional race discrimination in the jury selection process, and state court systems began to take steps to include Blacks in the jury pool. Congress took steps as well; in 1970 Congress adopted the system for selecting jurors randomly from lists of registered voters, making intentional racial discrimination more difficult. In 1975 the Supreme Court ruled that the Sixth Amendment mandates that a jury be drawn from a "cross-section" of the community (*Taylor v. Louisiana*, 1975). The cases that established this doctrine had involved the exclusion of women from juries, but the concept was immediately applied to the exclusion of Blacks from juries as well (Leipold, 1998). More recent reforms have attempted to broaden the jury pool by selecting names from lists of licensed drivers, welfare recipients, unemployment lists, and so forth.

Selection of the Jury: The Use of Peremptory Challenges

Techniques that create more representative jury pools (venire) do not address problems that may arise during the *voir dire* stage of jury selection wherein prospective jurors are questioned by the attorneys or the judge to determine their fitness as possible jurors. The judge may exclude any prospective juror "for cause" if the judge decides that the individual would be unable to serve as an impartial juror. Additionally, attorneys for each side may exclude a limited number of persons by utilizing a limited number of "peremptory challenges," usually between 5 and 20, depending on the type of case and the jurisdiction. Widespread concern about the *voir dire* process stems from the belief that the composition of the particular jury that emerges through *voir dire* can significantly affect the outcome of the trial. Legal analysts have long argued about the relative importance of the characteristics of the jurors in determining the outcome of jury trials, in comparison to the strength of the evidence, the skills of the attorneys, and other factors.

The *voir dire* process, inherited from British common law, has undergone many modifications in the American legal system. Historically, through the use of peremptory challenges, attorneys could systematically exclude jurors on the basis of race, gender, age, or whatever other characteristic they wished to focus on. Systematic exclusion of African-Americans from trial juries via peremptory challenges has remained a consistent policy in many parts of the US (Alschuler & Deiss, 1994). In *Swain v. Alabama* (1965), the Supreme Court stated that the use of peremptory challenges could not be used to systematically exclude Blacks from juries. However, the *Swain* ruling required that the defense prove a systematic pattern of discrimination that went beyond the present case. This is a difficult standard, as during the next 20 years there were only two cases nationwide in which the defense was able to successfully challenge the prosecution's systematic exclusion of Blacks from juries. Even Justice White, the author of the *Swain* opinion, publicly admitted that the decision had not solved the problem.

The Supreme Court revisited this issue in *Batson v. Kentucky* (1986). The Court shifted the burden of proof to the prosecution, who must convince the trial judge that systematic racial exclusion was *not* taking place. A subsequent decision outlawed systematic exclusion owing to gender (*J. E. B. v. Alabama*, 1994), and some appellate courts have outlawed jury-selection discrimination directed toward other "cognizable groups," such as Hispanics in Florida (*Florida v. Johans*, 1993). The *Batson* decision said that the prosecution must convince the trial judge that challenges were not based on race alone, but rather on some other characteristic(s). This has apparently been an easy standard to meet, as very few post-*Batson* challenges have been successful. Most judges seem ready to accept whatever alternative explanation the prosecution wishes to give (Cavise, 1999; Kressel & Kressel, 2002).

Some scholars and judges have suggested that peremptory challenges should be eliminated altogether (Abramson, 1995; Adler, 1994; King, 2000; Melilli, 1996). Justice Thurgood Marshall made such a suggestion in his concurring opinion in the *Batson* decision. Because the concept of peremptory challenges is not part of the Constitution, peremptory challenges could be eliminated by state legislatures, and in some states legislation has been introduced in recent years to reduce the number of peremptory challenges provided to each side (King, 2000). Other criticisms of the current *voir dire* system are that it may cause prospective jurors to become frustrated and cynical about the whole process, that it wastes time, and that it promotes "juror shopping" and reliance on "jury experts," an issue that will be discussed subsequently. However, others have suggested that reducing or eliminating peremptory challenges would not be a panacea, because attorneys would still attempt to continue "juror shopping" by making greater use of challenges for cause. At present, an estimated 15 to 25 percent of potential jurors are excused for cause (King, 2000).

Attorneys' Assumptions About Jurors

Some have claimed that the selection of the jury is the most crucial aspect of the trial process. Famed defense attorney, Clarence Darrow, once asserted, "Never forget, almost every case has been won or lost when the jury is sworn" (Kressel & Kressel, 2002, p. 8). In contrast, other observers have asserted that a jury's composition is a relatively minor determinant of the verdict, and that trials are usually decided by evidence and/or the skills of the attorneys (e.g., MacCoun, 1980; Saks & Hastie, 1978). But since juries have a split verdict prior to deliberation in 70 percent of criminal trials (Lempert, 1975), it appears likely that personal characteristics of the jurors, who must endeavor to deliberate from this split vote to a unanimous decision, can be important.

Traditionally, attorneys have relied upon their intuition and previous trial experiences, as filtered through their stereotypes and implicit personality theories, in evaluating prospective jurors. They may also seek guidance from others. The publication of jury selection guides for attorneys has a long history (see, e.g., Donovan, 1887/1985). Even in more recent times, trial practice writers "have published rather detailed, sometimes amusing advice, often replete with racist, sexist, ethnic, age, and other forms of bias" (Fulero & Penrod, 1990, p. 234). A study of how attorneys profiled jurors on the basis of juror similarity, using multidimensional scaling techniques, found that attorneys' judgments of juror similarity were based primarily on four characteristics: gender, age, attitudes toward legal technicalities, and ideological orientation (Penrod, 1979).

Some who have stressed the importance of jury composition have claimed that attorneys are highly skilled in "reading" prospective jurors. A former president of the Association of Trial Layers of America stated, "Trial attorneys have developed a perceptiveness that enables them to detect the minutest traces of bias or inability to reach an appropriate decision" (Begam, 1977, p. 78). But such perceptions may instead illustrate the "illusion of control" in a high-stakes situation in which learning about actual accuracy would be difficult or impossible. Fulero and Penrod (1990) asserted that, because attorneys cannot observe juror deliberations and almost never learn how a challenged juror might have voted, "If any learning [by attorneys] does take place in these conditions, it is likely to resemble the superstitious behavior of animals reinforced with food at fixed intervals" (p. 241).

The Evolution of "Scientific Jury Selection"

The term "scientific jury selection" (SJS) originated in the early 1970s to describe efforts by social scientists and trial consultants (who also may be called litigation consultants or jury consultants) to use empirical methods to aid their clients on jury selection. Scientific jury selection has been called the most controversial of all the domains in which psychology has been applied to legal practices (Cutler, 1990). Trial consultants are hired most often in civil cases, where substantial amounts of money may be involved, but their use is increasing in criminal cases as well, as in the murder trial of O.J. Simpson in 1994–1995 (Barak, 1996; Brigham & Wasserman, 1999; Clark, 1997).

Advocates of SJS make several basic assumptions. These are (1) demographic and broad personality characteristics of potential jurors can be accurately assessed; (2) these characteristics are related to their case-relevant attitudes; (3) these attitudes, in turn, will significantly influence the verdict that each juror will prefer. The final assumption is that (4) a skilled trial consultant can ascertain these characteristics more accurately than can attorneys, defendants, or litigants. Each of these assumptions can be characterized as "debatable" (Berman & Sales, 1977; Wrightsman & Fulero, 2005).

Broad *personality characteristics* that may seem relevant are a general tendency to have a pro-prosecution or pro-defense orientation in criminal trials, or a pro-plaintiff or pro-defense orientation in civil trials. Research indicates that "legal authoritarianism" is generally associated with a pro-prosecution orientation in criminal trials (e.g., see Davis & Follette, 2004; Kravitz, Cutler, & Brock, 1993). In a similar vein, a positive attitude toward the death penalty is associated with a pro-prosecution view in capital cases. Wrightsman et al. (2002, p. 200) suggested that, although general traits such as these have only a very limited relationship to verdicts in specific cases, "They are better than nothing, and they are probably better than most people's intuitions, but their predictive accuracy is low when it comes to verdicts by individual jurors." In civil trials, a general pro-plaintiff or pro-defense orientation may be related to attitudes about the "litigation explosion," about risk taking, about standard of care, about personal accountability, and about corporate responsibility (Bothwell, 1999; Wrightsman et al., 2002).

In contrast to this emphasis on general attitudes or personality factors, the *case-specific approach* focuses on factors found to be significant in a specific trial. This approach was taken by psychologists involved in the first instances of SJS in the early 1970s, in a series of politically charged trials involving people prosecuted for actions taken to protest the war in Vietnam (*United States v. Ahmad*, 1973). Social scientists surveyed community members and also used "information networks" in the community to find out which demographic variables were associated with favorable attitudes toward war protesters (Christie, 1976; Schulman, Shaver, Colman, Emrick, & Christie, 1973). SJS was also used in a number of other political trials in the 1970s (Moran, Cutler, & De Lisa, 1994).

Generally, the opportunities for assessing case-specific attitudes are limited. To provide attorneys with more detailed case-specific information, there has been increased use of *supplemental juror questionnaires* that are reviewed by the attorneys for both sides. The supplemental questionnaire used in the criminal trial of O. J. Simpson contained almost 300 questions and was 61 pages long (Gordon, 1997)! Such a lengthy, intrusive questionnaire raises issues of invasion of jurors' privacy and "informed consent," possibly violating the research standards of the APA, which stress the importance of obtaining informed consent from research participants. In one case, for example, a prospective juror refused to answer 12 questions (dealing with religion, income, and political party affiliation) on a 100-item supplemental juror questionnaire that had been authorized by the court. The trial judge found her in contempt and sentenced her to three days in jail (Wrightsman & Fulero, 2005).

The Efficacy of "Scientific Jury Selection"

Some trial consultants have made extravagant claims as to the effectiveness of their efforts. One consulting firm advertised, "To date, where our advice and recommendation have been employed, our clients have achieved successful results in over 95 per cent of the cases in which we have been involved." (ad quoted in Adler, 1989, p. 10) However, one set of researchers observed that, "The financial success of these firms seems exceeded only by the hyperbole of their claimed expertise" (Moran et al., 1994, p. 311). The Code of Ethics adopted by the American Society of Trial Consultants (ASTC, 1998) discourages the use of "won–lost" records in advertising. A decade ago, Moran and his colleagues summarized things thusly: "By the 1980s, SJS consultants were much like other professional psychologists—confident of their competence and at odds with academia. Meanwhile, empirical jury selection research has not sufficiently addressed the controversy" (1994, p. 312).

Indeed, empirical data on the effectiveness of SJS are scarce. Research has generally supported the first assumption, that demographic and broad personality variables are often related to attitudes. However, there has been much less support for the remaining assumptions—the notion that these attitudes can be accurately assessed, that these attitudes are systematically linked to jury verdicts, and that trial consultants can identify and measure them accurately. Studies have often found relationships between demographic characteristics and attitudes, but systematic connections between either demographic characteristics or attitudes and verdict preferences have been more difficult to find (Cutler, Moran, & Narby, 1992; Wrightsman et al., 2002). A number of studies have found that attitudes about specific case-relevant matters predict verdict preference in specific cases (e.g., Cutler et al., 1992; Moran, Cutler, & Loftus, 1990). This suggests that attitudes toward case-relevant factors are better predictors of juror verdict information than are broad demographic variables. Nevertheless, studies of actual cases have sometimes found significant relationships between demographic characteristics and verdicts. Demographic factors that are sometimes related to verdict preferences include age, gender, socioeconomic status, race, and education level (see, e.g., Mills & Bohannon, 1980a, 1980b; Moran & Comfort, 1986).

Other studies have suggested the value of focusing on cognitive factors, such as individuals' preferred cognitive processing strategies (Frederick, 1984; Fulero & Penrod, 1990). For example, Graziano, Panter, and Tanaka (1990) found verdict decisions affected by cognitive complexity, cognitive persistence, completeness of information processing (the number of reasons listed for a verdict decision), and need for structure. Further, these variables tended to interact with each other, meaning that information was lost if any variable was studied in isolation.

A research review (Fulero & Penrod, 1990) identified a modest relation between demographic/personality variables and verdict, with those variables accounting for approximately 5–15 percent of the variance in verdict preferences. While these percentages may seem small, such information could still be useful to an attorney. An attorney, who operated on a completely random basis with a jury pool in which 50 percent were favorable and 50 percent were unfavorable to the attorney's side, would correctly classify 50 percent of the jurors. However, if the attorney knew of a variable that accounted for just 5 percent of the variance in verdict preference, systematic use of that information would increase the attorney's accuracy rate to 61 percent correct classifications (Penrod & Cutler, 1985). Alternatively, if the variable had accounted for 15 percent of the variance in verdict preference, the attorney's accuracy of classification would increase to 69 percent. While a 10–20 percent improvement in assessing verdict preferences may not seem monumental, it is worth noting, for comparison purposes, that Rosenthal (1990) calculated that the best modern medical drugs improve effective treatment by about 12 percent, on average. Viewed from this perspective, a 10–20 percent improvement in selection of jurors does not seem too shabby! As Fulero and Penrod observed, "If the defendant has his or her life, or a corporation has millions of dollars at stake, the jury selection advantages conferred by SJS techniques may well be worth the investment" (1990, p. 252).

Attitude–verdict relationships tend to be case-specific (Moran et al., 1994). Variables that are important in one case may not have an effect in another case. Thus, a case-specific approach is important because findings regarding predictor variables may not consistently apply across cases or across jurisdictions (Patterson, 1986). A study of four different simulated trials (murder, rape, robbery, and a civil suit) found that the overall percent of variance accounted for by 21 attitude and demographic items ranged from 5 to 14 percent. However, different predictors were effective in different cases, and no single predictor worked in even three of the four cases, thereby giving no support to the concept of a general trait of conviction-proneness (Penrod, 1990).

Some more general attitudes, such as legal authoritarianism, may be useful (Moran et al., 1994). Research shows that in some situations attitudes can be more strongly related to verdicts. For example, in cases involving the death penalty, attitudes about the death penalty are particularly relevant (Nietzel & Dillehay, 1986). Given the findings that the relationship between demographic/personality variables and verdicts varies from case to case, trial simulations involving mock jurors or focus groups may be particularly valuable for assessing the relationship in any particular case.

On balance, the research to date indicates that information about prospective jurors' demographic characteristics, general personality characteristics, and especially case-specific attitudes, may be of some use in identifying those most likely to favor one side of any particular case. But the conclusion reached by Kassin and Wrightsman (1988) some time ago seems still warranted: "In short, contrary to the worst fears, scientific [jury] selection procedures cannot reliably tip the scales of justice" (p. 61).

Ethical Issues in Jury Selection

Trial consultants are not licensed or certified in any state, and therefore anyone can proclaim himself or herself a trial consultant (Wrightsman & Fulero, 2005). However, while in the role of applied researcher, a psychologist/trial consultant must follow professional standards for ethical research. Indeed, ethics complaints against psychologists who work in forensic contexts are among the most common made to licensing boards (Ogloff, 1999). The Ethical Code of the APA applies to forensic psychologists in all of their professional activities (American Psychological Association, 1992). The *Specialty Guidelines for Forensic Psychologists* (Committee on Ethical Guidelines for Forensic Psychologists, 1991), formulated by the American Psychology-Law Society (Division 41 of the APA), contain a more comprehensive analysis of ethical issues that forensic psychologists may face. However, while psychologists are obligated to adhere to the APA ethical principles, the Specialty Guidelines do not represent an official statement of the APA and are more "aspirational" in nature. The ASTC, formed in 1982, has propounded its own ethical standards. The first standards (American Society of Trial Consultants, 1998) were designed to address community surveys done in connection with requests for a change of venue (see Abbott, 1999).

Given the fact that the trial consultant may be an entrepreneur as well as a scientist, certain conflicts may arise. One ambiguous area concerns the sharing of data and ideas. It is a fundamental principle within the scientific community that empirical data and scientific ideas are shared among researchers. However, trial consultants may guard their ideas closely. Hence, sound research may disappear into the vaults of research consultants who feel compelled to protect trade secrets and other commercial interests (Fulero & Penrod, 1990).

While some see the use of trial consultants as a means of correcting attorneys' stereotypes and prejudices, others see it in a much less positive light. For example, Marcia Clark, lead prosecutor in the O.J. Simpson criminal trial, asserted: "As far as I'm concerned, they are creatures of the defense. They charge a lot, so the only people who can afford them are wealthy defendants in criminal trials or fat-cat corporations defending against class-action suits" (Clark, 1997, p. 138). (It should be noted that Clark also employed a trial consultant in the Simpson case, but disagreed with his analyses and eventually barred him from the courtroom.)

The question of the effectiveness of SJS raises ethical, as well as scientific, issues. On the one hand, if the SJS techniques are *not* effective, then consultants may be committing an ethical breach by advocating and accepting payment for providing a useless service. On the other, if the techniques *are* effective, this raises different ethical issues. Is SJS a high-tech form of jury-rigging, no more acceptable than cruder forms of jury tampering? Or does it merely substitute a new set of selection criteria, presumably scientifically based, for older criteria such as lawyers' stereotypes and intuitions (Strier, 1999)? When they are used to buttress one side of a case (presumably, the side that has more money or a more popular cause), producing a jury that is strongly biased in favor of that side, the procedure could be seen as threatening the ideal of a fair trial.

Where does the future of SJS lie? The negative way in which it is seen by many judges is captured in this portion of a speech given by US Supreme Court Justice Sandra Day O'Connor at the 1999 National Conference on Public Trust and Confidence in the Justice System:

> The process of selecting a jury out of the citizens called for jury service on a particular day has changed from a necessary safeguard against potentially biased jurors to a way for highly paid jury consultants to attempt to ensure a jury favorable to the side paying their fees.
>
> (quoted in Kressel & Kressel, 2002, p. 209)

Contemporary observers suggest that the trial consulting industry is moving away from reliance on SJS as its main focus, to a greater emphasis on trial strategy issues, as assessed by the use of mock juries, focus groups, and related research tools (Abbott & Batt, 1999; Kressel & Kressel, 2002). The study of effective persuasion strategies and techniques may show the best promise for the future application of psychological concepts and research strategies to the American legal system, for good or for ill.

A Note About Civil Juries

Analyses of civil juries involve additional questions that are beyond the scope of this chapter. Four common assumptions about civil juries have been recently identified (Hans & Albertson, 2003): (1) they are sympathetic to plaintiffs and hostile to corporations and insurance defendants; (2) civil jurors have trouble comprehending trial evidence and legal instructions in complex trials; (3) compensatory awards are erratic, capricious, and too high; and (4) punitive awards are arbitrary, capricious, and too high. Since the 1980s, these assumptions have underlain proposed legislation to place caps on awards for pain and suffering and/or punitive damages, and over 40 states have instituted limits (Saichek, 1996). However, a review of relevant research (Hans & Albertson, 2003) indicated that none of the four assumptions had been clearly supported, leading the researchers to conclude that, "the problems with the civil jury are overstated (p. 1522)."

JURIES AND THE DEATH PENALTY

Perhaps the most difficult task facing criminal juries in United States is deciding whether a convicted murderer should be put to death for the crime. About three-quarters of the states and the federal government presently authorize the death penalty. Only about 6–15 percent of defendants charged with a capital crime (i.e., generally, murder with aggravating circumstances) receive a death sentence, resulting in about 250 death sentences per year (Abramson, 1995). In most states, it is the jury and not the judge who decides whether the defendant should be sentenced to death.

Historically, the imposition of the death penalty has been strongly marked with the specter of racial injustice. The Supreme Court struck down the death penalty in 1972 in *Furman v. Georgia*, ruling that its application violated the Eighth Amendment's prohibition against "cruel and unusual punishment" because it was applied in an "arbitrary and capricious manner." Four years later, in *Gregg v. Georgia* (1976), the Supreme Court reinstated the death penalty by upholding Georgia's revised death penalty statute. The new law specified both aggravating and mitigating factors that were to be taken into account by jurors in deciding whether to impose the death penalty. The new procedures were intended to produce more consistent and case-specific judgments.

The issue of racial injustice did not go away, however. In 1987, data on racial disparity in death-penalty sentencing (once again, in Georgia) were presented to the US Supreme Court in *McCleskey v. Kemp*. A large-scale study of factors determining the imposition of the death penalty in over 2400 capital cases in Georgia from 1973 to 1979 found that a racial disparity in sentencing that was related more to the race of the *victim* than to the race of the defendant. Thus, defendants who had killed Whites were much more likely to receive the death penalty (in 11 percent of the possible cases) than were those who killed Blacks (in only 1 percent of the possible cases). Blacks who killed Whites were treated harshly, sentenced to death 22 percent of the time. Many researchers were hopeful that in this case the Supreme Court would finally acknowledge the value and relevance of social science research, as presented in *amicus* briefs. However, in a five-four decision, the Court upheld McCleskey's death sentence. The majority stated that they accepted the validity of the research data, but nevertheless would not overturn McCleskey's conviction because the group data did not show that *intentional* racial discrimination was operating specifically in McCleskey's case, during his conviction and sentencing. Critics of the decision noted that it would be difficult or impossible to prove the existence of intentional racial discrimination in any individual case.

Another issue facing juries in capital cases involves the jurors' feelings about the death penalty itself. Should citizens who do not believe that there should be a death penalty be seated on a capital jury? For many years, prospective jurors who had conscientious "scruples" against the death penalty were excluded from capital juries for cause, a procedure known as "death qualification." Under this procedure, potential jurors who expressed anti-death penalty attitudes that would affect their ability to reach a guilty verdict, or their willingness to ever vote for the death penalty, were automatically excluded for cause from capital juries.

A 1986 case that called this procedure into question, *Lockhart v. McCree* (1986), was especially interesting to many forensic psychologists because there appeared to be a significant corpus of relevant empirical research findings that might be taken seriously by the Supreme Court. Two decades earlier, in *Witherspoon v. Illinois* (1968), the Court had upheld the legality of the death qualification procedure in capital cases, but the Justices had also expressed concern about research that seemed to show that allowing death-qualified juries stacked the deck against defendants by removing relatively liberal, defendant-oriented jurors for cause, while not removing more conservative conviction-prone jurors. While the Court in *Witherspoon* described the research data to that point, based upon just three empirical studies, as "tentative and fragmentary," the decision stated that the Court might rule differently in the future if further research clearly demonstrated that death-qualified juries were not neutral with regard to guilt.

The results of 15 such studies carried out in the two decades after *Witherspoon* were summarized in an *amicus* brief submitted by the APA in the *Lockhart v. McCree* (1986) case. The brief concluded that (1) death-qualified juries are conviction-prone; (2) death-qualified juries are unrepresentative, thereby threatening the defendant's right to a jury composed from a fair cross-section of the community; and (3) death qualification interferes with the proper functioning of the jury. These findings appeared to clearly demonstrate that death-qualified juries were conviction-prone (see, e.g., Cowan, Thompson, & Ellsworth, 1984; Moran & Comfort, 1986; Thompson, 1989).

Despite these data, the Supreme Court upheld the death qualification process in a narrow five-four decision in *Lockhart.* Donald Bersoff, then general counsel for the APA, wrote, "It is now clear that even the most unassailable and methodologically perfect evidence would not have convinced the majority." But, he added, "even though the majority eventually concluded that the social science evidence was not germane to its decision, it did not ignore it either. It gave it a respectful hearing and, it must be said, echoed the objective critique APA provided in its *amicus* brief. The Court's emphasis on the admitted lack of perfection in the studies was of far greater import to it, however, than it was to APA" (Bersoff, 1987, p. 58).

State procedures that involve both the judge and jury in the death sentencing process were revisited in *Ring v. Arizona* (2002). The Supreme Court declared the death-sentencing laws of Arizona and four other states unconstitutional because the laws gave judges the final say on whether or not the death penalty was invoked. The majority opinion in *Ring* held that a death sentence where the necessary aggravating factors are determined by a judge, rather than by a jury, violates a defendant's constitutional right to a trial by jury. The decision said that the constitutional guarantees to a jury trial would be "senselessly diminished" if jurors did not decide whether a particular murder merits a life or death sentence. There were 168 death row inmates at the time in those five states. Left unclear was the constitutionality of death-penalty procedures in several other states, whose laws involved both judges and juries in the death-penalty decision.

CONCLUSION

The trial jury holds a revered place in the justice system of the United States, owing both to its important historical role in the events leading up to American independence from Great Britain, and to its continuing function as a means by which common citizens can determine the course of justice. While the institution remains sacrosanct, we can expect continuing tinkering with particular aspects of the jury. I have touched upon some aspects that are characteristic of the US jury, including jury size, voting rule, and particularly of concern in the American jury, the representativeness of the jury pool (venire), and the way that jurors are selected from the venire. In addition, I have discussed issues arising from the option of a death penalty. Issues regarding attorneys' use of peremptory challenges, and the usefulness and ethicality of input from trial consultants, have received particular attention in recent years. We can expect this attention to continue, as the courts struggle to adapt this venerable institution to the attributes of an ever-changing society.

REFERENCES

Abbott, W. F. (1999). Jury research: An inventory of findings. In W. F. Abbott & J. Batt (Eds.), *A handbook of jury research* (pp. 1-1–1-39). Philadelphia: American Law Institute-American Bar Association.

Abbott, W. F., & Batt, J. (Eds.) (1999). *A handbook of jury research*. Philadelphia: American Law Institute-American Bar Association.

Abramson, J. (1995). *We, the jury: The jury system and the ideal of democracy*. New York: Basic Books.

Adler, S. (1989, 24 October). Litigation science: Consultants dope out the mysteries of jurors for clients being sued. *Wall Street Journal*, p. 1.

Adler, S. J. (1994). *The jury: Trial and error in the American courtroom*. New York: Times Books.

Alexander, J. (1963). *A brief narrative of the case and trial of John Peter Zenger, printer of the New York Weekly Journal*. Cambridge, MA: Harvard University Press.

Alschuler, A. W., & Deiss, A. G. (1994). A brief history of the criminal jury in the United States. *University of Chicago Law Review*, *61*, 867–928.

American Psychological Association (1992). Ethical principles of psychologists and code of conduct. *American Psychologist*, *47*, 1597–1611.

American Society of Trial Consultants (1998, Spring). Proposed minimum standards for survey research in connection with motions to change venue. *Court Call*, pp. 1–6.

Apodaca, Cooper, and Madden v. Oregon, 406 US 404 (1972).

Ballew v. Georgia, 435 US 223 (1978).

Barak, G. (Ed.) (1996). *Representing O.J.: Murder, criminal justice, and mass culture*. Guilderland, NY: Harrow and Heston.

Batson v. Kentucky, 476 US 79 (1986).

Begam, R. G. (1977). Voir dire: The attorney's job. *Trial*, *13*, 3.

Berman, J., & Sales, B. D. (1977). A critical evaluation of the systematic approach to jury selection. *Criminal Justice and Behavior*, *4*, 219–240.

Bersoff, D. N. (1986). Psychologists and the judicial system: Broader perspectives. *Law and Human Behavior*, *10*, 151–165.

Bersoff, D. N. (1987). Social science data and the Supreme Court: *Lockhart* as a case in point. *American Psychologist*, *42*, 52–58.

Bothwell, R. K. (1999). The ethical factor in *voir dire*. In W. F. Abbott & J. Batt (Eds.), *A handbook of jury research* (pp. 10-1–10-11). Philadelphia: American Law Institute-American Bar Association.

Brigham, J. C., & Wasserman, A. W. (1999). The impact of race, racial attitude, and gender on reactions to the criminal trial of O.J. Simpson. *Journal of Applied Social Psychology*, *29*, 1333–1370.

Burch v. Louisiana, 441 US 130 (1979).

Cavise, L. L. (1999). The Batson Doctrine: The Supreme Court's utter failure to meet the challenge of discrimination in jury selection. *Wisconsin Law Review*, *3*, 501–522.

Cheff v. Schnackenberg, 384 US 373, 86 S. Ct. 1523 (1966).

Christie, R. (1976). Probability vs. precedence: The social psychology of jury selection. In G. Bermant, C. Nemeth, & N. J. Vidmar (Eds.), *Psychology and the law: Research frontiers* (pp. 265–281). Lexington, MA: Lexington Books.

Clark, J. (2000). The social psychology of jury nullification. *Law and Psychology Review*, *24*, 39–57.

Clark, M. (1997). *Without a doubt*. New York: Viking Penguin.

Committee on Ethical Guidelines for Forensic Psychologists (1991). Specialty guidelines for forensic psychologists. *Law and Human Behavior*, *15*, 655–665.

Committee on Professional Responsibility (New York) (1999). Report on jury nullification. *The Record*, *54*, 197–205.

Cowan, C. L., Thompson, W. C., & Ellsworth, P. C. (1984). The effects of death qualification on jurors' predisposition to convict and on the quality of deliberation. *Law and Human Behavior*, *8*, 53–79.

Cutler, B. L. (1990). Introduction: The status of scientific jury selection in psychology and law. *Forensic Reports*, *3*, 227–232.

Cutler, B. L., Moran, G., & Narby, D. J. (1992). Jury selection in insanity defense cases. *Journal of Research in Personality*, *26*, 165–182.

Davis, D., & Follette, W. C. (2004). Jurors CAN be selected: Non information, misinformation and their strategic use for jury selection. In W. T. O'Donohue, P. R. Laws & R. C. Hollins (Eds.), *Handbook of forensic psychology* (pp. 781–805). New York: Elsevier; Academic Press.

Donovan, J. (1985). *Modern jury trials and advocates* (4th ed.). New York: Fred B. Rothman & Company. (Original work published 1887)

Duane, J. J. (1996). Jury nullification: The top secret constitutional right. *Litigation*, *22*, 6–60.

Duncan v. Louisiana, 391 US 145 (1968).

Elwork, A., & Sales, B. D. (1985). Jury instructions. In S. Kassin & L. S. Wrightsman (Eds.), *The psychology of evidence and courtroom procedure* (pp. 280–297). Beverly Hills, CA: Sage.

Finkel, N. J. (1995). *Commonsense justice: Jurors' notions of the law.* Cambridge, MA: Harvard University Press.

Finkel, N. J. (2000). Commonsense justice and jury instructions: Instructive and reciprocating connections. *Psychology, Public Policy, and Law*, *6*, 591–628.

Florida v. Johans, 613 SO 2d 1319,1321 (1993).

Frederick, J. T. (1984). Social science involvement in voir dire: Preliminary data on the effectiveness of "scientific jury selection." *Behavioral Sciences and the Law*, *2*, 375–394.

Fulero, S. M., & Penrod, S. D. (1990). Attorney jury selection folklore: What do they think and how can psychologists help? *Forensic Reports*, *3*, 233–259.

Furman v. Georgia, 408 US 238 (1972).
Gordon, W. L. III (1997). Reflections of a criminal defense lawyer on the Simpson trial. *Journal of Social Issues*, *53*, 615–622.
Gormlie, G. F. (1996). Jury nullification: History, practice, and prospects. *National Lawyer's Guild Practitioner*, *53*, 49.
Graziano, S. J., Panter, A. T., & Tanaka, J. S. (1990). Individual differences in information processing strategies and their role in juror decision making and selection. *Forensic Reports*, *3*, 279–301.
Gregg v. Georgia, 428 US 153 (1976).
Hans, V. P., & Albertson, S. A. (2003). Empirical research and civil jury reform. *Notre Dame Law Review*, *78*, 1497–1523.
Hastie, R., Penrod, S. D., & Pennington, N. (1983). *Inside the jury*. Cambridge, MA: Harvard University Press.
Horowitz, I. A. (1988). Jury nullification: The impact of judicial instructions, arguments, and challenges on jury decision making. *Law and Human Behavior*, *12*, 439–453.
J. E. B. v. Alabama, 511 US 127 (1994).
Johnson v. Louisiana, 32 L.Ed.2d 152 (1972).
Kassin, S. M., & Wrightsman, L. S. (1988). *The American jury on trial: Psychological perspectives*. New York: Hemisphere.
King, N. J. (2000). The American criminal jury. In N. J. Vidmar (Ed.), *World jury systems* (pp. 93–124). New York: Oxford University Press.
Kravitz, D. A., Cutler, B. L., & Brock, P. (1993). Reliability and validity of the original and revised Legal Attitudes Questionnaire. *Law and Human Behavior*, *17*, 661–677.
Kressel, N. J., & Kressel, D. F. (2002). *Stack and sway: The new science of jury selection*. Boulder, CO: Westview Publishing.
Leipold, A. D. (1998). Constitutionalizing jury selection in criminal cases: A critical evaluation. *Georgetown Law Journal*, *86*, 945–1010.
Lempert, R. O. (1975). Uncovering "nondiscernible" differences: Empirical research and the jury-size cases. *Michigan Law Review*, *73*, 644–708.
Levy, L. W. (1985). *Emergence of a free press*. New York: Oxford University Press.
Lind, R. C. (1995). Defender of the faith in the midst of the Simpson circus. *Southwestern University Law Review*, *24*, 1215–1235.
Lockhart v. McCree, 106 S. Ct. 1758 (1986).
Loh, W. D. (1981). Perspectives on psychology and law. *Journal of Applied Social Psychology*, *11*, 314–355.
MacCoun, R. J. (1980). Experimental research on jury decision-making. *Science*, *244*, 1046–1049.
McCleskey v. Kemp, 107 S. Ct. 1756 (1987).
McKinley, A. E. (1905). *The suffrage franchise in the thirteen English colonies in America*. Philadelphia: Penn.
Meissner, C. A., Brigham, J. C., & Pfeifer, J. E. (2003). Jury nullification: The influence of judicial instructions on the relationship between attitudes and juridic decision-making. *Basic and Applied Social Psychology*, *25*, 243–254.
Melilli, K. J. (1996). *Batson* in practice: What we have learned about *Batson* and peremptory challenges. *Notre Dame Law Review*, *71*, 447–503.
Mills, C. J., & Bohannon, W. E. (1980a). Character structure and jury behavior: Conceptual and applied implications. *Journal of Personality and Social Psychology*, *38*, 662–667.
Mills, C. J., & Bohannon, W. E. (1980b). Juror characteristics: To what extent are they related to jury verdicts? *Judicature*, *64*, 22–31.

Moran, G., & Comfort, J. C. (1986). Neither "tentative" nor "fragmentary": Verdict preference of impaneled felony jurors as a function of attitude toward capital punishment. *Journal of Applied Psychology*, *71*, 146–155.

Moran, G., Cutler, B. L., & De Lisa, A. (1994). Attitudes toward tort reform, scientific jury selection, and jury bias: Verdict inclination in criminal and civil trials. *Law and Psychology Review*, *18*, 309–328.

Moran, G., Cutler, B. L., & Loftus, E. F. (1990). Jury selection in major controlled substance trials: The need for extended *voir dire*. *Forensic Reports*, *3*, 331–348.

Muniz v. Hoffman, 422 US 454 (1975).

Nietzel, M. T., & Dillehay, R. C. (1986). *Psychological consultation in the courtroom*. New York: Pergamon Press.

Ogloff, J. R. P. (1999). Ethical and legal contours of forensic psychology. In R. Roesch, S. D. Hart, & J. R. P. Ogloff (Eds.), *Psychology and law: The state of the discipline* (pp. 405–422). New York: Kluwer Academic/Plenum.

Patterson, A. (1986). Scientific jury selection: The need for a case-specific approach. *Social Action and the Law*, *11*, 105–109.

Patton v. United States, 281 US 276 (1930).

Penrod, S. D. (1979). *Study of attorney and 'scientific' jury selection models*. Unpublished doctoral dissertation, Harvard University.

Penrod, S. D. (1990). Predictors of jury decision making in criminal and civil cases: A field experiment. *Forensic Reports*, *3*, 261–277.

Penrod, S. D., & Cutler, B. L. (1985). Assessing the competence of juries. In I. Weiner & A. Hess (Eds.), *Handbook of forensic psychology* (pp. 293–318). New York: Wiley.

Pfeifer, J.E., Brigham, J.C., & Robinson, T. (1996). Euthanasia on trial: Examining public attitudes toward nonphysician-assisted death. *Journal of Social Issues*, *52*, 119–130.

Ring v. Arizona, 01-488 (2002).

Rosenthal, R. (1990). How are we doing in soft psychology? *American Psychologist*, *45*, 775–777.

Saichek, D. A. (1996). Putting the lid on caps. *The Wisconsin Lawyer*, *69*, 5.

Saks, M. J. (1977). *Jury verdicts: The role of group size and social decision rule*. Lexington, MA: Lexington Books.

Saks, M. J., & Hastie, R. (1978). *Social psychology in court*. New York: Van Nostrand Reinhold.

Schulman, J., Shaver, P., Colman, R., Emrick, B., & Christie, R. (1973, May). Recipe for a jury. *Psychology Today*, 37–44, 79–84.

Slovenko, R. (1994). Jury nullification. *Journal of Psychiatry and Law*, *22*, 165–175.

Sparf and Hansen v. United States, 156 U.S. 51 (1895).

Starr, V. H., & McCormick, M. (1993). *Jury selection* (2nd ed.). Boston: Little, Brown.

Strier, F. (1999). Whither trial consulting? Issues and projections. *Law and Human Behavior*, *23*, 93–115.

Swain v. Alabama, 380 US 202 (1965).

Taylor v. Louisiana, 419 US 522 (1975).

Thompson, W. C. (1989). Death qualification after *Wainwright v. Witt* and *Lockhart v. McCree*. *Law and Human Behavior*, *13*, 185–215.

United States v. Ahmad, 366 F.Supp. 1356 (1973).

United States v. Dougherty, 473 F.2d. 1113, 1130-1137 (D.C. Cir.) (1972).

United States v. Thomas, 116 F.3d 606 (2d Cir.) (1997).

Weinstein, J. (1998). The many dimensions of jury nullification. *Judicature*, *81*, 168–171.

Williams v. Florida, 399 US 78 (1970).
Witherspoon v. Illinois, 391 US 350 (1968).
Wrightsman, L. S., & Fulero, S. M. (2005). *Forensic psychology* (2nd ed.). Belmont, CA: Wadsworth.
Wrightsman, L. S., Greene, E., Nietzel, M. T., & Fortune, W. H. (2002). *Psychology and the legal system* (5th ed.). Belmont, CA: Wadsworth.

3

Cross-Border Diversity: Trial by Jury in England and Scotland

LORRAINE HOPE and AMINA MEMON

Although sharing the same island landmass within the United Kingdom, cross-border differences between jury systems in Scotland and England[1] are considerable. This chapter will present a comparative account of both jury systems, highlighting the particular characteristics of both before turning to focus on a number of unique features of the Scottish system. Of the two forms of jury system, it might be argued that the Scottish criminal jury differs most from the well-researched American jury on a number of key features including jury size, verdict options, and majority required for verdict. Clearly, such differences provide an interesting applied social psychological context and confirm the importance of conducting research beyond the standard North American jury model.

SCOTTISH AND ENGLISH JURIES: A COMPARATIVE OVERVIEW

In contrast with many of their European counterparts, juries in Scotland and England are located within an adversarial, as opposed to inquisitorial, system. However, it is at this point that the Scottish and English juries diverge in their similarity to the US jury system. For instance, neither jurisdiction enshrines any constitutional right to trial by jury and in both Scotland and England, only a very small percentage of all trials are heard by a jury (<1–2 percent). In England, a jury trial will only proceed in the Crown Court when the defendant pleads not guilty to a serious offense typically classified as "indictable only." Less serious offenses appear at a magistrates' court. A small number of offenses have been classified as "triable either way" meaning they may be tried in either court should the defendant plead not guilty. Recent recommendations by Lord Justice Auld (2001) in a review of the criminal justice system suggest that the "either way" option for defendants to appear before a jury may shortly be abolished. The situation in Scotland is considerably more straightforward. Crimes may be prosecuted under summary procedure (i.e., without a jury) or in the case of serious crimes, such as murder and rape, under solemn procedure (i.e., with a jury). A number of crimes may be tried under either procedure and for such crimes (e.g., assault, fraud), the public prosecutor decides the appropriate mode of trial. Civil juries are extremely rare in both jurisdictions. Curiously, Scottish civil juries mirror English juries in terms of size and verdict options and, therefore, embody none of the unusual characteristics of their criminal counterpart. Thus, for comparative purposes this chapter will focus on an examination of the criminal juries.

JURY SELECTION AND COMPOSITION

In both Scotland and England, jurors aged between 18 and 65 are randomly selected from the electoral roll. A residency criterion requires the prospective juror to have lived in the UK for at least 5 years beyond the age of 13. Individuals who have previously been sentenced to 5 or more years' imprisonment and those suffering serious mental disorders are immediately disqualified. Persons closely involved in the administration of justice (such as judges, police, and prison officers) are ineligible while a further category of individuals in particular public service occupations (such as doctors, chemists, members of the clergy, and armed forces) currently hold the right to refuse to serve on a jury. Again, however, recent recommendations striving to improve the representativeness of the jury may lead to the revocation of this right (Lord Justice Auld, 2001).

Both the Scottish and English systems differ quite radically from North America in terms of procedures to empanel the final jury for the trial. Once the random selection of jurors has been made there is very little opportunity to alter the original selection by either defense or prosecution. In both jurisdictions, there is no voir dire procedure equivalent to that observed in the US and peremptory challenges for the defense are no longer possible. Challenges for cause are permitted but, owing to the complexity inherent in identifying "cause" consistent with the notion of random selection, challenges of this type are extremely rare (Duff, 1999). Neither the Scottish nor English systems make a provision for alternate jurors but rather permit the jury to proceed with the loss of up to three jury members.

The first significant structural difference between the English and Scottish criminal juries concerns the number of empanelled jurors. While the English jury (and the Scottish civil jury) is made up of 12 individuals, 15 jurors are seated for a Scottish criminal jury. In his article, which describes the Scottish jury as a "very peculiar institution," Duff (1999) observes that a 15 member jury has been in place in Scotland since the end of the sixteenth century and evolved as such in tandem with two other unique features of the Scottish jury: the majority required for verdict and the availability of a third verdict option. The role of psychological research in relation to these and other features of the Scottish jury will command the focus of the current chapter.

MAJORITY VERDICT

In the United States, it is typically required that juries reach their verdict unanimously and, if unable to do so, the jury will be declared hung. Unanimity was also a requirement for English jurors until 1967 when the Criminal Justice Act decreed a majority verdict of ten to two acceptable. Currently, jurors are instructed at the outset of the trial that they must aim to reach a unanimous verdict. If, after 2 h of deliberation a unanimous verdict has not been reached, a majority verdict of ten to two for either conviction or acquittal may become acceptable after further instruction. Should the jury be unable to reach this majority (e.g., a nine to three verdict split), the jury will be declared hung and a retrial will take place.

The decision rule in Scotland is markedly different and the jury can return a verdict reflecting a bare majority (i.e., an eight to seven split) for either conviction or acquittal. As Duff (1999) points out, this eliminates the possibility of a hung jury as every trial results in a verdict for the defendant. Unlike in England, jurors in Scotland are not instructed to seek a unanimous decision but are informed at the outset that a majority vote will suffice to convict. Furthermore, when the foreperson returns the verdict they are simply required to indicate whether the verdict was unanimous or by majority. The size of the majority is never revealed in order to retain the confidentiality of deliberations in the jury room.

It is clear that a decision rule requiring such a slim majority is questionable for a number of reasons—particularly as execution following such a verdict was possible prior to the abolition of capital punishment. A review of psychological research on jury group decision-making also highlights potential implications of this particular decision rule. For instance, one of the first lay notions to be usurped by Kalven and Zeisel's (1966) initial findings is that the nature and content of the jury's discussion will be the ultimate determinant of the jury's verdict. In explaining their finding that the initial verdicts held by a majority of jury members are most influential, Kalven and Zeisel argue that group processes, such as the sequence and order of opinion polling, social and normative influence, and persuasion and individual preference, are important deliberation characteristics. In other words, jury deliberations will reflect the pattern of preference present among jury members and, as a result, be skewed in the direction of that preference.

The finding that the initially preferred verdict of the majority is likely to be the jury's final verdict (the *majority effect*) has been observed both in field studies (e.g., Sandys & Dillehay, 1995) and in simulation research (MacCoun & Kerr, 1988). Research has on the whole found support for variations on a "two-thirds majority, otherwise hung" decision rule (e.g., Stasser, Kerr, & Bray, 1982). In other words, if verdicts in a jury group fail to reflect a two-thirds majority in favor of a particular verdict, then it is unlikely that any verdict will be reached. In support of this conclusion, a meta-analysis conducted by MacCoun and Kerr (1988) found that when there is an initial two-thirds majority in favor of conviction, a guilty verdict was returned 67 percent of the time. This fits neatly with a standard group polarization outcome and is the typical consequence of a majority decision scheme. However, if the two-thirds majority favored acquittal then the defendant went free 94 percent of the time. In this respect, one variation of the decision rule cited above has been strongly supported, namely the "two-thirds majority, otherwise acquit" social decision scheme. MacCoun and Kerr's (1988) data suggest that the "critical threshold for conviction is between .75 and .83, while the threshold for acquittal is between .67 and .50."

Jurors in Scotland, however, only have to reach a majority of one to secure a verdict. Thus, it seems inevitable that this decision rule has clear implications for the nature of the jury deliberations. For instance, Hastie, Penrod, and Pennington (1983) suggest that decision rule impacts on the way in which opposing viewpoints are communicated during deliberations. Positions favored by the minority receive less discussion and, as a result, members of those minority factions participate and contribute less to the content of the deliberations when full jury agreement is not required (i.e., a majority vote is adequate). The authors also contend that a majority (or nonunanimous) rule results in a less thorough discussion and consideration of the evidence although they also concede that the effect of decision rule on accuracy might not be as drastic as these qualitative differences might predict. It has, however, been suggested that shortcomings associated with majority rule conditions may be improved by the adaptation of a particular deliberation style (ibid, p. 230).

Research has identified two distinct ways in which juries might approach their task (Cowan, 1984; Hastie et al., 1983). A "verdict-driven" deliberation style has been characterized by an initial public vote by jurors and the ensuing deliberations tend to be dominated by individual statements of verdict preference. Essentially, individual jurors take up a position in relation to their verdict and cite evidence in support of that position. In contrast, "evidence-driven" deliberation emphasizes group story construction, taking a ballot later in the process, with individual jurors submitting their recollection of the evidence without reference to a particular verdict in an attempt to recreate the most meaningful collective representation of the original crime event. These two contrasting deliberation styles, verdict- and evidence-driven, can exert a significant influence on the deliberative process. Verdict-driven discussions have been shown to create "adversarial factions preoccupied with winning the point and silencing the dissenters" (Marder, 1987, p. 602; see also Schein, 1969). One outcome of this style is the propensity for this type of deliberation to result in hung juries, with either side unlikely to relinquish their position having been polarized by the adversarial nature of the discussions (Hastie et al., 1983). However, evidence-driven discussions involve greater interaction and communication by all members of the group such that members feel they have had a fair chance to influence the decision outcome even if they hold a minority position (Schein, 1969). Thus, this evidence-driven style is clearly preferable for the courts. However, many juries adopt the verdict-driven style, which leads to the rapid formation of factions favoring opposing verdicts (Devine, Clayton, Dunford, Seying, & Pryce, 2001). Although no extant research has documented a particular deliberation style associated with a decision rule such as that favored in the Scottish systems, it is possible to speculate that the requirement of a slim majority promotes a verdict-driven style as the jury members seek to initially establish the distribution of initial verdicts. Without the unanimity (or a larger majority) requirement, it may be the case that deliberations involve less conflict resolution and in-depth discussion than may be observed in juries seeking unanimity or a greater majority to return a verdict. However, it may be the case that such juries end up as hung juries—an outcome which is not possible under the Scottish system. Proponents of the current decision rule contend that the Scottish requirement for corroborating evidence, the size of the jury, and the verdict options available protect against any potential limitations associated with a bare majority verdict. Clearly, further research by psychologists is warranted to examine the impact of this rather unusual decision rule.

However, any future research would need to also take into account what is probably the most unusual feature of the Scottish jury—the Not Proven verdict. Like jurors elsewhere in the UK and US, Scottish jurors can choose to convict or to acquit by means of a Guilty or Not Guilty verdict. However, they can also choose to return a Not Proven verdict.

THE NOT PROVEN VERDICT

The Not Proven verdict is actually a vote for acquittal and has the same legal effect as a Not Guilty verdict. In both instances, the defendant is acquitted and cannot be retried for the same crime. The difference between the verdicts is simply that a verdict of Not Guilty reflects quite categorically that in the jury's view the defendant did not commit the crime and is innocent while the Not Proven verdicts reflects a measure of doubt that the defendant's guilt has been adequately demonstrated by the prosecution (Connelly, 1999; Duff, 1999).

This unique verdict option has been part of the Scottish legal system for more than 300 years (Scottish Office Study, 1994). In 1660, judges in Scotland began the practice of issuing special directives to the jury, informing them of the precise facts that had to be proven by the Prosecution in order for the defendant to be convicted. The sole function of the jury at this time was to determine whether these facts had indeed been proven by the Prosecution while a judge subsequently determined guilt. As a result, the verdicts of Proven and Not Proven came into general use. A three-verdict system (Guilty, Not Guilty, Not Proven) and the inclusion of the jury in determining guilt were formalized in the early eighteenth century. Since then, juries have been charged with deciding whether the defendant should be convicted or acquitted, and the unusual Not Proven verdict option has remained as a third possibility. Thus, the occurrence of this verdict has been described as "pure historical accident" (Wilcock, 1966, p. 217).

More recently, the Not Proven verdict has typically accounted for between one fifth (Scottish Office Study, 1994) and one third (Duff, 1999) of all acquittals by Scottish juries. Recent Scottish court statistics indicate that of all persons acquitted in 2002, 21 percent had received a Not Proven verdict (Criminal Proceedings in Scottish Courts, 2002). Concerns have also been raised in recent years about both the meaning and implications of the Not Proven verdict. In particular, criticism has been directed at the apparent lack of logic inherent in the verdict. Duff (1999) points out that if the Prosecution cannot prove the case beyond reasonable doubt then the verdict should be Not Guilty as opposed to the somewhat second rate acquittal offered by the Not Proven verdict.

Experimental research on the Not Proven verdict has not been conducted until recently. With our collaborator, Edie Greene, we conducted two studies to determine how and when jurors use the Not Proven verdict.[2] In particular, we were keen to examine the impact (if any) of this third verdict on conviction.

We designed two jury simulation studies that manipulated the number of verdict options such that either two (Guilty, Not Guilty) or three (Guilty, Not Guilty, Not Proven) verdict options were available to mock jurors. In both studies, participants read a summary of a criminal case (either a physical or sexual assault) and received instructions on reasonable doubt and elements of the crime (and for jurors in the three verdict condition, an additional judicial instruction on the effect of a Not Proven verdict). Participants acting as jurors in the study were required to reach an individual verdict and completed a number of questions about the likelihood that the defendant committed the crime, their confidence in the verdict, the extent to which the evidence was sufficient to support their verdict, and implications of the Not Proven verdict.

In Study 1, which used a physical assault trial, there was a significant association between verdict choice and verdict availability such that the proportion of jurors selecting a Not Guilty with only two verdict options (i.e., Guilty vs. Not Guilty) dropped significantly as participants opted for the Not Proven verdict instead. Thus, while there was no impact of the not proven verdict on the actual conviction (or acquittal) rate in the current study, mock jurors showed a preference for the Not Proven verdict over the alternative acquittal verdict of Not Guilty.

Our results for Study 2, which used a sexual assault trial, resulted in a higher conviction rate but a very similar pattern of findings to Study 1 with respect to the Not Proven verdict. We saw a large shift from the use of the Not Guilty verdict to the Not Proven verdict when it was an available option. Contrary to our predictions, however, the Not Proven verdict was used less frequently by jurors in the sexual assault trial than the physical assault trial used in Study 1. An examination of the rationales for choice of verdict indicated quite clearly that in both studies the majority of participants choosing a Not Guilty verdict did so because they believed there was insufficient evidence to convict. Similarly, participants reaching a Not Proven verdict indicated that this was the main reason for their choice of verdict.

Governmental statistics suggest that the use of the Not Proven verdict varies by crime type. For instance, while just over 20 percent of acquittals during 2002 involved a Not Proven verdict, this figure ranged from 6 to 83 percent across different types of crime (Criminal Proceedings in Scottish Courts, 2002, 2004). For instance, for cases involving nonsexual crimes of violence (e.g., homicide, serious assault), 24 percent of all acquittals resulted from a Not Proven verdict. However, for cases involving a charge of rape or attempted rape, the Not Proven verdict reflected 38 percent of all acquittals. One possible explanation of the increased use of the Not Proven verdict in cases of sexual assault is that such a verdict may be more satisfactory to the victim than an outright acquittal because it reflects merely an absence of necessary proof rather than doubt about the reliability or honesty of the victim in cases with little or no compelling or corroborating evidence.

From a psychological perspective, our results suggest that it may be the case that it is relatively easier for jurors to reason that the prosecution's case was not proven than to assess whether they had a reasonable doubt about the defendant's guilt. The pre-deliberation instance of the verdict observed in our studies is higher than the observed actual use of the Not Proven verdict. This may be due to the interaction of the Not Proven verdict with jury group decision-making. To our knowledge, research has yet to be conducted to examine the use of the Not Proven verdict by a jury group. One potential study might investigate whether the availability of the third verdict becomes a tool of compromise between opposing factions favoring either a guilty or not guilty outcome.

INDICTMENTS IN THE SCOTTISH SYSTEM

While the peculiarities of the Not Proven verdict clearly demand further research to examine decision-making processes, there is a further feature of the Scottish juror experience that is psychologically interesting. Unlike the Not Proven verdict, however, this feature has rarely, if ever been remarked upon, much less been the subject of research. The Scottish system does not allow for opening speeches on behalf of the prosecution or defense at the outset of a trial but moves straight to witness testimony and exposition of the evidence. The Court Clerk typically reads the indictment to empanelled jurors at the beginning of the trial and provides them with their own copy of the charge(s) to retain throughout proceedings, including the deliberation phase. The indictment is a written accusation of the crime, re-stating the content of the original charge or summons and is signed by a member of court staff. Such indictments vary considerably in length depending on the nature of the crime and number of charges against the defendant. Therefore, an indictment provides the jury with some basic information concerning the charge that they will have to consider before the presentation of evidence. Presenting jurors with information such as this at the outset of a trial raises a number of interesting questions for psychologists.

Research has shown that the jury is more likely to recall information provided by the prosecution at the outset than that proffered by the defense (Young, Cameron, & Tinsley, 1999), a primacy effect. This finding is consistent with research on the cognitive processing of social targets, which suggests that unfavorable expectancies about a social target show primacy effects (Ybarra, Schaberg, & Keiper, 1999). Furthermore, research relating specifically to the processing of evidence indicates that the initial evidence items are processed at a deeper semantic level again resulting in a primacy effect (Kerstholt & Jackson, 1998). A biased indictment may be processed in a similar fashion. Thus, where this information is only provided in the form of an indictment, as is the case in Scotland, it is important that this information is not only accurate but also fair and impartial as it will be referred to by jurors throughout the trial.

Under the Scottish system, however, the information presented to the jury is not the straightforward statement of the charge against the defendant one might expect but instead a rather elaborately worded "accusation." An examination of a number of sample indictments suggest that the Scottish legal system tends to embrace rather archaic legal jargon in the production of indictments which may, at best, make it difficult for jurors to understand proceedings and, at worse, unduly influence the decision-making process. For example, a defendant charged with the assault of a policeman was indicted with the following information:

> On—January 19—, at the rear of the premises occupied by the—Public House at—Street, Aberdeen you did assault—, A Constable in—Police, then in the execution of his duty, and did struggle violently with him and repeatedly strike him on the head and body with a shovel or similar instrument to his severe injury.

It is unclear why this unnecessarily complex wording style is retained at such a crucial interface between the law and lay public, although it is most likely no more than an obligation to legal tradition. However, it has been noted that indictments generated within the Courts of England and Wales are skeletal by comparison with the wordy Scottish version. The impact (if any) of information presented to jurors in this way is unclear at present.

There are, however, findings in other areas of psychological research that offer insights on the potential effects of this type of information. A considerable body of literature on juror comprehension suggests that the format of legal documentation available to juries may not only hinder juror understanding of the case but may also affect a juror's impression of the defendant and ultimately beliefs as to culpability. For instance, Findlay (2001) in his review of legalese concluded that consistent features of a trial are likely to cause trouble for jurors in terms of the demands on concentration, comprehension, and decision-making but that these features are likely to be trial specific and interrelated. Furthermore, in a study conducted for the New Zealand Law Commission, Young et al. (1999) report widespread misunderstanding of legal matters and aspects of the law among jurors. Their results also suggested that these basic misunderstandings persisted through, and significantly influenced, jury deliberations despite clarifications provided during the course of the judges' summary. In addition to promoting hung juries or questionable verdicts, legal misunderstandings served to prolong deliberations and led individual jurors to "agree on a verdict on an erroneous basis" (ibid, p. 55). While the majority of these misunderstandings center on precise legal definitions and how they might be interpreted within a specific case in question, at least one source of misunderstanding documented by Young et al. (1999) emanated from court produced documentation available to jurors. In particular, the wording of the indictment was identified as a potential source of confusion.

In a similar vein, research concerned with the efficacy of judges' instructions to the jury (typically administered just before deliberation) has determined that "lofty language and strangely structured sentences create confusion among jurors" (Diamond, 1993; Lind, 1982 in Halverson, Hallahan, Hart, & Rosenthal, 1997, p. 591). Simplification of judicial instructions, which is essentially a standardized document read by the judge to the jury, has been shown to greatly improve jurors' understanding of fundamental points of law and reduce confusion within the jury (Charrow & Charrow, 1979; Elwork, Alfini, & Sales, 1982; Severance, Greene, & Loftus, 1984; Severance & Loftus, 1982). Research suggests that when in unfamiliar situations, a less qualified person will look to more qualified others or those clearly in a position of authority to determine the proper behavior under those circumstances (Kruglanski & Mayseless, 1990). In the courtroom such authority would undoubtedly be attributed to the judge, officers of the court, and, by extension, artifacts of the court, such as court-produced documentation. Therefore, we carried out a study to examine, not the misunderstanding caused by an inaccurate or complex indictment, but the extent to which an indictment (delivered in the Scottish style) promotes a prejudicial pretrial characterization of the defendant.[3] It was predicted that the elaborately worded Scottish-style indictment, closely modeling the wording of an actual indictment for a similar offense, would result in an immediate negative impression or characterization of the defendant. It was also hypothesized that any negative impression of the defendant facilitated by this pretrial information would generate preconceptions of the defendant's role and culpability in relation to that crime. In other words, it was anticipated that the processing of the indictment would bias the potential juror against the defendant resulting in both negative characterization and attributions of guilt prior to presentation of evidence.

In our study, 106 jury eligible participants read either an elaborately worded Scottish-style indictment concerning a physical assault or a simple statement of the charge against the defendant containing the same factual details. Participants were required to write down their initial impression of the defendant and then evaluate the defendant and the alleged assault on a number of measures. The results indicated that participants reading the Scottish-style indictment were less likely to report factual elements contained within the indictment (such as the age of the defendant or the date of the incident) but made significantly more negative attributions about the defendant's character and the crime event. They were also significantly more likely to believe that the defendant intended to kill the victim, conclude that he initiated the fight and ultimately, was guilty of murder. Meanwhile, respondents reading a simple statement of the charge against the defendant did not generate any such characterizations of the defendant or make attributions of guilt, despite also reading that he was charged with a fatal stabbing. On the contrary, they were more likely to refer to factual details contained within the charge and make reference to the due process of law and the importance of fairness and impartiality. This data suggest quite strongly that the elaborate indictment generates an immediate negative impression of the defendant and more dangerously, leads the juror to form opinions pertaining to the guilt of the defendant.

The data from this preliminary study direct us toward several interesting lines of inquiry. Firstly, and importantly, from the applied perspective, these data provide no evidence that the observed effect is anything more than an immediate and short-lived spontaneous impression. Nor do the results provide us with evidence that reading an elaborately worded indictment will have negative implications for the fair and impartial processing of evidence in the course of a trial. Thus, future studies should include presence of testimony for and against the defendant, with appropriate measures of evidence interpretation, organization, recall, and, of course, ultimate verdict. However, an interesting aspect of these data concerns impression formation and specifically, the way in which the information provided leads to the formation of a particular impression of an individual. The data suggest that knowing that the defendant has been charged with a particular crime will not necessarily lead to negative characterizations. Instead, it would appear that how this information is conveyed plays an important role in the formation of impressions about the defendant. In this study, both experimental groups were aware that the charge was one of murder. In fact, this charge was stated quite explicitly in the simply worded indictment and described as a "fatal stabbing" thereby also indicating the *modus operandi* of the crime. In the Scottish indictment, the charge was also stated, although somewhat obfuscated by the convoluted language of that indictment. Thus, although both groups knew that the defendant had been charged with committing a murder by stabbing, only one group generated negative characterizations of the defendant and was more likely to believe he was guilty as charged. This may imply that the singular activation of concepts such as "murder" does not always result in the activation of stereotypic notions about the kind of person who might commit such a crime. Instead, the activation of such concepts to a sufficient extent that they result in the generation of a stereotypic negative characterization may involve a specific form of semantic content, perhaps content that is of an emotive or evocative nature. It may even be the case that patterns of activation are selective depending on the nature of the original input. Drawing on the literature on impression formation and in particular, spontaneous trait inferences (STIs), is instructive. STIs occur when "attending to another person's behavior produces a trait inference in the absence of our explicit intention to infer traits or form an impression of that person" (Uleman, Newman, & Moskowitz, 1996, p. 211). For instance, the STI "smart" (or "clever" or "intelligent") might be activated after reading the description behavior "John gets an A for the test." When reading the indictment information, respondents were not aware of the subsequent impression formation task, thus the impressions formed may reflect the use of STIs.

Results of a study conducted by van Overwalle, Drenth, and Marsman (1999) might lend an interpretative framework with which to view the results of our Scottish indictment study. They examined whether implying a trait by means of a behavior description would be sufficient to result in the spontaneous encoding of the trait and the association of that trait with a particular target individual. Results suggested that the trait inferences made when exposed to trait-implying stimuli refer to an interpretation of the actor's behavior but also describe the actor's disposition. Thus, it may be the case that the elaborately worded Scottish indictment exerts a similar effect in that the language used serves to generate more negative traits. After the initial traits of the target are inferred, any remaining social information is encoded in a stereotype-maintaining way (Wigboldus, Dijksterhuis, & van Knippenberg, 2003). Research has also demonstrated that when perceivers make decisions about a social target they research their decisions more quickly and with less information when supplied with negative information about the target (Yzerbyt & Leyens, 1991). Skowronski and Carlston (1989) have argued that some behavioral information will be more informative, more diagnostic, and, thus, more influential for impression formation. In particular, extreme or negative behaviors will be usually perceived as more diagnostic than moderate or positive behaviors. The results of the Scottish indictment study would appear to support this interpretation. The impressions formed by respondents in the Scottish indictment are likely to be the result of exposure to more "informative" behavioral information. This information is also negatively valenced and the resulting characterizations are therefore more extreme. Of course, this is just one interpretation of these findings. It may simply be the case that the extra detail presented in the Scottish-style indictment acts as an information processing heuristic, whereby more detailed descriptions are considered more valid. Further research is clearly needed to separate the effects of priming and stereotype activations from the simple use of heuristics. Thus, while the current data do not suggest that this information goes on to bias jurors within a trial, it does highlight an implication of retaining legal tradition, particularly when the impartiality of the law might be better preserved with use of the contemporary vernacular.

The issue of pretrial bias raised in the previous section leads neatly to a final significant difference between the experience of Scottish and English jurors and their American counterparts. Pretrial publicity constitutes a relatively well-researched form of pretrial information in North America and, interestingly, the response to prejudicial pretrial publicity across jurisdictions is markedly different.

PRETRIAL PUBLICITY AND UK JURIES

Most studies investigating the phenomenon of pretrial publicity (PTP) have found support for a prejudicial effect on prosecution verdicts by potential juror samples exposed to negative pretrial information about the defendant (e.g., Bornstein, Whisenhunt, Nemeth, & Dunaway, 2002; Hoiberg & Stires, 1973; Honess, Charman, & Levi, 2003; Hope, Memon, & McGeorge, 2004; Kramer, Kerr, & Carroll, 1990; Ogloff & Vidmar, 1994; Sue, Smith, & Gilbert, 1974). In 1999, Steblay and her colleagues conducted a meta-analysis of PTP research, which incorporated 44 empirical tests and represented 5755 participants. Results indicated that "subjects exposed to negative PTP were significantly more likely to judge the defendant guilty compared to subjects exposed to less or no negative PTP" (Steblay, Besirevic, Fulero, & Jimenez-Lorente, 1999, p. 219).

Broadly speaking, the responses taken by contemporary legal systems can be categorized as preferential to the notion of upholding either a "free press" or a "fair trial." On the whole, English courts recognize the threat posed by prejudicial publicity and have imposed strict limitations on the press to limit the reporting or publication of potentially prejudicial information. However, it is not certain that these measures seeking to control the press actually achieve their aim. In Scotland, the Contempt of Court Act 1981 "makes it an offence of strict liability to publish, including broadcast, anything which creates a 'substantial risk' that the course of justice in an 'active' proceedings will be 'seriously impeded or prejudiced'" (Duff, 1999, p. 186). However, this Act cannot prevent the publication of potentially prejudicial information before legal proceeding or appeals have been initiated. Furthermore, it cannot restrict the release of information appearing in foreign newspapers available on English newsstands or articles appearing on the Internet. These limitations have led to a number of farcical episodes whereby the press and traditional media have been restricted from publishing details of high-profile incidents while details of the case became common knowledge among the general populace because of the availability of information on the Internet.

While the directions of the Contempt of Court Act also govern proceedings in Scotland, it has been observed that "its application in Scotland is so starkly different from that in England that it is difficult to believe that the two jurisdictions are dealing with the same statutory provisions" (Bonnington, 1995, p. 145). For instance, the Lord Advocate (Scotland's equivalent of England's Attorney General) is more likely than his English counterpart to act in accordance with this statute and ensure subsequent compliance in order to curtail pretrial information in the press. However, as Duff points out, the Scottish courts have chosen to interpret the direction that there must be "substantial risk" to constitute a breach of the legislation as incorporating "some risk, greater than a minimal one." Furthermore, an individual believing himself to have been the victim of biasing pretrial publicity can initiate proceedings under the act in Scotland, whereas a decision to begin or consent to such proceedings is at the discretion of the Attorney General in England. However, even such rigorous regard for the legislation does not guarantee the successful management of the PTP threat. For instance, one very contradictory example concerns the case of *Stuurman v H.M. Advocate* (1983). The courts imposed heavy fines on the media for the dissemination of adverse publicity likely, or with the potential, to prejudice legal proceedings. Yet just a few weeks after the evocation of the Contempt of Court Act, the imposition of the fines, and thus, the indirect acknowledgment that there had been some element of biasing pretrial information in the public domain and that this biasing information had the potential to alter the outcome of the case, the Court decided that a fair trial was possible and the case proceeded. Advocates of this decision argued that the time lapse between the publicity and trial was sufficient for any bias to wane and that, even if this was not the case, the judge's instructions to disregard this information would dissuade the jury from being influenced by the negative pretrial publicity. Thus, in many respects, the same criticisms of the approaches taken to manage the impact of pretrial publicity apply in both Scotland and England where "loopholes in the law and pressures from modern media" (Armstrong Brandwood, 2000, p. 1412) mean that harsh restrictions on the press do not necessarily guarantee a fair trial.

A number of studies have also demonstrated reluctance among the judiciary to accept that publicity might prejudice a trial, leading Studebaker and Penrod (1997) to conclude that "judicial common sense often reflects a misappraisal or misunderstanding by the courts of the capabilities and weaknesses of human inference and decision making. The courts' assumptions and expectations about jurors' decision-making processes and ability to disregard pretrial publicity are not consistent with social science findings concerning these matters" (p. 455).

FUTURE DIRECTIONS

The fairness, validity, and value of the jury system has been the subject of much debate with jury reform a matter of policy for the current administration in both English (Lloyd-Bostock & Thomas, 1999; Lord Justice Auld, 2001) and Scottish jurisdictions (Duff, 1999). Particular features of both the Scottish and English jury systems provide a rich vein for future research by psychologists interested in the way jurors process evidence and ultimately reach a group verdict. The current chapter highlights a number of these features and introduces jurisdiction-specific research, much of which is still in the very early stages. Reform of the jury system will also open new research avenues for those interested in the psychological aspects of jury decision-making. For instance, the recent Auld's Review of the Criminal Courts of England and Wales (2001) considers the possibility that the European Court of Human Rights may soon under Article 6 require juries to supply reasons for their verdicts (in order to assess the validity of the verdict reached and avoid so-called perverse verdicts). In response to this, Auld recommends that trial judges provide juries with a series of questions, the answers to which can only logically lead to either a verdict of guilty or not guilty (i.e., provide a reasoned verdict). Tailoring the decision-making of juries in this way may have important implications for the way in which they reach their decisions in the future. In some nations, the requirement of verdict justification is already in place, as in the presentation of critical questions to be answered by the jury (see, e.g., Chapter 5).

The greatest contribution that could be made to improving the validity and applicability of jury research would be permitting research on actual juries within the UK. Currently, any contact with jurors during or after a trial is strictly forbidden under the terms of the Contempt of Court Act 1981. Limited access to the deliberations of actual juries was recently granted during the Arizona Jury Project in the US as part of a study of changes to Arizona's civil procedures (e.g., Diamond, Vidmar, Rose, Ellis, & Murphy, 2003) and has recently been selectively granted in Australia. However, the prospect of a similar concession in the UK seems somewhat unlikely at present. While the Runciman Royal Commission (1991–1993) recommended that the Contempt of Court Act 1981 be amended to allow authorized research to take place in the jury room, Lord Justice Auld's recent review of the criminal courts (2001) was, unfortunately, somewhat less amenable.

Commentators frequently observe that the jury system is in decline—particularly in England where attempts have been made to limit the role of the jury and right of a defendant to a jury. Yet the jury retains "great symbolic significance and is still highly prized, not least because it continues to exercise its long-standing right to reach a verdict based on conscience, against the letter of the law, and occasionally in defiance of government" (Lloyd-Bostock & Thomas, 1999, p. 40). A greater understanding of how jurors evaluate evidence, interpret legal instruction, and ultimately reach their final verdicts can only contribute to the working of jury systems—irrespective of their global location.

NOTES

1. The United Kingdom incorporates three separate legal systems across Scotland, Northern Ireland, and England and Wales. England and Wales share legal—and consequently, jury—systems.
2. An article containing full details of this research is currently undergoing the review process.
3. This study forms part of the first author's doctoral dissertation.

REFERENCES

Armstrong Brandwood, J. (2000). You say: "Fair trial" and I say "free press". British and American approaches to protecting defendants' rights in high profile trials. *New York University Law Review*, *75*, 1412–1453.

Bonnington, A. J. (1995). Press and prejudice. *New Law Journal*, *1623*, 145.

Bornstein, B. H., Whisenhunt, B., Nemeth, R. J., & Dunaway, D. (2002). Pretrial publicity effects in a civil trial: A two-way street? *Law and Human Behavior*, *26*, 3–17.

Charrow, R. P., & Charrow, V. R. (1979). Making legal language understandable: A psycholinguistic study of jury instructions. *Columbia Law Review*, *79*, 1306–1374.

Connelly, C. (1999). Courts. In P. Duff & N. Hutton (Eds.), *Criminal justice in Scotland* (pp. 146–165). Aldershot, England: Dartmouth Publishing Co.

Cowan, C. L. (1984). The effects of death qualification on jurors' predisposition to convict and on the quality of deliberation. *Law and Human Behavior*, *8*, 53–80.

Devine, D. J., Clayton, L. D., Dunford, B. B., Seying, R., & Pryce, J. (2001). Jury decision making—45 years of empirical research on deliberating groups. *Psychology, Public Policy and Law*, *7*, 622–727.

Diamond, S. S. (1993). What jurors think: Expectations and reactions of citizens who serve as jurors. In R. Litan (Ed.), *Verdict: Assessing the civil jury* (pp. 282–305). Washington, DC: Brookings Institution.

Diamond, S. S., Vidmar, N. J., Rose, M., Ellis, L., & Murphy, B. (2003). Inside the jury room: Evaluating juror discussions during trial. *Judicature*, *87*, 54–58.

Duff, P. (1999). The Scottish criminal jury: A very peculiar institution. *Law and Contemporary Problems*, *62*, 173–201.

Elwork, A., Alfini, J. J., & Sales, B. D. (1982). Towards increasing the comprehensibility of jury instructions. *Judicature*, *65*, 432–443.

Findlay, M. (2001). Juror comprehension and complexity: Strategies to enhance understanding. *British Journal of Criminology*, *41*, 56–76.

Halverson, A. M., Hallahan, M., Hart, A. J., & Rosenthal, R. (1997). Reducing the biasing effects of judges' nonverbal behavior with simplified jury instruction. *Journal of Applied Psychology*, *82*, 590–598.

Hastie, R., Penrod, S. D., & Pennington, N. (1983). *Inside the jury.* Cambridge, MA: Harvard University Press.

Hoiberg, B. C., & Stires, L. K. (1973). The effect of several types of pretrial publicity on the guilt attributions of simulated jurors. *Journal of Applied Social Psychology*, *3*, 267–275.

Honess, T. M., Charman, E. A., & Levi, M. (2003). Factual and affective/evaluative recall of pretrial publicity: Their relative influence on juror reasoning and verdict in a simulated fraud trial. *Journal of Applied Social Psychology*, *33*, 1404–1416.

Hope, L., Memon, A., & McGeorge, P. (2004). Understanding pretrial publicity: Predecisional distortion of evidence by mock jurors. *Journal of Experimental Psychology: Applied*, *10*, 111–119.

Kalven, H. Jr., & Zeisel, H. (1966). *The American jury*. Boston: Little Brown.

Kerstholt, J. H., & Jackson, J. L. (1998). Judicial decision making: Order of evidence presentation and availability of background information. *Applied Cognitive Psychology*, *12*, 445–454.

Kramer, G. P., Kerr, N. L., & Carroll, J. S. (1990). Pretrial publicity, judicial remedies, and jury bias. *Law and Human Behavior*, *14*, 409–438.

Kruglanski, W. A., & Mayseless, O. (1990). Classic and current social comparison research: Expanding the perspective. *Psychological Bulletin*, *108*, 195–208.

Lloyd-Bostock, S., & Thomas, C. (1999). Decline of the 'little Parliament': Juries and jury reform in England and Wales. *Law and Contemporary Problems*, *62*, 7–40.

Lord Justice Auld (2001). *A Review of the Criminal Courts of England and Wales.* Retrieved from http://www.criminal-courts-review.org.uk

MacCoun, R. J., & Kerr, N. L. (1988). Asymmetric influence in mock jury deliberation: Jurors' bias for leniency. *Journal of Personality and Social Psychology*, *54*, 21–33.

Marder, N. S. (1987). Gender dynamics and jury deliberations. *Yale Law Journal*, *96*, 593–612.

Ogloff, J. R. P., & Vidmar, N. J. (1994). The impact of pretrial publicity on jurors—A study to compare the relative effects of television and print media in a child sex abuse case. *Law and Human Behavior*, *18*, 507–525.

Sandys, M., & Dillehay, R. C. (1995). First-ballot votes, predeliberation dispositions, and final verdicts in jury trials. *Law and Human Behavior*, *19*, 175–195.

Schein, E. H. (1969). *Process consultation Volume I: Its role in organization development.* New York: Addison-Wesley.

Scottish Executive National Statistics (2004). Criminal proceedings in Scottish Courts, 2002. *Statistical Bulletin*, CrJ/2004/1.

Severance, L. J., Greene, E., & Loftus, E. F. (1984). Toward criminal jury instructions that jurors can understand. *Journal of Criminal Law and Criminology*, *75*, 198–233.

Severance, L. J., & Loftus, E. F. (1982). Improving jurors' abilities to comprehend and apply criminal jury instructions. *Law and Society Review*, *17*, 153–197.

Skowronski, J. J., & Carlston, D. E. (1989). Negativity and extremity biases in impression formation: A review of explanations. *Psychological Bulletin*, *105*, 131–142.

Stasser, G., Kerr, N. L., & Bray, R. M (1982). The social psychology of jury deliberations: Structure, process, and product. In N. L. Kerr & R. M. Bray (Eds.), *The psychology of the courtroom* (pp. 221–256). New York: Academic Press.

Steblay, N. M., Besirevic, J., Fulero, S. M., & Jimenez-Lorente, B. (1999). The effects of pretrial publicity on juror verdicts: A meta-analytic review. *Law and Human Behavior*, *23*, 219–235.

Studebaker, C. A., & Penrod, S. D. (1997). Pretrial publicity: The media, the law and common sense. *Psychology, Public Policy & Law*, *3*, 428–460.

Stuurman v H.M. Advocate (1980). J.C. 111; 1980 S.L.T. 182.

Sue, S., Smith, R. E., & Gilbert, R. (1974). Biasing effects of pretrial publicity on judicial decisions. *Journal of Criminal Justice*, *2*, 163–172.

The Scottish Office (1994). *Juries and verdicts: Report on improving the delivery of justice in Scotland.* Edinburgh: Scottish Office.

Uleman, J. S., Newman, L. S., & Moskowitz, G. B. (1996). People as flexible interpreters: Evidence and issues from spontaneous trait inference. *Advances in Experimental Social Psychology*, *28*, 211–279.

van Overwalle, F., Drenth, T., & Marsman, G. (1999). Spontaneous trait inferences: Are they linked to the actor or to the action? *Personality and Social Psychology Bulletin*, *25*, 450–462.

Wigboldus, D. L. H., Dijksterhuis, A., & van Knippenberg, A. (2003). When stereotypes get in the way: Stereotypes obstruct stereotype-inconsistent trait inferences. *Journal of Personality and Social Psychology*, *84*, 470–484.

Wilcock, I. (1966). *The origins and development of the jury in Scotland.* Edinburgh: The Stair Society.

Ybarra, O., Schaberg, L. A., & Keiper, S. N. (1999). Favorable and unfavorable target expectancies and social information processing. *Journal of Personality and Social Psychology*, *77*, 698–709.

Young, W., Cameron, N., & Tinsley, Y. (1999). *Juries in criminal trials: A summary of the research findings.* Retrieved from http://www.law.com.govt.nz/documents/publications/PP37Vol2.pdf.

Yzerbyt, V. Y., & Leyens, J. P. (1991). Requesting information to form an impression: The impact of valence and confirmatory status. *Journal of Experimental Social Psychology*, *27*, 337–356.

4

Lay Participation in Legal Decision-Making in Australia and New Zealand: Jury Trials and Administrative Tribunals

JANE GOODMAN-DELAHUNTY and DAVID TAIT

INTRODUCTION

This chapter examines social psychological aspects of lay participation in criminal and civil cases in Australia and New Zealand, drawing on empirical research in those countries. The two major legal proceedings in those communities in which lay participation occurs are jury trials and a range of administrative tribunal hearings. The research review focuses on jury decision-making, grouped in three sections. First, the extent to which the research has supported the implementation of legal reforms to facilitate communication with jurors is examined. Second, studies of bias and prejudice in jury decision-making are presented, such as the role of preexisting attitudes, the impact of media publicity, and the influence of emotionally distressing or evocative evidence. Third, studies that examine the competence of lay participants to render legally appropriate decisions are reviewed, e.g., use of juries in cases involving complex evidence and expert testimony, methods of instructing jurors on the law and on deliberation processes to enhance their performance. Finally, future research directions are specified.

ORIGINS AND TYPES OF LAY PARTICIPATION IN LEGAL DECISION-MAKING IN AUSTRALIA AND NEW ZEALAND

All Australian states and territories and New Zealand allow for jury trials. This is not because Britain brought juries to Australia as part of the rule of its penal colonies; indeed it was not until 1833 that the Supreme Court of New South Wales first introduced juries of ordinary citizens to replace inquisitorial military panels in trials of serious offenses. Grand juries, common in the United States, were used for a short period in New South Wales in the 1850s, but their use in Australia was never widespread. Instead, other lay judicial decision makers, the magistracy, held committal hearings to decide if a case should proceed. Thus the term jury trial applies to the petit jury. Jury acts and procedures in each state and territory vary somewhat, but generally follow conventions in England and Wales rather than those prevalent in continental Europe or the United States. A detailed account of the history and procedures used in criminal jury trials in Australia was compiled by Chesterman (1999).

In addition to jury trials, a distinctive English import was the institution of the lay magistrates, who in panels of three, heard summary offenses and imposed sentences including imprisonment. This form of lay participation affected more people than jury service or jury trials, although recruitment into the ranks of the magistracy was primarily from the wealthier sectors of society. However, unlike England and Wales, Australian jurisdictions have largely abandoned this form of lay participation in judicial decision-making in favor of a professional corps of legally trained magistrates. In New Zealand, the term "magistrate" was abandoned altogether and the presiding officers in lower courts became known as district court judges.

On the contrary, several states made provisions for special purpose juries. Indeed, the first jury trial in Australia was a special purpose jury: in 1789, Anne Davis was questioned by a jury of 12 matrons to determine if she was pregnant (Waechter, 1997). Foreigners, or alien residents, could request a jury consisting half of overseas-born people, a jury *de medietate linguae* (section 85, South Australia Juries Act, 1927). This type of jury originated in medieval England to protect the rights of overseas merchants and Jews, and was used in the United States in cases involving Native American defendants. A judge rejected a request by a lawyer to apply this provision for Aboriginal clients, on the grounds that indigenous people were not aliens (*R. v Merridio and Nengavil*, 1841). One special purpose jury that survives in some states is the "coronial inquiry," invoked to investigate suspicious deaths, first conducted by 24 members in the first part of the nineteenth century (Waechter, 1997). A coronial inquiry has a similar function in some respects to a grand jury, to assess the sufficiency of evidence surrounding a death to warrant criminal prosecution. Coronial investigations may also include some inquisitorial aspects, and can be applied to systemic issues, such as a series of deaths resulting from lapses in workplace safety standards.

Many other English-speaking countries involve lay decision makers in some of the same areas. For instance, England and Wales have a Mental Health Tribunal; Ontario, Canada, has a Consent and Capacity Review Board. However, the Australians have developed the tribunal model quite extensively, particularly at the state level. Generally, all tribunals have an inquisitorial function, and some also have their own investigative capacity. There are three major types of tribunals in Australia: administrative, civil, and protective. Administrative tribunals review the decisions of government departments and all local councils, sometimes having power to overturn those decisions; otherwise to make recommendations. Civil tribunals resolve disputes between individuals, groups, or corporate bodies on topics such as housing, tenancy, small claims, and workplace discrimination. Protective tribunals make decisions in relation to vulnerable persons, such as those who lack decision-making capacity, need medical treatment for which they cannot give consent, or have a mental illness. At the Commonwealth level, federal tribunals such as the Commonwealth Administrative Appeals Tribunal, the Migration Review Tribunal, the Social Security Appeals Tribunal, and the Veterans Review Board are entirely administrative, because the Constitution reserves the exercise of judicial powers to courts in accord with the doctrine of separation of powers. The same constitutional restriction does not hold for the states, leading to a proliferation of lay tribunals, subsequently consolidated into super-tribunals, such as the Victorian Civil and Administrative Tribunal, and the New South Wales Administrative Decisions Tribunal. As a result, Australians are more likely to experience a tribunal than a court (Downes, 2004).

The expansive use of tribunals reflects in part the inability of existing courts to respond to new needs, in part the lack of any constitutional prohibition at the state level on such activity, but may also reflect recognition of the contribution that different professional groups can make to legal decision-making. Unlike jurors, most tribunal members are repeat players, who develop experience through regular tribunal participation. Most typically, one or three lay participants are appointed per tribunal panel, to serve on a full time or part-time basis, and the same individual continues to serve for a number of years. In general the lay participants are chosen because of their subject-matter expertise. Lawyers who have expertise in interpreting the law are often selected to chair tribunal panels, and encouraged to apply more informal rules of natural justice in tribunal proceedings rather than formal evidentiary rules. Psychologists and psychiatrists contribute to a range of protective and civil tribunals. For the most part, professional tribunal members continue their own practices while serving a few days a month on a tribunal panel.

While the form of many of these tribunals appears to be "lay" in practice, many of them resemble what in several European countries are considered "mixed panels" (or elsewhere in this volume, "mixed juries"). For example, the Victorian Civil and Administrative Tribunal is chaired by a Supreme Court Justice, who presides over some of the hearings and provides administrative oversight to the body. However, many tribunals include a "community member," someone with personal interests or knowledge of the particular topic, or someone who may represent consumer interests. In sum, the Australian tribunal system is best described as a hybrid of mixed panels, multidisciplinary decision-making, and popular participation. Tribunals are relevant to any consideration of juries because they demonstrate that although the "pure," citizen-only jury panel is retained for criminal cases, in many other areas of law, citizens are included alongside a range of professionals, and sometimes judges. Research that has examined disagreement among tribunal members revealed that most frequently, lay members would advocate for more stringent sanctions, the professionals for more interventions, and the legally trained tribunal members would undertake the role of resolving the differences on the panel (Ballenden, 1994).

Another innovative use of lay decision makers in the justice system can be found in the growing use of restorative justice and community conferencing. For example, both in Australia and New Zealand, court processes frequently involve respected indigenous elders, either sitting alongside a judicial officer, or replacing the formal court proceeding altogether. Unlike criminal jurors (but akin to sixteenth-century jurors) familiarity with the accused and their cultural background is highly valued. New Zealand makes extensive use of family group conferences both for juvenile and adult offenders.

As in England and Wales, criminal offenses are classified as nonindictable or summary offenses and indictable offenses. Summary offenses are relatively minor offenses, which, when committed by an adult, are dealt with by magistrates in the Local Courts without a jury, and usually cannot attract a penalty greater than a term of 2 years' imprisonment or a fine of AU$10,000. Indictable offenses as a group are more serious than summary offenses. When an indictable offense is committed by an adult, the case is usually tried by a judge and jury in a superior court, such as the Supreme Court of a state or territory, or an intermediate level District Court (Chesterman, 1999). Indictable offenses can result in penalties of greater than 1 or 2 years' imprisonment or AU$10,000. Only indictable offenses are eligible for trial by jury (section 80 of *The Constitution of the Commonwealth of Australia*, 1900), but in practice, most indictable offenses of a less serious nature are disposed of in the lower level courts. With the jurisdictional transfer of matters such as robbery to the lower courts, there are increasingly fewer jury eligible offenses. More serious indictable offenses usually include (1) homicide; (2) offenses punishable by penal servitude for life; (3) an offense arising under s. 61B of the Crimes Act 1900; (4) the offense of attempting to commit an offense arising under s. 61B of the Crimes Act; or (5) an indictable offense prescribed by the regulations as a serious indictable offense within the applicable criminal legislation. The relatively low incidence of jury trials is largely attributable to these practices. In four Australian jurisdictions, when a case reaches a higher level court, a defendant has the right to select a trial by judge alone (Chesterman, 1999), an option exercised most often when the offense is unpopular, e.g., pedophilia, or involves a particularly heinous crime. Plea bargaining and its more common cousins, charge negotiation or charge bargaining, reduce the frequency of jury trials by restricting the overall number of criminal trials. The potential exists for a jury trial in Commonwealth courts, but is almost never exercised. In general, use of the jury in Australia and New Zealand is declining. One scholar determined that juries are used in as few as 1 percent of all criminal cases, and only 4 percent of those cases in which a "not guilty" plea is entered (Chesterman, 1999).

In sum, in the criminal area, Australia uses lay decision makers for the most serious cases, meeting on a one-off basis in juries comprised only of lay members. However, in the civil area, lay decision makers are used widely in many areas of law and public policy, more rarely in civil juries than in the United States, but more frequently on multidisciplinary tribunal panels.

Jury Service in Criminal and Civil Trials

Information from jurors regarding their views of the experience is sparse. In New South Wales, approximately 140,000 people are summonsed annually of whom about 14,000 serve as jurors (Ryan, 2003). Approximately two thirds serve on generally shorter trials held in District Courts, and fewer (28 percent) in the more serious cases tried in the Supreme Court. Most individuals called to a jury in Australia and New Zealand serve on criminal trials, e.g., 95 percent of New South Wales jurors serve on criminal cases (Ryan, 2003). In 2003, in New South Wales, a survey of 2000 exiting jurors showed that most jurors (75 percent) served on trials lasting under 2 weeks. Results revealed moderate levels of satisfaction, i.e., 49 percent were satisfied that they had played their part in the legal process, and 38 percent felt positive about the overall experience (Ryan, 2003).

Civil juries are still in use in the State of Victoria, but are largely restricted to defamation cases in the five other jurisdictions in Australia, and in New Zealand. Reforms steadily eliminating the use of the civil jury have been implemented largely in the absence of empirical data (Horan, 2004). In Victoria, where juries serve on civil cases, a recent empirical study of 411 exiting jurors who served on 69 civil trials in 2001 revealed higher levels of juror satisfaction, i.e., 87 percent viewed the civil jury system favorably following their term of service, and 96 percent thought the experience was worthwhile (Horan, 2004). Most of the group (77 percent) was willing to serve again in 3 years if asked, once their period of exemption expired.

The Juries Act of 1981 in New Zealand restricts jury eligibility to persons aged 20–65 years. There is no upper age limit in any states or territories in Australia, although some concern has been expressed that the increasing length of jury trials restricts service to the unemployed (Dunford, 2004), such as retirees. Biases in the form of under-representation of indigenous persons and ethnic minorities on the jury roll have been reported both in Australia (Israel, 1998) and in New Zealand (Dunstan, Paulin, & Atkinson, 1995; New Zealand Law Commission, 2001). Indigenous persons are over-represented in trials as defendants and are rarely called or empanelled as jurors (Israel, 1998). This is partially attributable to under-representation of indigenous persons on the electoral roll, the limited geographical radius for jury districts from which jurors are summonsed, and practical problems with child care and transportation (New Zealand Law Commission, 2001).

Jury selection consists of two phases: (1) that which occurs outside of the courtroom, in selecting individuals from the jury roll or list of qualified, eligible jurors in the community; and (2) in-court selection, when a jury is formed for a particular case from individuals appearing on a panel. One striking feature is the brevity of jury selection in Australia and New Zealand. In New South Wales, for example, an average of only 30 min is devoted to jury selection (Weems, 1984). Prospective jurors may not be questioned (Horan, 2004). This provides little basis to challenge a juror for cause, so challenges for cause are rare. The prosecutor and the defense solicitor may exercise peremptory challenges (three to eight, depending on the jurisdiction). Peremptory challenges are reportedly exercised to remove all Aboriginal jurors or women from a jury being empanelled. However, procedures to reduce biases of this nature during the in-court jury selection phase have not been implemented (Israel, 1998).

In Australia, procedures to empanel alternate or reserve jurors are not always implemented. Concerns have been expressed that the system for alternate or reserve jurors needs amending to avoid inefficiencies: for example, when jurors drop out, mistrials are declared (North, 2000). For instance, about one-fifth of aborted trials are halted because a juror knows a trial participant. This could be avoided if better jury vetting procedures were implemented to identify inappropriate jurors, or to empanel alternate jurors so that one dropout did not require the termination of the trial. A study in New South Wales of criminal cases involving state offenses tried between 1997 and 2000 revealed that in this period 2268 jury cases reached a verdict, 273 were aborted and 230 were hung (Baker, Allan, & Weatherburn, 2002).

CURRENT JURY RESEARCH IN AUSTRALIA AND NEW ZEALAND

Experimental jury simulation studies have provided insight into the way in which juries in these communities may assess certain evidence, but these studies are most typically conducted using undergraduate samples as mock jurors, and the extent to which their views reflect those prevalent in the wider community is unknown. Thus, the information in this chapter is derived from a handful of court-approved jury surveys of actual jurors, and simulations or experimental studies using mock jurors.

Research by criminologists and sociologists has focused on archival data and survey methods, using real cases and actual trial participants, such as judges, lawyers, and jurors. By comparison, research by psychologists has tended to be more experimental in nature, using simulated trials and undergraduate students or citizens as research participants. All of these methods are useful, but each brings different strengths and weaknesses to the research process, as is highlighted by a review of studies on the impact of media coverage, or pretrial publicity on jury decisions (Steblay, Besirevic, Fulero, & Jimenez-Lorente, 1999) (see below).

COMMUNICATING WITH JURORS

Much recent, Australian and New Zealand jury research has examined the communication of information to jurors. This emphasis may reflect the fact that certain aspects of a jury trial, such as jury selection, are of short duration, whereas the trial length is increasing. The average length of criminal trials has increased by a factor of 10 in the past 50 years (1–2 days vs. 2 weeks or more) and the content has also become steadily more complex (Dunford, 2004). The longest civil trial in Victoria in 2001 lasted 20 days; the mean trial length was seven trial days (Horan, 2004). More than half the Victorian civil jurors who held negative views of their experience served on a trial in which deliberations continued for 2 days, whereas the average length of deliberation in other civil trials was one half-day (Horan, 2004). Some innovations aim to ease the burden on jurors, others aim to make the courtroom more hospitable to witnesses.

A recent survey of ex-jurors in New South Wales metropolitan and rural areas revealed that the greatest source of frustration and anxiety experienced by jurors arises from the legal process itself (Ryan, 2003). Similar data were forthcoming in New Zealand (Tinsley, 2001). These findings highlight the fact that scant attention has been paid to jurors as a source of information regarding ways to enhance their participation and improve their performance. While much information is directed at jurors, outside of returning a verdict, in general, jurors have limited opportunities to communicate reciprocally with the court, the parties, and the lawyers. A recent survey of practices among 131 judges presiding over criminal jury trials in New Zealand revealed that half the judges informed jurors at the commencement of the trial of their right to ask questions during the trial (Young, 2004). A survey of 136 Australian judges revealed that while 54% of the judges allowed jurors to ask questions, only 43% informed jurors of the procedure to follow to do so (Ogloff, Clough, Goodman-Delahunty, & Young, 2006).

Equally important is how the court communicates with jurors. Concern was expressed by an Australian High Court Justice that unless jury procedures were adapted to digital age, generation-Xers born between 1961 and 1981, who are accustomed to a high level of control over information technology, may find intolerable the often boring and tedious lengthy opening statements, expert testimony, and repetitive evidence summaries. He recommended that juries receive briefer directions, fewer descriptions of the evidence, simplified judicial directions on the law, and brisk proceedings designed to enliven their interest and participation (Kirby, 1998). Whether such recommendations will assist or impede jury understanding, without compromising the fairness of trial procedures remains to be tested.

Opening Remarks by Judges and Opening Statements by Lawyers

Most research on opening statements confirms that they are influential because they create a framework or schema in light of which jurors evaluate the evidence that follows (Pyszczynski & Wrightsman, 1981). A recent survey of judicial practices in New Zealand revealed that about half of the 131 respondents provided some discussion about the elements of the relevant substantive law in their opening remarks, but only 25 percent anticipated the defenses and included some directions to jurors on those defenses (Young, 2004). A survey of 136 Australian judges indicated that this practice was less common in Australia, i.e., approximately 24% of the judges included some instructions on elements of the relevant substantive law in the case in their opening remarks and directions to jurors, but only 7% anticipated defenses and provided directions on those (Ogloff et al., 2006).

A common practice in Australia and New Zealand is for the defense to reserve its opening statement until the case by the prosecution or plaintiff is closed, in light of the legal doctrine that unless the moving party establishes a case, the responding party need not present countervailing evidence. Some preliminary field research in New Zealand indicates that this causes problems for jurors and biases the case in favor of the prosecution. Postverdict interviews of jurors by Tinsley (2001) in 48 New Zealand criminal trials revealed that jurors found that the lack of an opening statement by the defense left them uncertain as to how to assess the evidence presented by the prosecution or the cross-examination of witnesses for the prosecution. The researchers concluded that jurors were actively processing the evidence from the outset, creating a story to account for the evidence. Although further research data are needed to confirm the operation of the story model (Byrne, 1995; Pennington & Hastie, 1992; Goodman-Delahunty, Bright, & Shanahan, 2004), a growing body of studies demonstrate that active processing by jurors of information needs to be taken into account in dealing with jurors (Diamond & Vidmar, 2003; Hannaford, Hans, & Munsterman, 2000). More recent research has confirmed predictions by Hastie and Pennington that emotional responses to evidence influence the content of stories constructed by jurors to account for the events in civil cases (Shanahan, 2006).

Some recent research in the US investigated the influence on mock jurors of different types of organizational strategies by plaintiffs and defense lawyers in their opening and closing statements (Spiecker & Worthington, 2003). A narrative or story type of organization was compared with a legal expository structure, and a third presentation format in which a narrative opening was paired with a legal expository closing statement (mixed strategy). In all cases, the opening statements were made by both parties at the start of the trial, before any witnesses testified. Results showed that plaintiffs benefited most from the mixed strategy, and defendants from either a mixed or a strictly legal expository strategy. The legal expository strategy most closely resembles judicial practices in Australia and New Zealand at the close of the trial in summing up the evidence and applying the judicial instructions on the law to the evidence to guide jurors in their deliberations.

Summing up by the Judge

At the close of the trial, in Australia and New Zealand, as is common practice in England, the judge orally summarizes the salient facts for the jury and outlines the way in which the relevant legal principles apply to those facts. After demonstration in a New Zealand study that a written summary of the law was desired by many jurors and that jurors who received a flowchart (two juries) used it systematically (Tinsley, 2001), many New Zealand judges incorporated these procedures in case summaries. A recent survey of judges showed that more than half provided a written copy of legal directions to the jury, 90 percent gave jurors a written list of the elements of the offense charged, and two thirds provided flowcharts or decision trees or a list of questions to guide jurors in their deliberations (Young, 2004). A similar survey administered to 136 Australian judges showed that juries in Australian courts were less likely to receive this assistance: 38% of the judges provided written copies of the legal directions, 51% provided a list of the elements of the offenses, and 27% provided juries with flow charts, decision trees, or a list of questions to assist them in reaching a verdict (Ogloff et al., 2006).

The Tradition of Orality: Examination and Cross-examination of Witnesses

One Australian High Court Justice noted that the orality of jury trials is at odds with the modern tendency for an increasing amount of evidence and argument to be presented in written form, often electronically (Gleeson, 1999). Although the emphasis in the adversarial system has been on the oral presentation of evidence, via questions from lawyers and answers by witnesses, some recent field research by Tinsley (2001) in New Zealand identified four particular problems that jurors experience with evidence presentations of this sort: (1) they have difficulty in concentrating on, absorbing, and recalling orally presented information, given few written or visual aids; (2) the slow pace of witness examinations creates a cumbersome and inefficient presentation of evidence, affecting their capacity to make reliable credibility assessments of witnesses; (3) evidence presented in a fragmented illogical (not temporal) sequence is more difficult to follow; and (4) the presentation of technical or specialized evidence, e.g., by expert witnesses, is hard to understand, often because it is ponderous and complicated.

Evaluating Witness Credibility

Several experimental studies examined various aspects of witness testimony that influences jurors' credibility assessments. For example, beliefs about witness behaviors, which could indicate a propensity to tell the truth or a lie, were assessed in a study in which responses of 119 mock jurors (aged 18–66 years) were compared with those of 67 police detectives and 41 prosecuting and defending lawyers. The study included 12 witness behaviors. All groups perceived nine of the behaviors to be indicators of inaccuracy, with the exception of overconfidence and recall of items not previously recalled (Potter & Brewer, 1999). The fact that research has not demonstrated that these very factors are reliable cues of deception or veracity (DePaulo, Lindsay, Malone, Muhlenbruck, Charlton, & Cooper, 2003; Sporer & Schwandt, in press) highlights the need to caution jurors against reliance on such factors in assessing witness credibility.

Other experimental research on how jurors reach decisions regarding inconsistent or contradictory evidence revealed that where the prosecution witness was inconsistent, jurors rated the witness less credible and found the defendant less likely to have committed the crime charged (Semmler & Brewer, 2002). Thus jurors' verdicts were sensitive to the controverted testimony. However, when mock jurors identified with the witness (belonged to the same in-group), witness group identity effects were powerful (Brewer, Hupfeld, & Schmidt, 2001). In an assault case, witnesses were in-group, out-group, or neutral to jurors, and the testimony was either consistent with earlier statements or contained contradictory information. Consistent testimony from an in-group or neutral witness was given more weight than consistent testimony from an out-group witness. Group identity influenced the judgments; the identity effect was weaker when the testimony was inconsistent and stronger when it was ambiguous (Brewer & Hupfeld, 2004). The authors concluded that the results supported the heuristic–systematic processing model (Chaiken, Liberman, & Eagly, 1989), because biased heuristic processing strategies were employed when evidence was unclear or ambiguous, manipulated in this instance through inconsistent testimonial statements.

Courts often encourage jurors to assess witness credibility by attending to their confidence level and to consistencies or inconsistencies in their statements. In a study that varied these factors in the context of an eyewitness identification case (Brewer & Burke, 2002) mock jurors heard an audiotape of an armed bank robbery trial, in which question and answers were given by witnesses responding to the prosecution and defense lawyers. Lack of witness confidence seldom produced a guilty verdict whether the testimony was consistent or inconsistent on direct and cross-examination. A significant main effect on verdict was obtained for witness confidence, but not for witness consistency; nor did the interaction between confidence and consistency attain statistical significance. These findings show that the impact of testimonial consistency is less persuasive than that of witness confidence. However, the researchers recommended additional studies on witness consistency–confidence interactions in which these variables are operationalized in other ways.

Procedural Innovations for Vulnerable Witnesses

A substantial body of research has demonstrated that child witnesses are ill equipped to cope in court (Cashmore, 2002). Analyses of court transcripts of sex abuse cases conducted in New Zealand in which the victims were children aged 5–13 years at the time of trial, showed that the questioning styles by lawyer for the defense were more complex, grammatically confusing, credibility-challenging, leading, and closed-ended than were questions by prosecution counsel. However, the children rarely sought clarification and often answered confusing, ambiguous questions. Many children (75 percent) changed one aspect or more of their testimony on cross-examination. Children showed a high rate of misunderstanding and compliance with the leading and closed-ended questions (Zajac, Gross, & Hayne, 2003).

As a consequence, procedural innovations to assist child witnesses in sex abuse trials have been implemented, such as alternatives to in-person appearances in court by the child (e.g., videolink testimony, video-depositions, and screens). However, evaluations of these innovations are needed (McAuliff & Kovera, 2002). Results of one study in Tasmania showed that the credibility of the child witness diminished with videolink versus either video-deposition or in-person testimony, and that defendants were more likely to be convicted when the child testified in court in person (Eaton, Ball, & O'Callaghan, 2001). In a study involving actual jurors in real trials in Western Australia in which closed circuit television (CCTV) was used, convictions were less likely when children testified in court with or without a screen (O'Grady, 1996). The researcher noted that conclusions from this field study were difficult to draw because a number of other legal procedural changes came into effect at the same time, and there were differences in age between children granted permission by the court to use CCTV and those who were not. Research to evaluate courts which routinely use these innovations is proceeding in New South Wales to explore how and why jurors may react more negatively to child witnesses who are "accommodated" by innovative and alternative testimonial procedures (Duda, 2004).

BIAS AND PREJUDICE IN LAY PARTICIPATION

Preexisting Attitudes

Some juror biases arise because of preexisting attitudes or cultural differences in the assessment of criminal conduct, and the explanations that laypersons generate to account for crime and delinquency. For instance, a survey of resident Australian adolescents aged 12–18 years revealed that participants with an individualistic cultural background (Australian Anglo-Celtic) rated juvenile criminal behaviors as less serious than did their counterparts with a collectivist cultural background (Asian ethnicity) (Tyson & Hubert, 2003). The perceived seriousness of the conduct increased with age among participants from a collectivist culture, but not among those from an individualist culture.

One experimental study of young Australians aged 18–30 years revealed some conservative attitudes to law and order, suggesting a possible link between attitudes and perceptions of the evidence in criminal cases. After expressing their views for or against the death penalty, 166 young Australians read one of four versions of a murder trial. Approximately 71 percent of the participants supported the death penalty, 29 percent were opposed. Young Australians who favored the death penalty were less likely to accept an insanity defense in a murder trial, recommended harsher sentences, found the conduct of the defendant more intentional, and rated the defendant as more dangerous in the future (ForsterLee, Horowitz, ForsterLee, King, & Ronlund, 1999). Capital punishment is not on the political agenda in Australia and New Zealand, and no executions have occurred since the 1960s.

The Influence of Gender Stereotypes in Sexual Offense Trials

Numerous researchers have examined reasons underlying low conviction rates in sexual assault cases (25 percent or less), despite the fact that much case attrition occurs before the trials commence (Esteal, 1998; Kelly, 2002). In some rural areas, acquittals are the norm (Henning, 2002). Stereotypical gender biases held by jurors regarding what constitutes genuine consent in heterosexual relationships was posited as a source of error in jury decisions in sexual offenses trials, as jurors tend to require evidence of physical injury and to think that women who have had past sexual contact with the accused lack credibility, and consequently seek corroborative evidence, although the law does not require this (Department of Women, 1996; Henning, 2002). Convictions are more common in cases in which there is physical or medical evidence of injury and where the perpetrator is a stranger (Henning, 2002).

Empirical researchers have demonstrated that rape myths influence responsibility allocations and verdict preferences (Dhaliwal & Goodman-Delahunty, 2004). Mock jurors who scored high on rape myth acceptance were more likely to acquit the perpetrator, to find the perpetrator more credible and the victim less credible, and the victim more responsible for the assault than mock jurors who scored low on rape myth acceptance. Older people and males were more prone to believe in rape stereotypes than were younger people and females. These findings demonstrate that commonly held preexisting beliefs about gender roles influence assessments of controverted evidence in acquaintance rape cases.

The Impact of Pretrial Publicity on Jury Decisions

Another potential source of bias in jury trials is media coverage of the issues. In response to concerns that the influence of the media on jury trials may be problematic, an investigation in New South Wales, Australia, on the influence of pretrial publicity on jurors in 41 criminal cases in the period 1997–2000 was conducted by a multidisciplinary research team (Chesterman, Chan, & Hampton, 2001). Data were collected using structured posttrial interviews of attorneys, judges, and jurors. As is often the case in field studies, methodological limitations generate data that may not be representative. For instance, constraints on the ability of the researchers to contact the ex-jurors resulted in a low and under representative juror response rate (36 percent, none in the age range 36–45 years). In some instances, the interviews were conducted as long as 3 years after the media coverage in issue. Nonetheless, the researchers adopted a model of bias that required jurors to recall the specific pretrial media coverage about the cases. The model of juror decision-making was not well informed by psychological research on the influence of pretrial publicity, which has shown powerful effects from generic as well as specific media publicity, although the strength of the effect of the latter is greater (Steblay et al., 1999). In this study, when a juror did not recall the pretrial publicity, the researchers concluded that no bias could occur. Approximately one third of the participants consciously recalled the publicity, and those jurors were spread across different cases. Psychological research indicates that considerable forgetting occurs in a time frame as lengthy as 3 years (Meeter, Murre, & Janssen, 2005), that much of the influence of pretrial publicity is unconscious, and that decision makers often lack insight into their own cognitions and decision-making.

Biasing media influence was assessed by asking legal experts (judges and lawyers familiar with the cases) if the ultimate jury verdicts were "safe" or if they controverted the thrust of the media coverage about the parties. Eight percent (3/41 cases) of the verdicts were regarded as influenced by publicity rather than the evidence. The researchers concluded that in general, the media influence was overrated and did not pose a problem in New South Wales, and that the process of deliberation overrode the biasing or negative influence of the media. This outcome suited courts reluctant to abort a trial after 6 or 7 weeks. However, the method and the psychological model of bias employed raise questions about the reliability of these conclusions.

Most courts realize that jurors cannot avoid exposure to all forms of pretrial publicity, and so instruct jurors to make sure, as best they can, that the media reports do not influence them (Chesterman et al., 2001). The study did produce extremely interesting findings about the extent to which jurors adhere to the court's directions. Notwithstanding social pressure to conform to the court's expectations, at least one juror admitted ignoring judicial instructions not to seek independent information from the media, and the interviews revealed that in 3 of the 41 trials, jurors used the Internet to seek information about the case during their term of jury service. As a consequence, in Queensland and New South Wales, legislation was introduced imposing up to 2-year jail sentences on jurors who conduct investigations on the Internet (Meade & Hart, 2005). The potential threat of access in-trial to websites and other media coverage has not received much attention from psychologists. These findings raise important psychological questions about the extent to which jurors are aware of and can consciously monitor and control their responses to media publicity.

Concerns about prejudicial media publicity are most acute in cases involving sensational or egregious facts. Some recent experimental research indicated that the subtle effects of sensation or emotionally evocative evidence (community reactions of shock and horror to victim death, support for her family, her good character references) can influence mock jurors' perceptions. The emotionally evocative evidence was more influential on mock jurors' recommended sentences than factual information contained in pretrial publicity about the accused (name, past convictions, bad character references, insinuation of guilt) (Douglas & ForsterLee, 2003). Significantly, harsher sentences were recommended in response to the first type of publicity than the second. A weakness of the study was that the victim-focused versus defendant-focused variables were confounded with the experimental manipulations, and there was no control group without publicity. Moreover, in real Australian cases, jurors do not participate in the sentencing phase of a criminal case. Thus, the findings cannot be accepted with certainty, and the study bears repeating with greater attention to conditions present in Australian courts.

Emotionally Distressing Evidence

Some experimental research has examined whether gruesome verbal or visual evidence biases mock juror decision-making and may prejudice a defendant's right to a fair trial. The potentially prejudicial effect of graphic violent evidence was tested in a mock juror study in which a 40-page written murder summary comprised the evidence (Thompson & Dennison, 2004). Graphically violent versions described the evidence in vivid details that evoked more visual images (e.g., "slashed" vs. "cut" and "blood droplets on the carpet" vs. "the evidence"). Standard jury instructions or instructions to use the evidence that was probative were provided. Defense-oriented jurors, identified by the Juror Bias Scale (Kassin & Wrightsman, 1983) reported significantly higher stress levels in response to the graphic evidence than did prosecution-oriented jurors, and they also applied a significantly more stringent threshold of proof (a mean of 97.8 percent certainty that the defendant committed the crime). The conviction rate and probability of commission were not higher in the response to the graphic evidence. Decisions in response to the variations in jury instructions were not statistically different.

These results neither support the Affect Infusion Model (Forgas, 1995) nor the action tendency model (Frijda, 2001) posited to account for previous findings of juror bias in response to graphic evidence.

In a between-subjects study, mock jurors reviewed a circumstantial criminal case in which the written evidence included gruesome versus neutral details of a homicide. Strength of the balance of the evidence was also varied, so that it was either legally sufficient or insufficient to sustain a conviction. The presence of gruesome written descriptions significantly increased the number of convictions, even when this evidence was presented in the context of a weak inculpatory case (Bright & Goodman-Delahunty, 2004). More guilty verdicts were returned in response to strong versus weak evidence (26.3 vs. 20 percent), but this difference was not statistically significant. There was a main effect of evidence strength on likelihood of guilt ratings (M=64.34 and 47.50 for strong and weak evidence conditions, respectively). However, no direct measure was taken of mock jurors' emotional states, so it cannot be seen whether the effects of the gruesome descriptions were mediated by emotional response.

In a follow-up study using realistic trial transcripts, both visual and verbal gruesome evidence was varied. Undergraduate students at the University of New South Wales read a 20-page trial transcript that included opening statements by counsel, excerpts from direct and cross-examination of key witnesses, a judicial summary of the evidence and judge's instructions on the law. The evidence included gruesome or nongruesome written details, accompanied by gruesome photographs, neutral photographs, or no photographs. In addition, an affect measure to assess mock jurors' anger, anxiety/fear, sadness, and disgust was administered before and after the presentation of the trial materials. The conviction rate when gruesome visual evidence was included was more than four times the conviction rate without photographic evidence. The highest conviction rate emerged when gruesome visual and gruesome written details were paired. Mock jurors exposed to the gruesome visual evidence rated the sufficiency of the prosecution evidence as significantly higher than mock jurors who saw no photographs. Mediational analyses confirmed that the gruesome photographs increased the level of anger aroused by the defendant's conduct, and also increased ratings of the sufficiency of the inculpatory evidence, which was awarded more weight (Bright & Goodman-Delahunty, in press). These studies tend to show that gruesome evidence, particularly when it is visual, may be prejudicial.

Finally, the effect of another emotion-inducing factor, victim impact statements, has received some attention. In a mock jury study, punishment assigned to male defendants in a heinous murder case was harsher than that assigned to female defendants when no impact statement was presented, but sentences for male and female defendants were in the same range when victim impact statements were included (ForsterLee, Fox, ForsterLee, & Ho, 2004). Note that Australian juries do not decide punishment, but the important point here is that in this study, impact statements evoked the emotional response of anger in mock jurors; it remains to be seen whether this heightened anger affects verdicts.

In another study, mock jurors were exposed to an audiotaped trial about the circumstances of an automobile accident in which witness testimony was either consistent or inconsistent and controverted. In addition, mock jurors received either a neutral or an emotionally evocative presentation of the evidence. The emotional information consisted of information about the impact of the accident on the driver and victim (explicit details of suffering) whereas the neutral version contained no such details. All mock jurors' levels of "sadness" were increased by listening to the case facts. The sad moods induced more careful detailed and analytic processing of the evidence and better recall of the evidence (Semmler & Brewer, 2002).

LAY JUROR COMPETENCE

In evaluating lay and mixed juries, the issue of lay juror competence is a strong theme, as witnessed in the recurring treatment of this issue in the national jury systems discussed in this volume. Issues of lay competence have centered on (1) the capacity to decide factually complex cases (e.g., involving expert witnesses and scientific evidence); (2) the capacity to decide legally complex issues (e.g., understand and apply judicial instructions in civil fraud cases); and more recently, (3) the capacity to reach reasoned decisions.

Juror Competence to Decide Factually Complex Cases

As elsewhere, the issue of jury competence to decide cases involving technical and scientific evidence has been vigorously debated in Australia and New Zealand. Jury detractors (such as large corporations) regard jurors as scientifically illiterate, irrational, and subject to emotional biases. Some believe that jury administration and court procedures can be enhanced to improve jury performance, e.g., by allowing jurors to take notes and ask questions, by providing transcripts of expert testimony (Gray & Thomson, 2001) and reports to the jury, and by adding visual aids on the technical issues (Young, 2003, 2004). Others believe judges must do more intensive screening of the junk science; and that jurors must be better trained in scientific literacy (Edmond & Mercer, 1999). Expert detractors (e.g., judges) favor "blue ribbon" panels, court-appointed experts, special masters, science courts, and more professional regulation of experts (Edmond & Mercer, 1997).

Numerous jurists have advocated eliminating jurors in cases involving complex evidence or issues. Recent criticism of a popular survey of judges' views on how jurors deal with expert evidence (Freckelton, Selby, & Reddy, 1999) demonstrated that the survey offers no direct insight into the way that jurors assess expert evidence (Edmond, 2005). Accordingly, before reforms are adopted, more careful empirical research is needed to examine sources of complexity, the relationship between complexity and comprehension of evidence, and the relationship between complex evidence and verdicts (Findlay, 2001). Researchers who have studied jury performance in complex cases conducted across Australia concluded that there was not as much disagreement between experts on the whole as is contended, i.e., the problems are not attributable to a battle of the experts or differences between two reasonable experts. Rather, the problems are systemic, within the adversarial system, e.g., lawyers who deliberately confuse the jurors (Wheate & Magnusson, 2002).

Researchers have noted that the choice as to whether a judge, other experts, or jurors should adjudicate between competing experts is political, and have classified defenders of the jury into four major camps: (1) moral/political defenders; (2) scientific competence defenders; (3) jury supporters conditional on enhanced judicial gate-keeping to screen out junk science; and (4) jury supporters conditional on improved scientific literacy. These schools of thought are most apparent in the current debate over jury performance in cases involving DNA evidence.

Many defendants fear that once DNA evidence is introduced at trial, a conviction is inevitable, as jurors often assume that once DNA evidence is found at the scene of a crime, the defendant is guilty (Wheate, 2002). DNA evidence is a crucial predictor of guilty verdicts in jury trials. A recent study of 200 sexual assault cases in Queensland revealed that jurors were 33 times more likely to convict in cases in which prosecutors introduced DNA evidence than in similar cases in which no DNA evidence was introduced (Briody, 2002). Jury understanding of DNA evidence is complicated by preconceptions and misconceptions about what criteria constitute a DNA "match" (Wheate, 2002). Difficulties jurors have in understanding the often-complex statistical information conveyed in expert testimony about DNA have also been documented (Magnusson & Selinger, 1990). A review of the Crimes (Forensic Procedures) Act 2000 in New South Wales included surveys administered to police prosecutors, prosecutors in the Office of the Director of Public Prosecutions and defense lawyers regarding DNA evidence obtained under the Act. Posttrial questionnaires were issued to trial counsel, judges, and jurors who served on selected trials. The final report confirmed that individual juries exposed to DNA evidence in the context of actual cases had difficulty understanding and applying its significance (Findlay & Grix, 2003). The Australian Law Reform Commission (2003) recommended that the judiciary take the lead in developing model jury directions to help judges and juries evaluate DNA evidence and the associated statistical calculations offered into evidence by expert witnesses (Australian Law Reform Commission, 2003). However, research on communicating accurate information to jurors is needed before the content of model jury instructions can be developed (Goodman-Delahunty & Newell, 2004).

Juror Competence to Decide Legally Complex Issues

In 1998, a study of 48 jury trials in New Zealand revealed that jurors reported high levels of satisfaction with the jury instructions they received, but in 35 of the 48 trials studied, some of the jurors misunderstood the law, especially elements of the offense charged (The New Zealand Law Commission, 2001). In recognition of difficulties juries experience following the court's directions on the law, researchers have explored ways to assist them: strategies or interventions to assist jurors, including providing them with flow charts, decision trees, and visual animations. One experimental study investigated the efficacy of a flow-chart supplement regarding instructions on self-defense in a murder trial, based on an actual case decided in South Australia. Jury comprehension of the oral instructions provided by the court orally (15 min) was assessed by the ability of jurors to reproduce the elements of self-defense. Verdicts were also assessed via accuracy of comprehension of instructions. The conviction rate increased as more elements of self-defense were understood correctly. The group without instructions was no worse than the group receiving standard trial directions from the court. Use of instruction plus a flowchart produced the most accurate performance, but the jurors had trouble applying the concepts to new scenarios (Semmler & Brewer, 2002).

Self-defense jury instructions are complex and are expected to be difficult for jurors to understand and apply. In another experimental study, jurors received one of three versions of self-defense instructions adapted from three different cases, each of which incorporated a different legal test (Thomson, 2002). Applying these different tests to the facts of a murder trial should have resulted in different verdict patterns in each group. However, no matter which instruction was provided, the percentage of jurors in each group who returned verdicts of murder, manslaughter, or not guilty verdicts was the same. Jurors appeared to assess the evidence in the same way, notwithstanding the legal standard provided. One interpretation of these results is that the jurors did not follow the legal instructions on self-defense.

In a simulated murder trial involving a self-defense plea, instructions were presented to mock jurors via audiotape (10 min) plus flowchart (13 min), or visual computer animations (10 min). Lay participants who were eligible jurors with low expertise performed significantly better with audio-visual judicial instructions than audiotapes alone. The standard instruction (judicial audiotape alone) produced very poor communication among community participants, like jury eligible citizens. With the animations, these participants showed a significant improvement in their comprehension, and reached the level of law students (Brewer, Harvey, & Semmler, 2004). However, the level of accuracy in their performance was still low, on average: 64 percent on a recognition task, 54 percent on recall, and 41 percent on applying the concept to a new task. A recent survey of New Zealand judges revealed that they had taken the advice to provide more assistance to juries on board: as many as two thirds of the judges routinely provided jurors with flowcharts, decision trees, or a list of questions to guide them in applying the legal directions to the evidence (Young, 2004).

Another type of jury instruction that has received attention from psychologists is limiting instructions, i.e., instructions to disregard evidence or limit its weight. In general, empirical studies that vary the presence and timing of these instructions show that the instructions are ineffective, or paradoxical, that the prejudicial effects are exacerbated (Devine, Clayton, Dunford, Seying, & Pryce, 2001; Edwards & Bryan, 1997; Kassin & Studebaker, 1998). Often, when gruesome photographic evidence is admitted in a criminal trial, jurors are instructed to be calm and rational in their examination of the photographs, and to use them only for certain purposes (Zammit, 1999). In an experimental study that examined the effects of gruesome evidence on the emotions and cognitions of 108 mock jurors, participants read a summary of a murder case, and received a limiting jury instruction either before or after exposure to gruesome or neutral photographs, or received no instruction. The gruesome photographs evoked significantly more sympathy for the victim and negativity toward the defendant than did neutral photographs, but did not bias the processing of the evidence or the verdict choice. The timing of the instructions had a significant effect on the conviction rate: preinstructed jurors were more biased in favor of the defendant and less inclined to convict (44 percent found the defendant guilty), whereas instructions at the close of trial were ineffectual (68 percent convicted). In line with other studies showing that jurors are active processors of the evidence throughout the trial, the results indicate that compliance with limiting instructions is facilitated by early presentation of that instruction in the evidence-processing task (Cush & Goodman-Delahunty, in press).

Notably, most of these mock juror studies have examined decision-making by individuals and not by groups. Deliberation is rarely included in the experimental research. Most inquiries into deliberations have come from posttrial interviews of actual jurors.

The Capacity of Juries to Reach Reasoned Decisions

The New Zealand study of postdeliberation interviews provided some insight into the method of deliberation used in the 48 trials (Tinsley, 2001). In 13 cases, an immediate straw poll was taken; in 13, there was a brief discussion of the issues followed by a straw poll; and in 21 cases, the jury had a full discussion of the evidence before voting. In all, 14 juries were unsystematic in their approach to reviewing the issue and evidence. The researchers concluded that the foreperson was crucial in establishing a structure for deliberations. Juror dominance occurred when the foreperson was weak, and in some cases, jurors felt intimidated by the dominant jurors in less structured deliberations. A follow-up survey of judicial practices in New Zealand shows that after learning of these studies, more judges are providing guidance to jurors on the selection of a foreperson. Forty percent of the judges now allow jurors more time to settle in, to get oriented, and become acquainted, acknowledging that if they do not, the information presented on the first day at the start of the trial is lost. All judges gave the jury some guidance on the role of a foreperson and on the process they might use to choose one. Over half the judges went further and provided some guidance on suitable candidates for the role of foreperson (Young, 2004).

One source of anxiety revealed by some exiting jurors is the interpersonal dynamics on the jury, such as bullying and capitulating jurors, jurors who bring past trauma to the deliberations, or jurors who refuse to participate (Ryan, 2003). Approximately 9 percent of the exiting jurors surveyed in New South Wales in 2003 reported jury dynamics as a source of anxiety (Ryan, 2003). This response was more common among jurors who served on longer trials, e.g., lasting 4 to 6 weeks, and from jurors who served on cases involving murder charges in which a guilty verdict was returned (Ryan, 2003). Jurors interviewed in the New Zealand study also reported that pressure to reach a decision came from other jurors, from the court, and from circumstances, e.g., the desire to finish the trial (Young, 2004). A common strategy was to focus on a dissenting juror, asking that person to explain their disagreement with the majority. Others reviewed the evidence until consensus was reached.

If one accepts that one of the functions of a jury is to serve as a check on unpopular laws, then it is acceptable for jurors to nullify, or fail to convict in the face of clear, cogent evidence of guilt, as occurred in Australia in the trials of those involved in the Eureka Stockade in 1854–1855, and in the early 1960s, in trials for censorship (Dunford, 2004). Thus, judge–jury agreement is not necessarily the best measure of jury competence. The safety or questionable nature of jury verdicts was assessed in a New Zealand study of 48 trials (Tinsley, 2001). Three of 48 cases produced questionable verdicts (not supported by judge, independent assessor, and researchers). Judge–jury agreement occurred in half of the cases. Where disagreement occurred, the jury view was often supported by the evidence, leading the researchers to caution that the view of the trial judge should not necessarily be adopted as the standard against which jury performance is assessed.

A growing body of evidence tends to show that hung juries tend to arise not so much because of one rogue or unreasonable juror, but because a reasoned basis for a dissenting opinion exists based in part on juror understanding of the evidence. For instance, in the recent documentary, "Secrets of the Jury Room," two volunteer juries observed the same live simulated trial evidence presented in a Sydney courtroom by real barristers, expert witnesses, and a judge. The two juries were committed to the process, despite knowledge that the case was simulated. Videotapes of the deliberations showed how the two juries reached different verdicts, both of which were reasoned and justifiable (Russel, 2004). This outcome further highlights the fact that standards to assess jury performance must be carefully assessed (Cassidy, 2000).

CONCLUSIONS

Various researchers have called for more evidence-based reforms before the jury in Australia is abandoned (Nolan, 2003). A recent survey of communications by Australian and New Zealand judges to juries revealed considerable variation in practices adopted by judges who preside over jury trials (Ogloff et al., 2006). Judges are increasingly willing to provide jurors with a framework and tools to guide their decision making. These include providing better introduction/training than a brief video, written aids to jurors, guidance on selection of a foreperson, and on ways to avoid deadlock in deliberations; access to transcripts of testimony, making deliberations more transparent, requiring juries to give reasons for their verdicts, and increasing use of special verdict forms. Many of these recommendations remain to be tested, and many findings do not clarify the best policy approach in response to the findings. For instance, if research confirms that jurors widely misuse evidence of past conduct, or propensity evidence, should the law be reformed or should this evidence be prohibited, or should we search for better means of enforcing limiting instructions?

New topics for researchers are also emerging. For instance, studies of juror experiences, and ways to minimize juror stress and discomfort are relatively new. Juror misconduct is also attracting attention, e.g., juror access to the Internet during deliberations and juror visits to the crime sites.

At times, it seems no amount of research is enough to warrant a reform. At other times, reforms that contradict the research trends are implemented. For example, despite the findings that reform of the jury decision rule from unanimous to majority verdict is not warranted by data on hung juries, political pressures militate and the majority decision rule has been adopted in some states. The recent support for an annual jury research and practice conference bringing together members of different disciplines in the Australian and New Zealand communities may assist in ensuring that academic researchers address topics of concern to the practitioner and that practitioners acquaint themselves with the research findings that bear on their questions.

REFERENCES

Australian Law Reform Commission (2003). Essentially yours: The protection of human genetic information. *Briefing note: Law enforcement* (Vol. 2, Part J). Sydney, Australia: Author.

Baker, J., Allan, A., & Weatherburn, D. (2002). Hung juries and aborted trials: An analysis of their prevalence, predictors and effects. *Crime and Justice Bulletin*, *66*, 1–19.

Ballenden, N. (1994). *The balance of power: An analysis of the Victorian Mental Health Review Board's decision making.* Unpublished Masters Thesis, Department of Criminology, University of Melbourne, Melbourne, Victoria.

Brewer, N., & Burke, A. (2002). Effects of testimonial inconsistencies and eyewitness confidence on mock-juror judgments. *Law and Human Behavior*, 26, 353–364.

Brewer, N., Harvey, S., & Semmler, C. (2004). Improving comprehension of jury instructions with audio-visual presentation. *Applied Cognitive Psychology*, 18, 765–776.

Brewer, N., & Hupfeld, R. M. (2004). Effects of testimonial inconsistencies and witness group identity on mock-juror judgments. *Journal of Applied Social Psychology*, *34*, 493–513.

Brewer, N., Hupfeld, R. M., & Schmidt, C. A. (2001). How evidence and social identity interact to affect jurors' judgments. *Law in Context*, 17, 130–147.

Bright, D. A., & Goodman-Delahunty, J. (2004). The influence of verbal gruesome evidence on mock juror verdicts. *Psychiatry, Psychology and Law*, *11*, 154–166.

Bright, D. A., & Goodman-Delahunty, J. (in press). Gruesome evidence and emotion: Anger, blame and jury decision making. *Law and Human Behavior*.

Briody, M. (2002). The effects of DNA evidence on sexual offence cases in court. *Current Issues in Criminal Justice*, *14*, 159–181.

Byrne, M. D. (1995). The convergence of explanatory coherence and the story model: A case study in juror decision. In J. D. Moore & J. F. Lehman (Eds.), *Proceedings of Seventeenth Annual Conference of the Cognitive Science Society* (pp. 539–543). Mahwah, NJ: Lawrence Erlbaum.

Cashmore, J. (2002). Innovative procedures for child witnesses. In H. Westcott, G. M. Davies, & R. Bull (Eds.), *Children's testimony: A handbook of psychological research and forensic practice* (pp. 203–218). Chichester: Wiley.

Cassidy, B. (2000). Juries speaking: Some thoughts on removing the 'gag' on jury deliberations. *Alternative Law Journal*, *25*, 9–13.

Chaiken, S., Liberman, A., & Eagly, A. H. (1989). Heuristic and systematic information processing within and beyond the persuasion context. In J. Uleman & J. Bargh (Eds.), *Unintended thought* (pp. 212–252). New York: Guilford.

Chesterman, M. (1999). Criminal trial juries in Australia: From penal colonies to a federal democracy. *Law and Contemporary Problems*, 62, 69–102.

Chesterman, M., Chan, J., & Hampton, S. (2001). *Managing prejudicial publicity: An empirical study of criminal jury trials in New South Wales.* Sydney, Australia: Justice Research Center, Law and Justice Foundation of New South Wales.

Cush, R., & Goodman-Delahunty, J. (in press). The influence of limiting instructions on processing and judgments of emotionally evocative evidence. *Psychiatry, Psychology and Law*.

Department of Women (1996). *Heroines of fortitude: The experiences of women in court as victims of sexual assault*. Sydney, Australia: New South Wales Department of Women.

DePaulo, B. M., Lindsay, J. J., Malone, B. E., Muhlenbruck, L., Charlton, K., & Cooper, H. (2003). Cues to deception. *Psychological Bulletin*, *129*, 74–112.

Devine, D. J., Clayton, L. D., Dunford, B. B., Seying, R., & Pryce, J. (2001). Jury decision making: 45 years of empirical research on deliberating groups. *Psychology, Public Policy, and Law*, *7*, 622–727.

Dhaliwal, S., & Goodman-Delahunty, J. (2004, November). *Mock-juror judgments of sexual assault: Effects of perpetrator intoxication and judicial instruction*. Poster presented at the Third Australasian Conference on Jury Research and Practice, Melbourne, Victoria.

Diamond, S. S., & Vidmar, N. J., (2003). Jury discussions during civil trials: Studying an Arizona innovation. *Arizona Law Review*, *45*, 1–81.

Douglas, K. M., & ForsterLee, L. (2003). Pre-trial publicity in Australian print media: Eliciting bias effects on juror decision making. *Australian Studies in Journalism*, 12, 104–128.

Downes, G. (2004). Tribunals in Australia: Their roles and responsibilities. *Australian Law Reform Commission Journal*. Retrieved December 6, 2004, from http://www.aat.gov.au/CorporatePublications/speeches/downes/tribunals.htm

Duda, N. (2004). *Child sexual assault specialist jurisdiction: Controlling cross-examination through judicial intervention*. Unpublished Masters Thesis, University of New South Wales, Sydney, Australia.

Dunford, Hon. J. (2004, July). *Looking forward: The direction of criminal law*. Keynote Address at the Criminal Law Conference, Sydney, Australia.

Dunstan, S., Paulin, J., & Atkinson, K. A. (1995). *Trial by peers? The composition of New Zealand juries*. Wellington, New Zealand: Department of Justice.

Eaton, T. E., Ball, P. J., & O'Callaghan, M. G. (2001). Child-witness and defendant credibility: Child evidence presentation mode and judicial instructions. *Journal of Applied Social Psychology*, *31*, 1845–1858.

Edmond, G. (2005). Judging surveys: Experts, empirical evidence and law reforms, *Federal Law Review*, *33*, 95–139.

Edmond, G., & Mercer, D. (1997). Scientific literacy and the jury: Reconsidering jury competence. *Public Understanding of Science*, *6*, 329–357.

Edmond, G., & Mercer, D. (1999). The politics of jury competence. In B. Martin (Ed.), *Technology and public participation* (pp. 85–112). Wollongong, Australia: University of Wollongong.

Edwards, K., & Bryan, T. S. (1997). Judgmental biases produced by instructions to disregard: The (paradoxical) case of emotional information. *Personality and Social Psychology Bulletin*, *23*, 849–864.

Esteal, P. (Ed.) (1998). *Balancing the scales: Rape, law reform and Australian culture*. Sydney, Australia: Federation Press.

Findlay, M. (2001). Juror comprehension and complexity: Strategies to enhance understanding. *British Journal of Criminology*, *41*, 56–76.

Findlay, M., & Grix, J. (2003). Challenging forensic evidence? Observations on the use of DNA in certain criminal trials. *Current Issues in Criminal Justice*, *14*, 283–298.

Forgas, J. P. (1995). Mood and judgment: The affect infusion model (AIM). *Psychological Bulletin*, *117*, 39–66.

ForsterLee, L., Fox, G. B., ForsterLee, R., & Ho, R. (2004). The effects of a victim impact statement and gender on juror information processing in a criminal trial: Does the punishment fit the crime? *Australian Psychologist*, *39*, 57–67.

ForsterLee, L., Horowitz, I. A., ForsterLee, R., King, K., & Ronlund, L. (1999). Death penalty attitudes and juror decisions in Australia. *Australian Psychologist*, *24*, 64–69.

Freckelton, I., Selby, H., & Reddy, P. (1999). *Australian judicial perspectives on expert evidence: An empirical study.* Carlton, Australia: Australian Institute of Judicial Administration.

Frijda, N. H. (2001). The laws of emotion. In W. Parrot (Ed.), *Emotions in social psychology* (pp. 57–59). Philadelphia: Psychology Press.

Gleeson, M. (1999). The state of the judicature. *Law Institute Journal*, *73*, 67–74.

Goodman-Delahunty, J., & Newell, B. (2004). One in how many trillion? *Australasian Scientist*, *25*, 14–17.

Goodman-Delahunty, J., Bright, D. A., & Shanahan, C., (2004). *Jury work: Deliberation and decision making*. Professional Development Seminar for the Australian Psychological Society, New South Wales College of Forensic Psychologists, Sydney, New South Wales, Australia.

Gray, S., & Thomson, D. M. (2001, November). *Enhancing juror decision-making through provision of transcripts*. Presentation at the 21st Psychiatry, Psychology, and Law Annual Conference, Melbourne, Australia.

Hannaford, P. L., Hans, V. P., & Munsterman, G. T. (2000). Permitting jury discussions during trial: Impact of the Arizona reform. *Law and Human Behavior*, *24*, 359–382.

Henning, T. (2002). Beyond "beyond reasonable doubt": Wrong decisions in sexual offences trials. *Australian Journal of Law and Society*, *15*, 1–41.

Horan, J. (2004). *The civil jury system: An empirical study*. Unpublished Doctoral Dissertation, University of Melbourne School of Law, Victoria, Australia.

Israel, M. (1998). Ethnic bias in jury selection in Australia and New Zealand. *International Journal of Sociology of Law*, *26*, 35–54.

Kassin, S. M., & Studebaker, C. A. (1998). Instructions to disregard and the jury: Curative and paradoxical effects. In J. Golding & C. MacLeod (Eds.), *Intentional forgetting: Interdisciplinary approaches* (pp. 413–434). Hillsdale, NJ: Lawrence Erlbaum.

Kassin, S. M., & Wrightsman, L. S. (1983). The construction and validation of a juror bias scale. *Journal of Research in Personality*, *17*, 423–442.

Kelly, E. (2002). *A war of attrition: Recent research on rape.* Retrieved February 7, 2005, from http://www.cwasu.org/warattrition1.htm

Kirby, Hon. M. (1998, July). *Speaking to the modern jury: New challenges for judges and advocates.* Paper presented at the Worldwide Advocacy Conference, Inns of Court School of Law, London, England.

Magnusson, E., & Selinger, B. (1990). Jury comprehension of complex scientific evidence: The inference chart concept. *Criminal Law Journal*, *14*, 389–400.

McAuliff, B., & Kovera, M. B. (2002). The status of evidentiary and procedural innovations in child abuse proceedings. In B. L. Bottoms, M. B. Kovera, & B. D. McAuliff (Eds.), *Children, social science and the law* (pp. 412–445). Cambridge: Cambridge University Press.

Meade, K., & Hart, C. (2005, January 26). Judge demands trial web blackout. *The Australian*, 3.

Meeter, M., Murre, J. M. J., & Janssen, S. M. J. (2005). Remembering the news: A forgetting study with 14,000 participants. *Memory and Cognition*, *33*(5), 793–810.

New Zealand Law Commission (1999). *Juries in criminal trials, Part 2, Volume 2: A summary of research findings.* Wellington, New Zealand: Author.
New Zealand Law Commission (2001). *Juries in criminal trials,* Report 69. Wellington, New Zealand: Author.
Nolan, M. A. (2003). More creativity, less criticism: An "evidence based" approach to jury reform. *Legaldate*, 15, *3.*
North, J. (2000). The jury system. *Law Society Journal*, *38*, 5.
Ogloff, J. R. P., Clough, J., Goodman-Delahunty, J., & Young, W. (2006). *The jury project: Stage 1 – A survey of Australian and New Zealand judges*. Melbourne, Australia: Australian Institute of Judicial Administration Incorporated.
O'Grady, C. (1996). *Child witnesses and jury trials.* Perth: Western Australia Ministry of Justice.
Pennington , N., & Hastie, R. (1992). Explaining the evidence: Tests of the story model for juror decision making. *Journal of Personality and Social Psychology*, *62*, 189–206.
Potter, R., & Brewer, N. (1999). Perceptions of witness behavior-accuracy relationships held by police, lawyers and jurors. *Psychiatry, Psychology and Law*, *6*, 97–103.
Pyszczynski, T., & Wrightsman, L. S. (1981). The effects of opening statements on mock jurors' verdicts in a simulated criminal trial. *Journal of Applied Social Psychology*, *11*, 301–313.
R. v. Merridio and Nengavil (1841). Supreme Court of New South Wales, Burton J., 14 May.
R. v. Zammit (1999). NSWCCA, 65 (28 May 1999).
Russel, J. (Executive Producer) (2004, July 15). *Secrets of the jury room.* [Television broadcast.] Sydney, Australia: Special Broadcasting Service. Retrieved January 23, 2005, from http://www.secretsofthejuryroom.com
Ryan, S. (2003, October). *Jury debriefing and stress*. Paper presented at the Second Annual Jury Research Conference, Sydney, Australia.
Semmler, C., & Brewer, N. (2002). Using a flow-chart to improve comprehension of jury instructions. *Psychiatry, Psychology and Law, 9*, 262–270.
Shanahan, C. (2006). *Psychological processes underlying juror decision making in tort law.* Unpublished doctoral dissertation. School of Psychology, University of New South Wales, Sydney, Australia.
Spiecker, S. C., & Worthington, D. L. (2003). The influence of opening statements/Closing argument organizational strategy on juror verdict and damage awards. *Law and Human Behavior*, *27*, 437–456.
Sporer, S. L., & Schwandt, B. (in press). Paraverbal correlates of deception: A meta-analysis. *Applied Cognitive Psychology*.
Steblay, N. M., Besirevic, J., Fulero, S. M., & Jimenez-Lorente, B. (1999). The effect of pretrial publicity on juror verdicts: A meta-analytic review. *Law and Human Behavior*, *23*, 219–235.
The Constitution of the Commonwealth of Australia (1900). Section 80.
The New Zealand Law Commission. (2001). *Juries in criminal trials*. Wellington, New Zealand: The New Zealand Law Commission.
Thompson, C. M., & Dennison, S. (2004). Graphic evidence of violence: The impact on juror decision-making, the influence of judicial instructions and the effect of juror biases. *Psychiatry, Psychology and Law*, *11*, 323–337.
Thomson, D. (2002). *A comparison of jury understanding of self-defence instructions in Viro, McManus and Zekevic*. Presentation at the Australian Jury Research Conference, Melbourne, Victoria.

Tinsley, Y. (2001). Juror decision-making: A look inside the jury room. In R. Tarling (Ed.), *Selected proceedings: Papers from the British Society of Criminology Conference, Leicester, 2000* (Vol. 4). Retrieved December 6, 2004, from http://www.britsoc-crim.org/bccsp/vol04/Vol04.htm

Tyson, G. J., & Hubert, C. J. (2003). Cultural differences in adolescents' perceptions of the seriousness of delinquent behaviours. *Psychiatry, Psychology and Law, 10*, 316–328.

Waechter, R. (1997). Jury service in Victoria. *Law Reform Commission final report* (Vol. 3, pp. 1–73). Victoria, Australia: Parliament.

Weems, P. R. (1984). A comparison of jury selection procedures for criminal trials in New South Wales and California. *Sydney Law Review, 10*, 330–347.

Wheate, R. (2002). Expert evidence: Law, practice, procedure and advocacy, *Sydney University Law Review, 4*, 24.

Wheate, R., & Magnusson, E. A. (2002). *Experts, admissibility practices and jury responses*. Presentation at the First National Jury Research and Practice Conference, Melbourne, Australia.

Young, W. (2003). Summing up to juries in criminal cases—What jury research says about current rules and practice. *Criminal Law Review, October*, 665–689.

Young. W. (2004, November). *Judges' assistance to jurors*. Presentation at the Third Australasian Jury Conference, Melbourne, Victoria, Australia.

Zajac, R., Gross, J., & Hayne, H. (2003). Asked and answered: Questioning children in the courtroom. *Psychiatry, Psychology and Law, 10*, 199–209.

5

Psychological Perspectives on Spanish and Russian Juries

ANA M. MARTÍN and MARTIN F. KAPLAN

Existing jury laws were approved in Russia in 1993[1] and in Spain in 1995.[2] Both laws provide for the reestablishment of a jury composed exclusively of laypersons. Previous Russian lay juries, introduced in 1864 by Alexander II, were abolished by the Bolsheviks in 1917. Soviet "mixed courts" (Thaman, 2001, p. 325) were in force until the constitutional reform initiated by Gorbachev during the *perestroika* culminated in the Russian jury law. But these mixed courts cannot be considered juries to the extent that they were tribunals composed of a judge and two "people's assessors" who, although laypersons, were elected and controlled by the communist party (Thaman, 1999).

In Spain, the jury law was restored as part of the democratization process that followed the end of Franco's dictatorship. Spanish lay juries were first established by Napoleon in 1808 during occupation and periodically appeared and disappeared, coinciding with more liberal or more conservative political systems, until after the Spanish Civil War when Franco suspended juries, among other citizens' rights. The Spanish law of jury was one of the last acts of the socialist party, Partido Socialista Obrero Español (PSOE), which had led the three consecutive governments from 1982 to 1996, until the right-wing Partido Popular (PP) took the baton in 1996. Article 125 of Spanish Constitution of 1978 provided for citizen participation in the administration of justice via the jury institution, but the law to govern this participation took 17 years to become a reality, for many different reasons (see Kaplan & Martín, 1999a).

Thus, both juries' lay systems, composed exclusively of laypersons, deviate from the general trend in Europe toward panels of professional judges or mixed juries, which decide on facts, law, verdict, and penalty.

In Spain, although mixed juries have never been in force, the German and French systems of mixed panels were used as models in some of the many drafts considered before the final version of the jury law was approved (Cuesta-Martínez, 1992), and even today the mixed system is favored by many professional judges, academics, and by the PP ("El jurado pasa la revália," 2002;

García, de la Fuente, & de la Fuente, 2002; Gómez-Colomer, 1999). The electoral program of this party for the 2000 elections proposed changing to a mixed system. But once in the government, the PP compromised with the PSOE over reforming the justice system, and agreed to keep the lay jury for the moment, with the option of instituting mixed juries if future evidence warrants the change (García et al., 2002). Conversion to a mixed jury is not likely in the near future now that the PSOE is again in power after the elections of March 14, 2004.

The purpose of this paper is to analyze the issues raised by the Spanish jury system, and given the similarities stressed by Thaman (1999, 2000, 2001), by the Russian system as well. The issues lend themselves well to analysis from a social psychological perspective, and at the same time, the perspective can provide suggestions for further empirical research. To reach this goal, we will first describe the core characteristics of these jury systems.

CHARACTERISTICS OF SPANISH AND RUSSIAN JURIES

Spanish and Russian juries, although composed exclusively of lay jurors, share special features that differentiate them from the classical Anglo-Saxon jury. These features are related mainly to jurisdiction, composition, the decision rule, the form and content of the required judgments, and the need to give rationales for verdict.

Jurisdiction, Composition, and Decision Rule

In relation to jurisdiction, Russian juries try all cases in "regional or territorial courts," which are second-level courts of original jurisdiction. These cases include mainly capital crimes of aggravated murder and rape. When charged with any of these cases, defendants can choose among three-judge panel, a traditional court of lay assessors (mixed jury) or a lay jury.

In Spain, juries act as the "Audiencia provincial," provincial courts that are also second-level courts of original jurisdiction, and in which sentences to prison are between 5 and 20 years (there is no life sentence or death penalty in Spain). Note that cases involving sentences under 5 years are tried by judges only, hence the designation "second level" for trial courts potentially involving juries. But juries do not try all cases between these sentence limits, being restricted by law to particular types of offenses. According to the Consejo General del Poder Judicial (General Council of Judicial Power, herein CGPJ), offenses most commonly tried by Spanish juries since 1996 are crimes against life (57. 6 percent), burglary (19.5 percent), failure to help (8.4 percent), threats (6.7 percent), and offenses related to administration (5.1 percent) (CGPJ, 1998, 1999). Appeals and other offenses carrying this range of sentence are tried by a panel of three professional judges, and less serious offenses are tried by one judge. Contrary to the Anglo-Saxon system, Spanish law grants the citizen's right to participate in the administration of justice as jurors, but not the citizens' right to be tried by a jury. Thus, the law determines which offenses are tried by a single judge, a panel of judges, or a jury, and the defendant has no option with regard to the triers of fact.

Russian juries are composed of 12 members whereas Spanish juries include nine. In both cases there are two alternates. Potential jurors are randomly selected from voter registration lists by public officers. In Spain, the minimum age for jurors is 18, whereas in Russia it is 25. Certain public officials, as well as officials in the legal and law enforcement professions, are automatically exempt, and discretionary excuse from service can be granted on the basis of age, hardship, or illness. Once exemptions have been granted, at least 20 (Russia) or 36 (Spain) prospective jurors are called to court on the day of trial. Then, the trial judge questions each juror's ability to be fair and impartial in the case. The law in both countries allows both the prosecution and the defense to exercise challenges either for cause, or peremptorily, for a limited number of prospective jurors (two for each side in Russia, and four for each side in Spain).

In Spain, juries vote on not only the verdict, but on several questions that are proposed by the court (see the following section). Seven of the nine votes are required to consider any proposition as "proved" against the defendant, whereas only five votes are needed to accept any proposition as in favor of the accused. After all the propositions are decided, the jury takes a vote on the overall verdict. Verdicts of "guilt" require seven votes, and "not guilty" verdicts or recommendation of suspension of sentence and clemency require only five. In Russia, although propositions are not voted upon separately, the decision rule is even more complex. The jury decides under the unanimity rule during the first three hours and then, if a unanimous verdict is not reached, a "guilty" decision requires only 7 of the 12 votes, and a "not guilty" or "not proved" decision requires six votes.

Jury Judgments and the Requirement to Provide Justification

In both Russian and Spanish law, juries are asked to give, not only a general verdict of "guilty" or "not guilty," but answers to a "questions list" of propositions about the case, as in the French model (Planchadell-Gargallo, 1999). The purpose of the questions list is to provide trial judges with a sequence of facts that allow them to justify the sentence for future appeals. This justification requirement follows from the legal principle in both countries that verdicts and sentences must have a factual foundation. Relying on the jury's answers, the task of the trial judge is to legally qualify the facts proved by the jury and to impose a sentence afterward. However, the nature of the questions may also unintentionally enable jury nullification, as will be discussed below.

In Spain, the questions list is specifically called "el objeto del veredicto" (the object of the verdict). It is elaborated by the trial judge and includes a list of propositions, each explicitly identified as "favorable" or as "unfavorable" to the defendant. The members of the jury have to deliberate about each, to decide whether it has been proved or not proved during the trial, and to vote on each following a different rule, as was described above. These propositions refer to the facts alleged by the parties during the trial, and include the elements of the crime charged, the conditions which exclude guilt, and the legal factors that allow aggravating or mitigating defendant's criminal responsibility. If the jury finds for guilt, it is also asked whether it wants to recommend a suspended sentence or a complete or a partial amnesty for the offense.

The object of verdict submitted by the trial judge must be approved by defense and prosecution in that their objections to the questionnaire could sustain future appeals to superior courts. A basic problem for the questionnaire elaboration is that both the Spanish and the Russian jury are supposed to decide only about facts, keeping questions of law for the trial judge. But to separate law from facts is not a simple matter, as has been shown in the debate about what type of jury (pure vs. mixed) fits better with the Spanish Constitution (Gisbert, 1990).

In Russia, the questions list is even more restrictive and queries are aimed to determine whether during the trial it has been proved the criminal acts, the identity of the perpetrator, and his/her guiltiness. This separation among the three types of questions allows jury nullification. Judges are not able to ask questions involving any legal consideration, including those related to *mens rea*, being exclusively limited to the facts of the case. However, juries are instructed in the substantive law as if they were required to apply it. If the trial judge considers that the answers to the questions are incomplete or contradictory, he or she returns the questions list to the jury to continue the deliberation.

Spanish trial judges have been asked to avoid the use of legal terms, and it seems that they have been quite successful when questions are related to guilt, but not when questions refer to mitigating and aggravating circumstances (Thaman, 2001). The latter questions are often posed in legal terms directly, or by inserting definitions in legal language of the legal meaning of mitigation and aggravation. Thaman (2001) cites as examples propositions as to whether an act has been "committed intentionally, recklessly, with gross negligence, with simple negligence or accidentally"(p. 340). In Spain, there is a "strict [...] 'anti-nullification' approach" (Thaman, 2001, p. 341) to the extent that if there is any contradiction between the answers given to questions related to facts to be proved and guiltiness of the perpetrator, it is considered a "defect" in the answers to the questions list and the trial judge returns it to the jury to "correct" it. If the judge returns to the jury three times to correct verdict defects and they fail to do so, s/he may dissolve the jury and retry the case before a new jury. This control over juries by judges contrasts with the fact that in the questions list juries can be asked about complete excusal of penal responsibility (e.g., owing to diminished capacity or temporary insanity) as questions of facts, allowing an acquittal when a jury is confused by the task, as in the Otegui case[3] (Thaman, 2001).

Besides separately voting on each proposition of the questions list, the Spanish jury is also asked to give a succinct rationale for their answers, indicating the evidence for finding a particular proposition proved or not proved. This requirement is very important in that cases have been reversed by Superior Court of Justice based on the insufficiency of the rationales given by the jury (CGPJ, 1998), again as in the Otegui case.[4]

To facilitate the difficult tasks of answering each question on the list and providing a rationale for each answer, Spanish juries are instructed by trial judges before deliberation with respect to (1) the jury's function; (2) the content of the questions list; (3) the nature of the facts under discussion, including those that determine the circumstances constituting the crime(s) charged, and those that refer to allegation of exclusion and modification of guilt; (4) the rules of deliberation and voting; (5) the form of their final verdict; (6) not considering any evidence declared inadmissible at trial; and (7) resolving doubts in favor of the defendant. On the other hand, Russian judges are required to summarize the evidence and the position of the parties and to instruct the jury on the substantive law as it applies to the acts imputed to the defendant, although as has already been said, juries are not allowed to apply the law to the facts.

QUESTIONS FORMULATED AND/OR ADDRESSED BY PSYCHOLOGICAL RESEARCH

Looking at the Spanish and Russian juries broadly, the key issues that seem to be both appropriate and interesting for social psychology relate to the nature of the questions posed to the jury, the common requirement for sentence justification, and the power conferred to the trial judge during and after the trial. In addition to the consequences of these central characteristics, public and professional perceptions are also relevant for our purposes. Other aspects of these systems, such as jurisdiction, composition, size, and decision rule, although important, have been extensively studied in the United States and in Spain (for works with Spanish mock juries on these issues see e.g., Arce, Fariña, Vila, & Novo, 1998; Arce, Novo, & Real, 1999; De Paúl, 1996; Sáinz & Sáinz, 1990), and their effects are well known. Thus, our discussion will center on the rather unique but characteristic aspects of the Spanish and Russian jury.

Public and Professional Perceptions of the Spanish Jury

Evidence about public and professional perceptions of juries is readily available for Spain, but not for Russia. Perles, Canto, and San Martín (2000) concluded that there were no definitive attitudes for or against the jury institution in May 1999, but earlier polls by the Centro de Investigaciones Sociológicas (Center of Sociological Research, herein CIS), showed that 63 percent of Spanish respondents favored juries but, on the other hand, 60 percent said that they would not want to serve on a jury (CIS, 1996). Nearly 60 percent thought that judges' decisions are fairer owing to their training and experience and, not surprisingly, preferred to be tried by judges (CIS, 1997).

Spanish legal professionals, however, think differently about juries. According to reports:

1. Academics think that juries have difficulty: (a) understanding trial judges' instructions and the questions list, (b) voting on each proposition in the questions list, (c) deliberating, and (d) justifying the verdict (Gómez-Colomer, 1999).
2. Professional judges worry that if questions are not precise enough, the Superior Court may find "lack of motivation" (reasoning for decisions) for sentences and reverse many of them, and that trial judges feel that they must lecture lay jurors as though they were first year college students. Professionals suggest that mixed juries would solve most of these problems (El jurado pasa la reválida, 2002).

3. Superior Courts consider that juries deliberate and answer many questions (e.g., in the Otegui case there were 95) that "imply an exercise of reflection and discussion more thorough than those technical tribunals go on most of the times" (El jurado pasa la reválida, 2002).
4. Reports by the CGPJ point out that professional judges reject the jury due to their belief that the jury law has many technical faults (CGPJ, 1998, 1999). Some of these faults reflect the complexity and ambiguity of the propositions included in the questions list, as well as lack of clear separation between favorable and unfavorable facts. The most difficult questions are those related to the intention to kill, mitigating circumstances and different degrees of criminal responsibility (García et al., 2002).

Generally, comments by the public and legal professionals find severe fault with lay jurors, much the same as documented in other countries discussed in this volume. However, difficulties associated with the questions list are also prevalent among legal professionals and are supported by social psychological research cited below.

The Questions List

The question list contains propositions with dichotomous (yes/no) answers. In preparing this questionnaire, which is specific for each trial case, judges should avoid misleading questions, and consider the possibility of acquiescence and social desirability biases. The logical structure of the questionnaire is also very important. Flowcharts can be useful to ensure that alternative answers are feasible and accessible, that it is possible to reverse the flow of reasoning, and that there are no dead-ends (Rechea, 1989). But even if all these structural precautions are taken, it is still possible that the content and very existence of detailed questioning can impact the juries' reasoning and hence, verdicts.

In looking at potential biasing effects of question list composition, only one empirical study of Spanish mock juries is available. De la Fuente, de la Fuente, and García (2003; see also De la Fuente, García, & de la Fuente, 2003) presented two homicide cases differing in the strength of the evidence (pro-prosecution and ambiguous) to jurors along with questions lists. The authors found, as in previous research with traditional lay juries, that guilty verdicts were higher in prosecution-biased mock juries, and lower in defendant-biased mock juries, both before and after deliberation. Pretrial bias was independently assessed by a Spanish translation of the Juror Bias Scale (Kassin & Wrightsman, 1983). What is important is the fact that juror bias was also reflected in the answers to individual questions in the list, specifically to questions related to "intention to murder" in the pro-prosecution case, and "propositions which are difficult to answer on the basis of the evidence presented in the trial" in the ambiguous evidence case (p. 207). No systematic classification of the items was made, and therefore one cannot reach a conclusion about the effect of a questions list on verdict, but it can be seen that answers to the questions list can themselves be biased by preexisting attitudes, and therefore the requirement of responding to judicially imposed questions about specific aspects of the case is not necessarily a safeguard against the intrusion of biases. At this writing, there is no study directly assessing the effect of having a list, or of its contents, on juror decisions. Conclusions may be drawn, however, from three related research domains: verdict-driven versus evidence-driven style of deliberation, penalty phase in capital cases, and heuristic and systematic processing.

Verdict-Driven versus Evidence-Driven Deliberation Style The use of a questions list instead of asking for a simple verdict could enhance an evidence-driven, as opposed to a verdict-driven style of deliberation (Hastie, Penrod, & Pennington, 1983). The latter is characterized by (1) deliberation which starts with a public ballot; (2) individual jurors advocating only one verdict position at a time; (3) citing evidence only in support of a specific verdict position; and (4) deliberation which contains many statements of verdict preferences and frequent polling. On the other hand, in evidence-driven deliberation: (1) the first public ballot occurs late in deliberation; (2) jurors may cite testimony or instructions with reference to alternative verdicts or (3) the evidence is reviewed without any reference to the verdict categories; and (4) deliberation focuses on reviewing the evidence rather than defending preferred verdicts. Evidence-driven juries, in contrast to verdict-driven juries, are relatively less hurried, less cursory on testimony-law connections, more respectful of their own and others' persuasiveness and open-mindedness, and more vigorous in discussion. It is expected then that juries using the questions list would show an evidence-driven style of deliberation and, therefore, be more oriented to the facts of the case and less to individual opinions and preferences.

In her early work, De Paúl (1995) hypothesized that, given the special requirements, Spanish juries would display a more evidence- than verdict-driven style of deliberation.

However in a study by Arce, Tortosa, and Alfaro (2003), Spanish mock juries referred more to verdicts, and less to evidence and its reliability than did judge panels, behaving more as verdict-driven juries. But in this study lay juries were compared to judge panels, which may be more evidence-driven in general, and not to lay juries without questions lists. Thus, while this study provides evidence that lay juries are more verdict-driven than judge panels, it does not speak of whether provision of a questions list to pure juries promotes an evidence-driven style in such juries. If comparisons are made between lay juries with or without questions lists, the former may prove to be more evidence-driven (or at least less verdict-driven) than the latter, although, as Arce et al. demonstrate, neither would be as evidence-driven as judge panels. Moreover, to more completely assess deliberation style, analyses of deliberations might go beyond a count of references to verdicts and evidence to a content analysis of factual versus normative argumentation (e.g., Kaplan, 1989; Kaplan & Martín, 1999b).

Research on the Penalty Phase of Capital Cases Another source of evidence on the effects of the questions list may be studies on capital cases. The death penalty hearing differs from the guilt phase in American lay juries (Rose & Ogloff, 2001), but in some ways is similar to the task of Spanish and Russian juries.

In the United States, most jurisdictions establish a set of instructions to categorize penalty phase evidence into aggravating and mitigating factors. Jurors are asked to reach a verdict, considering both types of factors. But in Texas and Oregon, the procedure is different; jurors must answer specific questions, not unlike the questions list posed to Spanish and Russian juries, in order to recommend a death sentence. Virginia employs a hybrid of the two models (Haney & Lynch, 1997).

Empirical research on the penalty phase has shown that, in general terms, guidelines given to capital juries are difficult to comprehend. The concept of mitigation produced the greatest amount of confusion, and individual factors that jurors were supposed to identify as either aggravating or mitigating were often misconstrued as their opposites (Haney & Lynch, 1994). In another study (Wiener, Hurt, Thomas, Sadler, Bauer, & Sargent, 1998), participants failed to balance aggravating and mitigating circumstances in the manner prescribed by law. Sentences were not assigned by using mitigation to qualify aggravation, but by summing the effects of both types of factors, which were treated independently. And the less participants understood the rule for considering mitigating circumstances, the more likely they were to invoke the death penalty. However, in cases such as the previously cited Otegui case, it has been shown that when jurors are not able to decide on aggravating versus mitigating factors, they are biased in favor of the defendant.

It is better, though, to remediate jurors' understanding of mitigation and aggravation than to hope for a leniency bias owing to confusion. But Haney and Lynch (1997) showed that a revised version of capital penalty instructions was no better understood than those used previously, despite the fact that the new instructions included legal definitions of aggravating and mitigating circumstances that were presumably intended to enhance juror comprehension. The concept of aggravation continued to be better understood than either mitigation or extenuation. The same results have been found in studies using mock jurors (Wiener, Pritchard, & Weston, 1995) or qualitative interviews of jurors after they decided the sentence in actual first-degree murder trials (Haney, Sontag, & Costanzo, 1994). Haney (1995) suggested that aggravation is related more to the details of the crime, hence its easier comprehension and greater effect. Consequently, if instructions increase jurors' attention to the circumstances of the crime by defining both concepts in more detail, aggravation is better understood, and more likely to be used than mitigation (Haney & Lynch, 1997). Simply enhancing the definition of mitigation and aggravation in sentencing instructions may not solve the difficulties of Spanish and Russian juries with the questions list.

Another line of research has shown that persons excluded from capital juries are those more likely to understand mitigating factors and less likely to take into account the aggravating circumstances (Blakenship & Luginbuhl, cited in Wiener et al., 1998). They are also more likely to endorse nonstatutory mitigation (Butler & Moran, 2002). Given that people use those categories that are more accessible and more available (Tversky & Kahneman, 1974), jurors who better understand the category of aggravation, i.e., death-qualified jurors, and therefore are able to access more aggravating than mitigating exemplars, are more likely to overestimate the amount of aggravation in a given case (Haney & Lynch, 1997). Thus, it is reasonable to expect that this severity bias would occur in both Russian and Spanish juries. While there is no death penalty in Spain, it is relevant to note that use of aggravating more than mitigating factors when answering the questions list may be enhanced by specific personality profiles as, for example, death qualification and perhaps authoritarianism. In turn, a preponderance of replies to the questions list that favor aggravation may provoke a more severe sentence by the trial judge.

Heuristic and Systematic Processing The core query is whether the questions list, and the subsequent rationales for verdict, evoke a more systematic or more heuristic (biased?) form of processing, and whether one or the other would produce better decisions. Theorists have identified the importance of the relative care we take in scrutinizing the central points of the persuasive message for the process of persuasion. If clear and accessible information is lacking, or if there is a deficit in motivation or ability to process the information, decision makers are more influenced by irrelevant or peripheral cues (Petty & Cacciopo, 1986). The prime distinction in processing styles lies in careful, effortful, and detailed thought about points that are central and relevant to the decision (systematic reasoning) versus less effortful use of peripheral (nonrelevant) cues, most notably "heuristics," or simplifying (but perhaps invalid) decision rules. Chaiken (1987) describes several heuristic cues that decision makers may rely upon when they are unable or unwilling to systematically process relevant information: length and number of arguments, presentation style (e.g., vivid vs. pallid), the attractiveness, reliability, and/or prestige of the source. Extrapolating to jury decision-making, we suggest that if jurors are unable or unwilling to systematically scrutinize the propositional content of the questions list, they would be influenced by irrelevant cues or heuristics. Anything that prevents jurors from careful attention to the questions, or more precisely, from effortfully generating relevant and elaborated responses to what the court considers the central aspects of the case, will detract from the persuasiveness of case facts, thus leading to more capricious decisions. In place of the informed and carefully reasoned deliberations and decisions intended by trial law, jurors will fall back on simpler heuristics. What can interfere with systematic attention and processing of the trial evidence and questions list? Some likely candidates are length, complexity and density of the trial and questions list, difficulty of concepts (see, for example, the preceding discussion of juror comprehension of mitigation and aggravation), strong emotional arousal, limited experience and/or intellectual capacity, and strong disagreements over the meaning of evidence vis-à-vis the verdict.

Is there much danger of lay juries subverting the intent of the questions list by engaging in heuristic reasoning? This is ultimately an empirical question yet to be tested in jury settings, mock or otherwise. Even if Spanish and Russian juries, owing to length, complexity, or opaqueness of the questions list, abandon systematic processing, will this ultimately affect verdicts and sentencing? Psychological research is not unanimous about the superiority of systematic reasoning in making better decisions. On the one hand, it appears intuitively obvious that careful, systematic processing would produce more accurate judgments (Chen & Chaiken, 1999), and conversely, when individuals are motivated to make accurate judgments, they would undertake a more systematic examination of available information (Chaiken, Giner-Sorolla, & Chen, 1996). However, the hallmark of systematic processing, which is to ponder the validity and strength of information by a detailed scrutiny of the option's attributes, may, at its worst, produce obsessive over-analysis, leading to confusion and poor judgments (Wilson & Schooler, 1991). Moreover, there are many instances where use of heuristics that have high base-rate probability actually improves decision-making over careful consideration of all information (Meehl, 1954; Shanteau & Phelps, 1977).

The combination of questions lists and the requirement of rationales for the verdict may provoke jurors, individually and collectively, to think in greater depth and breadth about the evidence. But in the Russian experience, it is not uncommon for lists to contain nearly 90 questions, with the largest on record having 1047 propositions (Thaman, 1999). In the Otegui case in Spain there were 95 questions (Thaman, 2001). In being forced to attend to multiple attributes, people are less able to concentrate on information most relevant and central to the decision (Tordesillas & Chaiken, 1999). Thought induced by an overabundance of questions can disrupt the core benefit of systematic processing by diverting deep processing from critical information, in the sense of needlessly increasing cognitive load (Chaiken et al., 1996).

In the Otegui case, for example, 64 of the 95 questions posed to the jury referred to the defendant's diminished capacity caused by intoxication and rage provoked by alleged police harassment. This imbalance could well have distracted the jury from the evidence relevant to intentional murder.

The Trial Judge's Power

Besides the effects of the questions list, the second characteristic of the Spanish and Russian jury systems addressed in this chapter is the power of the trial judges. As in other countries with continental law, "judges [...] resemble more the priest figure" (Thaman, 2000, p. 68), and as authority figures they are able to influence jurors' opinion, both intentionally and unintentionally. Social psychological research on experimenter effects, expectations, and obedience show how laypeople are willing to follow the lead of authorities, even when these indications are not explicitly formulated (see Kaplan & Martín, 1999a, 1999b; Martín, Kaplan, & Álamo, 2003).

Unintentional influences of judges via their behavior toward attorneys have been extensively addressed (Kerr, 1982). But also both Spanish and Russian laws give ample prerogatives to the trial judges that permit direct influence, such as returning the questions list to the jury for further explication, dissolving the jury if the verdict is not "appropriate," and issuing specific instructions. Instructions are especially important in the Spanish and Russian jury context because they involve concepts of substantive law that juries must integrate into their response to questions regarding "naked" facts.

Jurors dealing with a traditional "guilty/not guilty" decision have repeatedly said that they make a "good faith effort" to comply with judges' instructions (Steele & Thornburg, 1988–89). However, such effort is sometimes wasted because jurors are often unable to comprehend and/or follow instructions (Spackman, Belcher, Calapp, & Taylor, 2002).

Psychological research has demonstrated that trial judge instructions are poorly understood in a variety of procedural and substantive content areas (Wiener et al., 1998). Elwork and Sales (1985) found that the level of comprehension in the studies they reviewed was 50 percent or less, with juries misunderstanding the most important legal issues. As noted earlier, capital sentencing instructions are no exceptions to this general rule (Haney & Lynch, 1997).

Possible explanations for this lack of comprehension of trial judge instructions include (1) legal language is convoluted, technical, and full of legal jargon with which laypeople are unfamiliar (Hartley, 2000); (2) some instructions, although technical, are vague; and (3) structural features of the trial, including written instructions and the possibility of asking questions are unfavorable (Reifman, Gusick, & Ellsworth, 1992). However, beyond the text itself, comprehension is also related to how carefully people read documents, and other external factors (e.g., time constraint, individual differences, and social pressures) (Howe & Wogalter, 1994, 1995). None of these circumstances seem to be more prevalent in Spanish and Russian juries as opposed to traditional lay juries; therefore it is reasonable to expect that their level of understanding is the same as that of North American juries.

Legal comprehension via instructions may be influenced by the type of law being described: declarative versus procedural. Smith (1988) defines "declarative knowledge" as related to meaning- and content-based information stored as semantic concepts, schemata, script, or prototypes, whereas "procedural knowledge" refers to active components of the cognitive systems that operate on the declarative knowledge stored in long- and short-term memory. Wiener et al. (1998) focused on the manner in which people construe law in terms of declarative and procedural knowledge, showing that declarative knowledge is more difficult to master than procedural knowledge. Reifman et al. (1992) also found that rewriting jury instructions could improve jurors' comprehension of procedural but not of substantive law. As we have said, the core of judges' instructions in the Spanish and Russian juries is of substantive nature, especially in relation to guilt and circumstances that modify or exclude criminal responsibility. Given that Spanish judges have different views of how they should instruct juries on the legal elements of the charged crimes (Thaman, 2001), and that it is difficult to answer the list questions in light of these elements, it may be important to study the factors that could improve understanding of instructions in general, and of substantive law in particular.

Because criminal verdicts may be reversed by appellate courts on the basis of improper jury instructions, trial judges in the United States generally adhere to legalistically framed, "patterned" instructions. But this is not the solution to the problem, because even standard instructions are difficult for laypeople to understand (Reifman et al., 1992). It is true that some authors have shown that written instructions can improve legal comprehension (Kramer & Koenig, 1990). However, Heuer and Penrod (1989) found that while jurors preferred written instructions, they benefited little from the practice, in that neither were they more satisfied with the trial process, nor was deliberation time reduced (see also Greene & Johns, 2001; Reifman et al., 1992). The only modification of standardized instructions that seems to facilitate comprehension, at least in the instance of self-defense criteria, is the use of a flowchart (Semmler & Brewer, 2002).

A COMMENT ON HISTORICAL AND CULTURAL FRAMEWORKS

There are circumstances in which whether jurors understand instructions or not makes no difference in verdicts (Spackman et al., 2002). Jurors who understand instructions may act as though they are ignorant of them because they construe instructions in a manner consistent with their own commonsense ideas about criminal justice (Finkel, 1995, 2000; Haney & Lynch, 1997; Smith, 1991, 1993). Smith (1991) has shown that laypersons have prototypical representations of crimes, for example, what constitutes a typical kidnaping. Jurors base their verdict on the extent to which the facts of the case fit their crime prototype and not on whether the evidence fits the legal definition of the crime as detailed in the jury instructions. Prior knowledge about law also influences factual recall and punishment preferences (Stalans, 1993), as well as susceptibility to misleading information during the fact-finding process (Smith & Studebaker, 1996).

As the only pretrial exposure to law most jurors have had is through informal sources such as mass media, it seems that these commonsense ideas are socio-culturally based (Smith, 1993). Thus, it may be that Spanish and Russian jurors are different from North American jurors. In fact, the lay jury itself is a new experience for the citizenry of Spain and Russia. Unlike countries with a long and continuous experience with lay juries and public trials, in a democracy (e.g., the UK and North America), the citizens of these nations may have a different conception of the nature of trial process, or even of the jury itself. Preconceptions of the jury process in Spain and Russia may differ radically from those of other countries given both their recent history and their cultural background. In these countries, lay participation in the jury institution was considered the last step in the democratization process. But in the collective memory of citizenry still lies the image of Spanish "popular tribunals" (Alejandre, 1981) or Russian "laypeople assessors" (Thaman, 1999), which were political instruments to justify executions or other form of political control, subordinated to particular ideologies.

Whether Spanish and Russian lay preconceptions differ from those of North American jurors, and whether these differences change the jury dynamics in those countries, are empirical questions. If true, research is needed to develop instructions that can replace cultural/historically based legal preconceptions with standard concepts and definitions provided by the law. Smith (1993) found that an instruction that refuted people's misconceptions, feature by feature, about what actions did and did not constitute kidnaping, enabled jurors to more accurately determine whether case scenarios involved kidnaping when compared to a mere admonition to disregard their own notion of kidnaping. Similarly, instructions are more effective when they explain to jurors how the law wishes them to treat the evidence and why (Wissler, Rector, & Saks, 2001).

CONCLUSIONS

Spanish and Russian jury systems seem to be hybrids that integrate the advantages of the Anglo-Saxon lay juries and the European mixed juries. On the one hand, they are composed entirely of laypersons, without the influence of high status co-jurors. But like mixed juries, they can qualify the sentence, by considering the circumstances that modify and/or exclude criminal responsibility, by asking for a suspension of sentence, or for a complete or a partial amnesty for the offense. Furthermore, they have the constitutional requirement of sentence motivation, giving the trial judges the facts on which the verdict was based and the rationale for that verdict.

Thus, while judging case facts as a pure jury, they are required to fully explain and justify their findings. The questions list, the rationales for verdict, the judges' instructions, and the possibility that trial judges may "correct" jury answers to the list serve as a strong check on irrationality and jury nullification. These very mechanisms to improve jury rationality can be a two-edged sword, enhancing systematic reasoning but also unintentionally confusing juries and leading to use of simplifying strategies.

The role of social-psychological research is to specify as much as possible the effects of these features on the decision process, the decision itself, and citizens' and participants' perceptions of both. This chapter has discussed empirical studies that suggest how evidence-driven deliberation, systematic information processing, and comprehension of aggravating and mitigating circumstances may be enhanced. Research on the difficulties of comprehending and adhering to the trial judge's instructions was reviewed in light of reported deficits in Spanish juries. In addition to forecasting possible consequences of existing conditions and suggesting some remedies, we also identified issues for future research clarification. Underlying this exposition are the beliefs that whether the functioning of the system is "good" depends on the standards against which it is compared, and that valid standards are those freely established by the citizens of each community, even in a globalized world.

ACKNOWLEDGMENTS

The authors thank Juan Antonio Pérez Lledó (Universidad de Alicante, Spain) for his documental support at the outset of our studies on Spanish juries, and Benito Reverón Palenzuela (Universidad de La Laguna, Spain) for providing us, more recently, with valuable legal references on European and Spanish Jury Laws.

NOTES

1. As obviously the Russian jury law is in Russian, and involves more than one document, we refer to Thaman (2001, p. 322, footnote 13) for the complete reference.
2. Ley Orgánica 5/1995, de 22 de mayo, del Tribunal del Jurado. BOE núm 122, de 23 de mayo de 1995, pp. 15001–15021. This law was amended by the Ley

Organica 8/1995, de 16 de noviembre, por la que se modifica la Ley orgánica 5/1995, de 22 de mayo, del Tribunal del Jurado. BOE núm. 275, de 17 de noviembre de 1995, pp. 33162–33165.

3. Mikel Otegui, a Basque nationalist, murdered two Basque policemen and was acquitted by a jury in 1997. The Superior Court of Justice of the Basque Country reversed the verdict based on the insufficiency of rationale, considering that the jury made a wrong use of the reasonable doubt principle. The Spanish Supreme Court confirmed the reversal. This case provoked a strong reaction of Spanish public opinion against the jury system, which was reflected by the main mass media of the country.
4. See Note 3.

REFERENCES

Alejandre, J. (1981). *La justicia popular en España* [The popular justice in Spain]. Madrid: Universidad Complutense.

Arce, R., Fariña, F., Vila, C., & Novo, M. (1998). The jury decision rule: An empirical study of four methods. In J. Boros, I. Münnich, & M. Szagedi (Eds.), *Psychology and criminal justice* (pp. 152–159). Berlin: De Gruyter.

Arce, R., Novo, M., & Real, S. (1999). Reconstrucción de hechos, errores e inferencias de jurados según el tamaño y la regla de decisión [Reconstruction of juries' facts, errors and inferences depending on the size and decision rule]. *Psicología Política, 19*, 85–99.

Arce, R., Tortosa, F., & Alfaro, E. (2003). Veredicto y análisis del contenido de las deliberaciones de los Tribunales de Jueces y Jurados en el contexto jurídico español [Verdict and content analysis of deliberation of the Panels of Judges and Juries in the juridical Spanish context]. *Psichothema, 15*, 127–135.

Butler, B. M., & Moran, G. (2002). The role of death qualification in venirepersons' evaluations of aggravating and mitigating circumstances in capital trials. *Law & Human Behavior, 26*, 175–184.

Centro de Investigaciones Sociológicas (CIS) (1996). Estudio 2.217. Madrid: CIS.

Centro de Investigaciones Sociológicas (CIS) (1997). Estudio 12. Madrid: CIS.

Chaiken, S. (1987). The heuristic model of persuasion. In M. P. Zanna, J. M. Olson, & C. P. Herman (Eds.), *Social influence: The Ontario symposium* (Vol. 5, pp. 3–39). Hillsdale, NJ: Lawrence Erlbaum.

Chaiken, S., Giner-Sorolla, R., & Chen, S. (1996). Beyond accuracy: Defense and impression motives in heuristic and systematic information processing. In P. M. Gollwitzer & J. A. Bargh (Eds.), *The psychology of action: Linking motivation and cognition to behavior* (pp. 553–578). New York: Guilford.

Chen, S., & Chaiken, S. (1999). The heuristic-systematic model in its broader context. In S. Chaiken & Y. Trope (Eds.), *Dual-processes theories in social psychology*. New York: Guilford.

Consejo General del Poder Judicial (CGPJ) (1998). *Informe sobre la aplicación de la vigente LOTJ* [Report on the application of the LOTJ in force]. Madrid: CGPJ.

Consejo General del Poder Judicial (CGPJ) (1999). *Informe sobre la aplicación de la vigente LOTJ* [Report on the application of the LOTJ in force]. Madrid: CGPJ.

Cuesta-Martínez, A. (1992). Proyectos legislativos sobre el jurado en España: Aspectos políticos [Legislative projects on the jury in Spain: Political aspects]. *Proceeding of the Jornadas El jurado sí: 'Pero cómo y cuándo'* (pp. 127–141). Barcelona: Centre d'Estudis i Formacio Especialitzada.

De la Fuente, L., de la Fuente, E., & García, J. (2003). Effects of pretrial juror bias, strength of evidence and deliberation process on juror decisions: New validity evidence of the juror bias scale scores. *Psychology, Crime & Law*, *9*, 197–209.

De la Fuente, L., García, J., & de la Fuente, E. (2003). Validez de la escala de sesgo del jurado en relación con las decisiones grupales de jurados simulados [Validity of the juror bias scale in relation to the group decision of mock juries]. *Psicothema*, *15*, 148–154.

De Paúl, P. (1995). *El tribunal del jurado desde la psicología social* [The jury tribunal from social psychology]. Madrid: Siglo XXI.

De Paúl, P. (1996). The influence of size and decision rule in jury decision-making. In G. Davies, M. McMurran, S. Wilson, & S. Lloyd-Bostock (Eds.), *Psychology, law, and criminal justice*. Berlin: De Gruyter.

El jurado pasa la reválida de los 6 años [The jury pass the final examination of the six years] (2002, April 7). *El País*, p. 28.

Elwork, A., & Sales, B. D. (1985). Jury instructions. In S. Kassin & L. Wrightman (Eds.), *The psychology of evidence and trial procedure* (pp. 280–297). Beverly Hills, CA: Sage.

Finkel, N. J. (1995). *Common sense justice: Jurors' notion of the law*. Cambridge, MA: Harvard University Press.

Finkel, N. J. (2000). Common sense justice and jury instructions: Instructive and reciprocating connections. *Psychology, Public Policy, & Law*, *6*, 591–628.

García, J., de la Fuente, L., & de la Fuente, E. (2002). Una visión psicojurídica del jurado español desde sus fundamentos y funcionamiento [A psycho-juridical view of Spanish jury from its foundations and functioning]. *Psicología Política*, *24*, 67–94.

Gisbert, A. (1990). *El futuro tribunal popular español* [The future Spanish popular tribunal]. Barcelona: PPU.

Gómez-Colomer, J. L. (1999). Aplicación práctica de la Ley del Jurado [Practical application of the Jury Law]. In J. Montero-Aroca & J. L. Gómez-Colomer (Eds.), *Comentarios a la Ley el Jurado* (pp. 1159–1180). Pamplona, Spain: Aranzadi.

Greene, E., & Johns, M. (2001). Jurors' use of instructions of negligence. *Journal of Applied Social Psychology*, *31*, 840–859.

Haney, C. (1995). The context of capital murder: Social histories and the logic of mitigation. *Santa Clara Law Review*, *35*, 547–609.

Haney, C., & Lynch, M. (1994). Comprehending life and death matters: A preliminary study of California's capital penalty instructions. *Law and Human Behavior*, *18*, 411–436.

Haney, C., & Lynch, M. (1997). Clarifying life and death matters: An analysis of instructional comprehension and penalty phase closing arguments. *Law and Human Behavior*, *21*, 575–595.

Haney, C., Sontag, L., & Costanzo, S. (1994). Deciding to take a life: Capital juries, sentencing instructions, and the jurisprudence of death. *Journal of Social Issues*, *50*, 149–176.

Hartley, J. (2000). Legal ease and "legalese". *Psychology, Crime & Law*, *6*, 1–20.

Hastie, R., Penrod, S. D., & Pennington, N. (1983). *Inside the jury*. Cambridge, MA: Harvard University Press.

Heuer, L., & Penrod, S. D. (1989). Instructing jurors: A field experimenter with written and preliminary instructions. *Law and Human Behavior*, *13*, 409–430.

Howe, J. E., & Wogalter, M. S. (1994). The understandability of legal documents: Are they adequate? *Proceedings of the Human Factors and Ergonomics Society*, *38*, 439–442.

Howe, J. E., & Wogalter, M. S. (1995). On making legal documents understandable: Objective and subjective measures. *Proceedings of the Human Factors and Ergonomics Society*, *39*, 430–434.

Kaplan, M. F. (1989). Task, situational, and personal determinants of influence processes in group decision making. In E. J. Lawler & B. Markovsky (Eds.), *Advances in group processes* (Vol. 6, pp. 87–105). Greenwich, CT: JAI Press.

Kaplan, M. F., & Martín, A. M. (1999a). The influence of expert and non-expert members of juries: The Spanish jury as an illustration. In S. Nagel (Ed.), *Handbook of Global Legal Policy* (Chapter 12, pp. 209–222). New York: Marcel Dekker.

Kaplan, M., & Martín, A. M. (1999b). Effects of differential status of group members of juries on process and outcome of deliberation. *Group Processes and Intergroup Relations*, *2*, 347–364.

Kassin, S. M., & Wrightsman, L. S. (1983). The construction and validation of a juror bias scale. *Journal of Research in Personality*, *12*, 423–442.

Kerr, N. L. (1982). Trial participants' behavior and jury verdicts: An exploratory field study. In V. J. Konečni & E. B. Ebbesen (Eds.), *The criminal justice system. A social psychological analysis* (Chapter 10, pp. 261–290). San Francisco: Freeman.

Kramer, G., & Koenig, D. (1990). Do jurors understand criminal jury instructions? Analyzing the results of the Michigan Juror Comprehension Project. *University of Michigan Law Review*, *23*, 409–438.

Martín, A. M., Kaplan, M. F., and Álamo, J. (2003). Discussion content and perception of deliberation in Western European vs. American juries. *Psychology, Crime & Law*, *9*, 247–263.

Meehl, P. E. (1954). *Clinical vs. statistical prediction.* Minneapolis: University of Minnesota Press.

Perles, F., Canto, J. M., & San Martín, J. E. (2000). Aspectos ideológicos de la actitud hacia el Jurado Popular [Ideological aspects of the attitude to the Popular Jury]. *Boletín de Psicología*, *66*, 69–82.

Petty, R. E., & Cacciopo, J. T. (1986). The elaboration likelihood model of persuasion. In L. Berkowitz (Ed.), *Advances in experimental social psychology* (Vol. 19, pp. 123–205). San Diego, CA: Academic Press.

Planchadell-Gargallo, A. (1999). El escabinato francés [The French escabinato]. In J. Montero-Aroca & J. L. Gómez-Colomer (Eds.), *Comentarios a la Ley el Jurado* (pp. 95–111). Pamplona, Spain: Aranzadi.

Rechea, C. (1989). El jurado: Relaciones del juez hacia el jurado [The jury: Judge's relations to the jury]. In C. Rechea (Ed.), *La criminología aplicada II* (pp. 131–163). Madrid: Consejo General del Poder Judicial.

Reifman, A., Gusick, S. M., & Ellsworth, P. C. (1992). Real jurors' understanding on the law in real cases. *Law and Human Behavior*, *16*, 539–554.

Rose, V. G., & Ogloff, J. R. P. (2001). Evaluating the comprehensibility of jury instructions: A method and an example. *Law and Human Behavior*, *25*, 409–431.

Sáinz, E., & Sáinz, J. (1990). Estrategias de decisión de un jurado bajo condiciones de simulación [Jury decision strategies under simulation conditions]. *Estudios de Psicología*, *42*, 5–28.

Semmler, C., & Brewer, N. (2002). Using a flow-chart to improve comprehension of jury instructions. *Psychiatry, Psychology & Law*, *9*, 262–267.

Shanteau, J., & Phelps, R. H. (1977). Judgment and swine: Approaches and issues in applied judgment analysis. In M. F. Kaplan & S. Schwartz (Eds.), *Human judgment and decision processes in applied settings* (pp. 255–272). New York: Academic Press.

Smith, R. E. (1988). Impression formation in a general framework of social nonsocial cognition. In R. S. Wyer, Jr., & T. K. Srull (Eds.), *Advances in social cognition* (Vol. 1, pp. 165–176). Hillsdale, NJ: Lawrence Erlbaum.

Smith, V. L. (1991). Prototypes in the courtroom: Lay representations of legal concepts. *Journal of Personality and Social Psychology, 61*, 857–872.

Smith, V. L. (1993). When prior knowledge and law collide: Helping jurors to use the law. *Law and Human Behavior, 17*, 507–536.

Smith, V. L., & Studebaker, C. A. (1996). What do you expect?: The influence of people's prior knowledge of crime categories on fact-finding. *Law and Human Behavior, 20*, 517–532.

Spackman, M. P., Belcher, J. C., Calapp, J. W., & Taylor, A. (2002). An analysis of the effects of subjective and objective instruction forms on mock-juries' murder/manslaughter distinctions. *Law and Human Behavior, 26*, 605–623.

Stalans, L. J. (1993). Citizens' crime stereotypes, biased recall, and punishment preferences in abstract cases: The educative role of interpersonal sources. *Law and Human Behavior, 17*, 451–470.

Steele, W. W., & Thornburg, E. G. (1988–89). Jury instructions: A persistent failure to communicate. *North Carolina Law Review, 67*, 77–119.

Thaman, S. (1999). El jurado ruso [The Russian jury]. In J. Montero-Aroca & J. L. Gómez-Colomer (Eds.), *Comentarios a la Ley el Jurado* (pp. 116–130). Pamplona, Spain: Aranzadi.

Thaman, S. (2000). La política y la ciencia del control judicial de los jurados: El caso ruso y español [The politics and the science of the judicial control of juries: The Russian and Spanish case]. *Boletín de Psicología, 20*, 67–84.

Thaman, S. (2001). Europe's new jury systems: The case of Spain and Russia. In N. J. Vidmar (Ed.), *World jury systems* (Chapter 9, pp. 319–351). Oxford, UK: Oxford University Press.

Tordesillas, R. S., & Chaiken, S. (1999). Thinking too much or too little? The effects of introspection on the decision-making process. *Personality and Social Psychology Bulletin, 25*, 623–629.

Tversky, A., & Kahneman, D. (1974). Judgment under uncertainty: Heuristics and biases. *Science, 211*, 453–458.

Wiener, R. L., Hurt, L. E., Thomas, S. L., Sadler, M. S., Bauer, C. A., and Sargent, T. M. (1998). The role of declarative and procedural knowledge in capital murder sentencing. *Journal of Applied Social Psychology, 28*, 124–144.

Wiener, R. L. Pritchard, C. C., & Weston, M. (1995). Comprehensibility of approved jury instructions in capital murder cases. *Journal of Applied Psychology, 80*, 455–467.

Wissler, R. L., Rector, K. A., & Saks, M. J. (2001). The impact of jury instructions on the fusion of liability and compensatory damages. *Law and Human Behavior, 25*, 125–139.

Wilson, T. D., & Schooler, J. W. (1991). Thinking too much: Introspection can reduce the quality of preferences and decisions. *Journal of Personality and Social Psychology, 60*, 181–192.

6

American Military Courts-Martial: Processes and Procedures of Trials and Decisions

VERLIN B. HINSZ, JORDAN M. HENKEL, and R. SCOTT TINDALE

As this volume illustrates, juries take many forms in the world. This chapter examines a unique type of jury: the jury that makes decisions in military justice systems. In particular, we will examine courts-martial, which serve as the deliberative and decision-making body for many aspects of the American military justice system. Similar courts-martial bodies exist for other military justice systems in the world (Schlueter, 1999); however, we will focus on particular aspects of the American military justice system. One reason for this focus on the American military justice system is that there is one set of legal documents that apply to all service branches in the American military: the Uniform Code of Military Justice (UCMJ). Courts-martial in the American military justice system are also of interest because they differ in important ways from juries in the American criminal justice system. Consequently, courts-martial are a separate type of jury that coexist with criminal juries under the same American governmental and judicial systems. Initially, we will outline the basis and purpose of the American military justice system within which courts-martial occur. Then we will consider the procedures by which a case comes to the attention of members of courts-martial. The processes by which the members are selected and seated for the court-martial will be described. We then consider aspects of the procedures and processes that courts-martial follow in deliberation and decision for the charge(s). We will then also consider the ways that justice is dispensed in the military justice system. Throughout this analysis of courts-martial in the American military justice system, we will discuss the implications of psychological research for the practice of justice in this system.

THE AMERICAN MILITARY JUSTICE SYSTEM

The American military justice system has been established by the military, US Congress, and the courts, to provide a separate system of justice in order to maintain good order and discipline, which are deemed to be essential components to the success of the military. There are several documents that serve as the governing documents for the American military justice system. Specifically, the US Congress enacted the UCMJ as the main element and documentation for the military justice system. The various articles of the UCMJ serve to describe substantive and procedural law. The UCMJ is a public document that can be found online and in the manual for courts-martial (MCM; 2002). The military rules of evidence (MRE) and the rules for courts-martial (RCM) are also included in the MCM. Our discussion of the American military justice system and courts-martial draws heavily upon the UCMJ, MCM, and RCM. We will not reference particular sections of these documents as we discuss the details of courts-martial in the American military justice system, but refer the interested reader to these documents for further discussion of these topics.

COMMANDERS OF THE ACCUSED AND THE CONVENING AUTHORITY

In the military, commanders are responsible for the performance of their subordinates. With this responsibility, they are given the power to exercise prosecutorial discretion. The commanding officer of the accused is typically authorized to make the first decision about what action will be taken regarding the offense. Usually they are also considered to be the accuser. Moreover, the commander decides whether the disposition of an offense will be done administratively or referred to trial by court-martial. If the commander determines a trial by court-martial is warranted, then the commander may forward charges to a superior commander for disposition. When the commanding officer of the accused is also the accuser, a special or general courts-martial must be convened by another competent superior authority. Charges may be forwarded up the chain of command for disposition by a superior commander, which includes a recommendation from the subordinate commander regarding whether to convene a court-martial.

The convening authority then is a superior commander of the accused, as long as they are not the accuser (for general court-martial or special court-martial). The convening authority plays a key role in the courts-martial process because they create the courts-martial. That is, the convening authority appoints the court members and refers the case to them for consideration (Roan & Buxton, 2002). Consequently, authorization for hearing cases is only given in military courts when they have been referred to it by the convening authority (Schlueter, 1999).

TYPES OF COURTS-MARTIAL

The American military justice system provides for three different types of courts-martial that vary in jurisdiction, types of punishment allowed, procedures, etc. The three types of court-martial are summary court-martial, special court-martial, and general court-martial. Characteristics and differences among these three types of

TABLE 6.1 Characteristics and Differences among Different Types of Courts-Martial

Type	Composition	Confinement	Forfeitures	Punitive discharge
Summary	One commissioned officer on active duty not below grade of lieutenant	Max of 1 month (may only impose confinement and hard labor without confinement on persons in certain lower grades)	2/3 pay per month for 1 month	None
Special	Military judge alone At least three members and military judge	12 months (may not impose confinement on enlisted persons)	2/3 pay per month for 12 months	Bad-conduct discharge
General	Military judge alone At least five members and military judge	See table of maximum punishments in Appendix 12 of the MCM	Total forfeitures (pay and allowances)	Bad-conduct or dishonorable discharge Dismissal
Capital	At least 12 members and military judge	May only impose the death penalty when authorized by the MCM and when charges are referred to a general court-martial as a capital case by the convening authority		

court-martial are summarized in Table 6.1. We will provide only a brief discussion on the processes and procedures of the summary court-martial because the decisions are made by individuals (e.g., military judges) and do not have any court members, which is our main focus (see Chapter 13 and Appendix 9 of the RCM in the MCM for specific information regarding the summary courts-martial).

Summary Court-Martial

A summary court-martial is a disciplinary proceeding used to address minor offenses through a process that includes one commissioned officer who presides over the hearing. With a summary court-martial, the accused have no right to counsel, but they may choose to hire a civilian attorney (Schlueter, 1999). Only enlisted members may be tried by summary court-martial, and there are strict limits on the punishment that can be imposed (see Table 6.1). A summary court-martial is the lowest level of court in the military, and is considerably different from special and general courts-martial. For example, more constitutional and procedural protections are given to the accused facing trial by general and special court-martial as compared to trial by summary court-martial (Roan & Buxton, 2002).

Special Court-Martial

A special court-martial stands in between the summary and general court-martial in the military justice system. This disciplinary proceeding includes, at the accused's discretion, either a military judge and at least three members, or a military judge alone. At this level of trial, a trial counsel and defense counsel represent the government and the accused (Roan & Buxton, 2002). Enlisted members or officers may be tried by the government for any noncapital offense, and the punishment may include a bad-conduct discharge, a maximum of 1 year confinement, forfeiture of two thirds pay for 12 months and a reprimand. The accused may request that enlisted members serve as members of the court, in which case at least one third of the court members will be enlisted members that are senior to the accused.

General Court-Martial

A general court-martial is the highest level of trial in the military judicial structure. The general court-martial is very similar to the proceedings of the special court-martial. An additional requirement, however, is that a thorough and impartial pretrial investigation of all the matters regarding the offenses shall be conducted before a general courts-martial is convened by a commissioned officer. This trial includes a military judge and not less than five members, or if requested by the accused, in a noncapital offense case, a military judge alone. As of 2003, the US Congress requires that for capital cases there must be 12 court members (Schlueter, 1999). As with the special courts-martial, the accused may request that one third of the court members are enlisted members. This type of court-martial is imposed for the most serious types of crimes and the punishment may include death or life in prison (Military Justice Overview, 2003).

COURTS-MARTIAL JURISDICTION

The nature of the courts-martial is strictly disciplinary. For a court-martial to hold jurisdiction, the accused must have been subject to the UCMJ both at the time of the offense and at the time of trial (Schlueter, 1999). Another requirement for the application of a court-martial is that it must have jurisdiction over the offense. For offenses that are strictly military offenses, the courts-martial holds sole jurisdiction. For offenses that are against both the UCMJ and a civilian code, jurisdiction in both the military and civilian communities may exist; in such cases there is an important issue regarding the offenses that could also be tried in state, federal, or foreign courts (Schlueter, 1999).

Personal jurisdiction occurs when the accused serves with the legal status as a service member, or is a person otherwise that is subject to the UCMJ. Controversy exists regarding when civilians fall subject to the code. Generally, in wartime, civilians have been subject to court-martial jurisdiction if they are "serving or accompanying an armed force, in the field, in a time of war" (Schlueter, 1999). This is the case with foreign fighters in the Afghanistan conflict that are detained by American authorities in Guantanamo base.

PREFERRAL OF CHARGES

If an offense is deemed triable by court-martial, the commander who has been referred the case initially may decide to prefer charges, which is the formal process of accusation. Preferral of charges occurs when an accuser signs and swears that they have investigated the charges or have personal knowledge of them and that the charges are true. Preferral occurs through charges and specifications. A charge is the formal statement that refers to a specific violation of the UCMJ. A specification is the facts and circumstances surrounding the alleged violation of the code.

The convening authority of a court-martial has a number of options for disposing of the case. They can chose to dismiss the case, refer charges to a lower or higher level court-martial convening authority, or order an investigation of the charges. American military courts differ from American criminal trials in that for more severe charges, an official investigation of the charges is conducted to produce demonstrable evidence of the charges. This investigation is similar to court mandated investigations that occur in justice systems in other nations (e.g., Germany, France).

PRETRIAL

An investigation of all matters regarding the case must occur for a trial to be referred to a general court-martial. The pretrial investigation evaluates the truth of the charges and provides a recommendation in terms of justice and discipline. At the conclusion of the investigation, the investigating officer makes conclusions, recommendations, and reports them to the directing commander and then to the accused.

After formal statement of the charges, the court generally holds a preliminary pretrial session, which is usually referred to as the Article 39 pretrial session (in reference to that article of the UCMJ). This is an out of court proceeding that is held for administrative purposes, addressing the rights of the accused, arraignment of the accused, handling pretrial motions, and taking the plea of the accused. With this, the accused are informed that they have the right to be tried by a panel of members serving on the court-martial or by a military judge alone.

Arraignment is typically the next step in the proceedings. The military judge addresses the potential maximum punishment for the charge and asks how the accused pleads. At this time the accused enters a plea of guilty or not guilty to the charges. The court must find guilt beyond a reasonable doubt when a plea of "not guilty" is entered. A guilty plea is equivalent to a conviction. Before a guilty plea is accepted, the military judge must conduct a providency inquiry. This inquiry occurs because when the accused plead guilty, their rights against self-incrimination, to trial by court-martial, and to confront and cross-examine witnesses are waived. If the accused has entered a plea of guilty to the charges, the court members are informed and their duty is then to determine an appropriate sentence (Schlueter, 1999). If the accused does not enter any pleas of guilty, the Article 39 pretrial session is basically concluded and trial proceedings take place with the court members present.

COMPOSITION OF THE COURT

For a court-martial to have appropriate jurisdictions for an offense, it has to have proper composition. A properly composed court-martial includes the military judge, counsel, and court members. The military judge must meet qualifications such as being a commissioned officer of the armed forces, a member of the bar of a federal court or a member of highest court of a State, and be certified as a military judge by that armed force's Judge Advocate General. The military judge is assigned to a separate trial judiciary command, and so is usually not a member of the convening authority's command (Schlueter, 1999).

A minimum of at least one trial counsel and one defense counsel is included in each court-martial. An assistant trial and defense counsel may additionally be included in the court-martial (Schlueter, 1999). Under the supervision of the counsel, any commissioned officer may serve at a general court-martial or special court-martial as assistant trial or assistant defense counsel. The accused can be represented by civilian counsel and an individually requested military counsel. Counsel can be disqualified for conflicts of interest, such as when the counsel has acted as an accuser or investigating officer for the charge.

Composition of a court-martial includes court members who are the military equivalent to jurors in the civilian jury. It is the duty of the members of a court-martial to determine whether the accused is guilty and determine a proper sentence if necessary. The members are expected to have equal voice and vote when deliberating. In the military justice system, court members may question witnesses, which is not true of jurors in the civilian justice system. Court members each must be a service member on active duty and must hold a position that authorizes them to hear cases involving officers, warrant officers, and enlisted personnel. Moreover, members of the court cannot be junior in rank or grade to the accused. The implication is that the court members will always have higher status than the accused. Consequently, it is not truly a jury of one's peers, which does not bode well for the defendant. Research on social influence has argued that people are more influenced by similar as opposed to dissimilar others (McGuire, 1969), and find similar others less blameworthy than dissimilar others for negative outcomes: the more negative the outcome, the greater the perceived difference in blameworthiness (Burger, 1981).

Unlike some civilian court systems, neither is random selection a requirement for selection of court members, nor must the court members be representative of the entire military sector (Schlueter, 1999). The personnel office typically has prepared a pool of names from which the convening authority selects individuals to serve as court members (Schlueter, 1999). The convening authority selects individuals to sit as court members based on age, education, training, experience, length of service, and judicial temperament, which is determined at the opinion of the convening authority. If the accused requests that enlisted members be appointed, then at least one third of the court-martial membership must be comprised of enlisted personnel, provided they are not in the same unit as the accused. Noncommissioned officers with lengthy service are typically the enlisted members selected to serve as court members (Schlueter, 1999).

The power and process of selecting the court members is one of the most criticized components of the military justice system. Although research on the effects of jury selection on final verdicts is mixed and controversial (Filkins, Smith, & Tindale, 1998; Saks, 1976; Tindale & Nagao, 1986), the limited research suggests that the convening authority could have a major effect on verdicts because they can select the potential panel members. Much of the research to date has questioned whether attorneys and/or consultants can really predict how an individual juror will vote in most trial contexts (Horowitz, 1980; Olczak, Kaplan, & Penrod, 1991; Saks, 1976). However, a military commander with direct knowledge of the potential jurors' predispositions could lead to the selection of biased court members that suit the commander's views of the case. Such biases could be either intentional or incidental by-products of cognitive processes (Martin & Tesser, 1992). Even if actual bias is rare, research on procedural justice indicates that if the defendant is afforded a greater degree of process control, he/she would have a greater "perception" of fairness (Thibaut & Walker, 1975).

A panel member's eligibility and appointment may be challenged in court. Consequently, the convening authority usually appoints more than the minimum number of court members (Schlueter, 1999). A "voir dire" examination of the members is allowed to obtain information for challenging members. The process of examination of members is conducted at the discretion of the military judge and specific grounds for excusing a member from the court are listed in the MCM. Unlimited challenges for cause are granted to each side. Additionally, one member may be challenged peremptorily by each party (Rule 912(g)(1)). Discussion of the MCM notes that there really is no reason for a peremptory challenge. Since peremptory challenges serve as the main mechanism for the defense to reduce potential bias among the court impaneled (Hans & Vidmar, 1982), the restrictions on this process could lead to both real and perceived injustices.

It is interesting to note that in the US civilian system, courts have ruled that a jury of less than six members denies an accused their right to a trial jury, and that a unanimous verdict must be cast when the jury composition is equal to six persons (Schlueter, 1999). The military holds court proceedings of less than six court members and does not need a unanimous verdict, except in cases of death penalty. The courts have concluded that the "jury" system of the military does not violate rights of due process or trial jury (Schlueter, 1999). Although this issue has raised some controversy, addressing it has been declined by the Court of Appeals for the Armed Force and the Supreme Court (Schlueter, 1999); however, it is a matter of practice for convening authorities to appoint more court members than are required.

Jury size and decision rule have received a fair amount of research attention ever since the US Supreme Court first found that juries of less than 12 members and using less than unanimous decision rules are not necessarily unconstitutional (*Apodaca et al. v. Oregon*, 1972; *Ballew v. Georgia*, 1978; *Williams v. Florida*, 1970). Empirical research on these issues is equivocal in relation to their effects on verdicts. Much of the research has found no significant differences in terms of verdicts as a function of either jury size or assigned decision rule (Davis, Kerr, Atkin, Holt, & Meek, 1975; Hastie, Penrod, & Pennington, 1983). However, simulations based on mathematical models that have been shown to well represent data from mock jury decision studies predict that both size and decision rule should make a difference under certain circumstances. For example, research has shown that if two thirds of the members of a jury begin deliberation favoring a particular verdict, the jury is very likely to reach consensus on that verdict (Davis et al., 1975; Tindale & Davis, 1983). Such a process argues that larger relative to smaller juries, on average, should have higher conviction rates when evidence is strongly against the defendant (i.e., jurors generally prefer guilt after hearing the evidence) and lower rates when the evidence is rather weak (Nagao & Davis, 1980).

Similar modeling simulations also show that group size and decision rule interact in somewhat counterintuitive ways to influence verdicts (Tindale & Vollrath, 1992; Vollrath & Davis, 1979). In a study of proposed changes to the grand jury system, Vollrath and Davis (1979) showed that different decision rules led to higher indictment rates at some group sizes, and lower rates for other group sizes. A simple example can demonstrate this point. For a five-person jury, a simple majority requires that 60 percent of the jurors (three) agree on a particular verdict. The same majority rule for a four-person jury requires 75 percent of the members (three) to agree. Thus, a five-person jury, in essence, involves a less stringent decision rule under simply majority than does a four-person group. However, for a two-thirds majority rule, the four-person jury still needs 75 percent of the members to agree while a five-person jury needs 80 percent (four of five) to meet the two-thirds criterion. Thus, one can demonstrate that a five-person jury is more conviction prone than a four-person jury under a simply majority rule, yet becomes less conviction prone under a two-thirds majority rule. Given that military courts-martial can have as few as three members, and can vary in size, it can be argued that the current rules of courts-martial do not guarantee equal protection under the law.

Empirical evidence also points to other potential differences owing to jury size and decision rule. Saks and Marti (1997), based on a meta-analysis of research on jury size, reported that six-, as opposed to twelve-person juries are less diverse, deliberate for shorter periods of time, and recall trial evidence somewhat less well. Six-person juries are also less likely to hang than are twelve-person juries, but a hung jury cannot occur in the military justice system. Thus, one of the few empirically supported advantages of smaller juries is irrelevant in this context. Hastie et al. (1983) showed that decision rules less than unanimity led to shorter deliberations and occasionally, less error correction in terms of misstatements of judge's instructions during deliberation. Given that military court members should be more familiar with legal concepts, this may be less of an issue in military juries.

PRELIMINARY SESSION

Before the court-martial is called to order, the members are given preliminary instructions by the military judge, which might include discussing the members' duties. The military judge may also describe procedures for questioning of the witnesses, or on taking notes. The general nature of the charges is then addressed. The military judge then states the plea(s) the accused made earlier, which the members are required to reach decisions upon. The type of plea(s) that was entered generally dictates the proceedings that follow. If the accused entered a plea of guilty to all of the charges, then the judge states this and the trial continues with the members of the court determining the sentence. Alternatively, the consideration of the facts of the trial begins.

TRIAL PROCEEDINGS

The actual trial begins with the prosecution and defense making opening statements, if they choose to do so. The prosecution, then the defense, presents their case and questions witnesses. Once both parties are finished with questioning of a witness, the military judge and court panel members are allowed to ask questions. Members' questions are collected and each question is then examined by both trial and defense counsel, and then given to the military judge. Any objection to the presentation of these questions is raised in a separate Article 39 session.

Again the questioning of witnesses that have been called continues. With this the trial counsels continue to present their case, including presentation of any evidence that has been approved. The defense is then allowed to call any of the witnesses who they want to be questioned. Again the military judge and panel members are given the opportunity to ask additional questions. Allowing jurors to ask questions is rare in civilian trials, but very limited research evidence has shown that the procedure neither harmed nor benefited either side in the proceedings (Penrod & Heuer, 1998). The presentation of both the trial and defense cases is followed by the closing arguments of each side.

In cases where an objection to an improper argument is sustained, the military judge should immediately instruct the members to disregard it. There are cases where an improper argument could be grounds for a mistrial (RCM 915). Although never studied in a military context, a fair amount of research evidence shows that jurors are unable to ignore improper arguments or inadmissible evidence in most circumstances (Kassin & Studebaker, 1998). In fact, simply being told that information is inadmissible for procedural reasons may actually increase its influence on juror judgments, while information inadmissible for reasons of unreliability tends to have little, if any, influence (Kassin & Sommers, 1997). However, Sue, Smith, and Caldwell (1973) found that giving people the reasons for ruling inadmissibility (e.g., unreliability, invalidity) and reliable evidence helps reduce the effect of inadmissible evidence.

There is some evidence that juries are less influenced by improper or inadmissible evidence than are individual jurors. Kerwin and Shaffer (1994) found that jury conviction rates were lower in conditions where some of the incriminating evidence was defined as inadmissible as opposed to admissible, whereas jurors were equally likely to convict in both conditions. Kaplan and Miller (1987) also found that deliberating juries were less influenced by extralegal factors than were individual jurors. However, recent theoretical and empirical work has questioned whether such effects will always occur or only under circumstances where natural group processes exacerbate other tendencies working against the influence of the improper evidence (Kerr, MacCoun, & Kramer, 1996; Kerr, Niedermeier, & Kaplan, 1999).

DELIBERATION AND DECISIONS

Deliberation and voting of the members is done in a closed session of only the members. Superiority of rank of the members is not allowed to be an influencing factor in the control of the deliberation or vote. However, the president of a court-martial is the member who is senior in rank and acts in some ways comparable to the civilian jury foreperson. The president leads over closed sessions (such as deliberations) and is the spokesperson for the members of the court. Although all court members are supposed to be equal in voice and vote, this deference to the senior member as the president allows rank to potentially produce more influence for those of higher rank. Recent research supports the idea that status can have multiple influences on multiperson interactions without these influences being intentional or conscious (Keltner, Gruenfeld, & Anderson, 2003; Ridgeway, 2001). For example, people having higher status or power tend to pay less attention to social norms and focus less attention on those with whom they interact. Thus, higher ranking members of the court may be less influenced by lower status members even without their direct awareness. Lower ranking members will tend to focus their attention toward the high-status members searching for cues as to how best to respond in the situation. Thus, all members may be equal in vote, but it is unlikely they will be equal in voice. Evidence of the influence of more authoritative jury members on deliberation has been reported (Strodtbeck, James, & Hawkins, 1957) and is also found in several chapters dealing with mixed juries in this volume.

An interesting aspect of military courts-martial is that members are allowed to take notes and use them during deliberations. They are also allowed to take copies of submitted evidence and judge's instructions into deliberation. Although note taking has become less rare in civilian juries, jurors are often not allowed to use their notes during the deliberation. However, research has shown that note taking and having access to such notes has little if any effect on deliberations or verdicts (Penrod & Heuer, 1998). Interestingly, it also does not appear to aid juror recall, though research on this is scarce (Penrod & Heuer, 1998). There is even less research on whether access to evidence and instructions during deliberations influences jury performance, but there is some evidence based on nonlegal groups that access to information during discussion can be useful (Sawyer, 1997; Sheffey, Tindale, & Scott, 1989).

After due deliberation, members vote on each charge and specification, by secret written ballot. For all offenses for which the death penalty is not mandated, two thirds of the present members must find the accused guilty. For offenses that require a mandatory penalty of death, all members must vote for a guilty finding. A finding of not guilty results if less than the required two-thirds (or unanimous) vote occurs by the present members. At least three-fourths of the members must vote for a sentence that includes confinement for life, with or without eligibility for parole, or more than 10 years. A summary of these mandated decision rules is presented in Table 6.2.

A majority vote is also required of the members present when the lack of mental responsibility of the accused is an issue. In such cases, two thirds of the members must first vote that the prosecution proved the elements of the case beyond a reasonable doubt and then, if necessary, they proceed with the vote regarding the mental responsibility of the accused. If a majority of the members vote that the accused has proven lack of mental responsibility by clear and convincing evidence, then "not guilty by reason of lack of mental responsibility" is the finding that results. The members determine the issue of lack of mental responsibility for each specification that it is an issue.

If a finding of not guilty has been determined for the greater offense, members then vote on a lesser offense. Members will vote on each lesser included offense charged until they reach a finding of guilty or until they reach a finding of not guilty for all the included offenses. Moreover, members vote on each included offense in order of severity. Before the corresponding charge is voted on, each specification is voted on by the members and the president determines the order of voting on several specifications or charges, unless the members object with a majority vote. The members' ballots are collected and counted by the junior member of the panel, and the president verifies the count and informs the other members of the result.

All multiple component decisions must involve some order of uptake, but research has shown that taking up the most severe charges first can increase the likelihood of juries convicting on lesser charge (Davis, Tindale, Nagao, Hinsz, & Robertson, 1984). Also, research has shown that voting on each element of a charge separately may lead to different outcomes than voting on the charge overall (Kameda, 1996; Lombardero, 1996). Given that the president sets the order elements are voted on, there is some possibility that he/she could influence the outcome by altering the order. However, such effects would be difficult to predict and are probably small.

TABLE 6.2 Decision Rules Applied for Decisions Regarding Different Types of Offenses

Required vote regarding findings	When needed
2/3 vote of members	All offenses for noncapital cases
Unanimous vote all members	Offenses that require a mandatory penalty of death
Majority vote is required by members	Lack of mental responsibility of the accused
Majority vote of the members	Reconsideration of any finding of not guilty
1/3 vote of members	Reconsideration of guilty findings
One vote	Reconsideration when the death penalty is mandatory
1/3 vote of members	Reconsideration of the finding of guilty of the elements in cases of any finding of not guilty by reason of lack of mental responsibility

Reconsideration of any finding may occur before it is announced in open session. Any member may make the proposal for reconsideration of a finding. Findings of not guilty are reconsidered if a majority of the members vote in favor of doing so. More than one third of the members must vote in favor of reconsideration of guilty findings. Only one member needs to be in favor of reconsideration when the death penalty is applied. One third of the members must vote in favor of reconsideration of the finding of guilty of the elements, in cases of any finding of not guilty by reason of lack of mental responsibility, and a majority of the members must vote in favor of the issue of mental responsibility. The initial deliberation and voting procedures are conducted again if the required vote in favor of reconsideration stands. This reconsideration is an interesting way in which the court has an opportunity to continue deliberation if a new argument or interpretation of events arises. It is also interesting to note that a reconsideration of a decision nominally requires the same number of votes such that, upon reconsideration, the original decision would not have achieved the decision rule criterion.

The president is the member of the court who informs the military judge that the panel has reached findings on each charge and specification. The president does not disclose any specific number of votes for any finding. If the panel members found the accused not guilty of all charges and specifications, then the court-martial typically is adjourned, otherwise the trial proceeds with the presentencing procedure.

PRESENTENCING

The presentencing procedure begins with the prosecution, then the defense, presenting matters to the court that will aid the court-martial in determining a sentence. This may include information from the accused's personal records, or evidence of previous convictions, aggravations, and rehabilitation potential (see Rule 1001 of the MCM for a complete discussion on matters presented by both the prosecution and defense).

Following this presentation, the military judge will typically conduct an Article 39 session to determine the instructions that will be given to the members of the court before they deliberate and vote on the sentence. These instructions are given to the court members before deliberation and must include statements of sentencing deliberation and voting procedures, a reminder that they alone are responsible for determining the appropriate sentence, and that the members should consider all matters in extenuation, mitigation, and aggravation. Members may have any of their notes, allowed exhibits, and written instructions with them while deliberating.

DELIBERATION AND VOTING ON SENTENCING

The sentence the court-martial determines may be the maximum punishment, or less, or no punishment at all. (Rule 1003 of the MCM discusses the punishments that the court-martial is authorized to adjudge, and also any limitations regarding specifics of punishment.) After deliberation regarding sentencing for a charge, a proposal for a specific sentence is made in writing by any member. The junior member collects the sentence proposals and submits them to the president. Even if a member initially voted that the accused was not guilty, every member must vote for a sentence for each offense the accused was found guilty. The sentence proposals are voted on in order of severity, beginning with the least severe and moving to the next least severe as necessary. Voting is done by secret ballot and in writing. The junior member collects and counts the ballots. The president verifies the count and informs the other members of the result. The fact that the same jurors who decide guilt also decide punishment is significant, and deviates from civilian trial procedure except for capital cases in some jurisdictions. Research has shown that when jurors also decide punishment they are more likely to find for guilt (compared to when an authority decides punishment) when the evidence is weak and potential punishment is moderate to severe (Kaplan & Krupa, 1986).

These sentencing procedures would tend to aid in protecting the defendants in ways that may not be directly apparent. First, research on anchoring and adjustment (Tversky & Kahneman, 1974) would argue that starting with the least severe sentence would tend to lead to less severe sentences overall, since the first sentence considered would by definition serve as an anchor. Second, allowing members who voted not to convict but to continue their participation during sentencing could result in more lenient sentences owing to their doubt about the accused's guilt in the first place.

All members must vote in favor of the penalty in order for a sentence of death to be declared. Owing to the severity of the potential punishment, there are additional procedures that are taken when dealing with capital cases. For example, before arraignment the defense is informed of the aggravating factors that the prosecution intends to prove, and the accused is allowed broad latitude to introduce evidence regarding extenuating and mitigating circumstances. A death sentence may be adjudged if the members find beyond reasonable doubt that one of aggravating factors occurred and outweighs any extenuating or mitigating circumstances. The military judge informs the members that they must take all the extenuating and mitigating evidence into consideration before they can adjudge death. The members first vote by written secret ballot on the existence of each aggravating factor and then vote on a sentence for a charge. A summary of the decision rules applied to charges with different levels of potential penalties is presented in Table 6.3.

A minimum of three-fourths of the members must endorse a sentence that includes confinement for life, with or without parole, or more than 10 years for it to be assigned. For all other sentences at least two thirds of the members must vote in favor in order for it to be adjudged. A sentencing mistrial may be called if the members do not agree on a sentence after a reasonable effort to do so. In such instances, the case is returned to the convening authority that can impose a no punishment sentence, or order a rehearing of the sentence.

The members may reconsider a sentence at any time provided it is done before the sentence is announced to the court. Any member of the court may propose to reconsider a sentence. A majority of the members must vote in favor of reconsidering the sentence when it would result in increasing the sentence. At

TABLE 6.3 Different Types of Decision Rules for Different Types of Potential Penalties

Required vote regarding sentence	When needed
Unanimous vote of members	Adjudging sentence of death
3/4 vote of members	Adjudging sentence that includes confinement for life, with or without parole, or more than 10 years
2/3 vote of members	Adjudging all other sentences
Majority vote of members	Reconsidering the sentence when it would result in increasing the sentence
One vote	Reconsideration when it would mean decreasing the sentence in cases that the sentence includes death
1/4 vote of members	Reconsideration in cases that the sentence includes confinement for life with or without parole, or more than 10 years
1/3 vote of members	Reconsideration of decreasing other sentences

least one member must vote in favor of reconsideration when it would mean decreasing the sentence that includes death. One fourth of the members must vote in favor of reconsideration in cases that the sentence includes confinement for life, with or without parole, or more than 10 years. For reconsideration that would decrease other sentences, more than one third of the members must vote in favor of the reconsideration. If a vote in favor of reconsideration stands, then the initial deliberation and voting procedures are conducted again. After agreement has been reached regarding the sentence, the court-martial is reopened. The president informs the military judge that the members have reached an agreement regarding the sentence and announces the sentence to the court. In cases in which the members decide on a punishment of death, the president also will announce which aggravating factor(s) they found. After the announcement of the sentence, the members are typically excused from the court.

There are a number of interesting aspects to the procedures outlined in Tables 6.2 and 6.3. As mentioned previously, both jury size and decision rule vary as a function of charge, and decision to be made. Thus, it is possible that very similar offenses may be tried by court panels with very different predispositions for certain types of outcomes. However, many of the more obvious implications are meant to lead to more accurate judgments and to protect the defendant. First, more stringent voting rules are required for more serious charges and sentences. Thus, greater levels of proof via higher levels of consensus are necessary for conviction and sentencing as the consequences for the defendant become more severe. In addition, the voting rules for reconsideration are always less stringent than those necessary for initial conviction. The inclusion of a procedure for reconsideration should also help to counteract the potential of rushing to judgment and pressures toward conformity. In the most serious cases (those involving the death penalty), even one member with a lingering doubt can force the court to reconsider the decision to convict. Such reconsideration options have been proposed in other contexts as a defense against defective initial decision processes (e.g., groupthink; Janis, 1982).

POSTTRIAL PROCEEDINGS

The court is not adjourned until the accused is informed of their rights concerning posttrial and appeal. The accused is first informed that the convening authority takes final action on the case. Moreover, the convening authority may approve the sentence given, a lesser one, or disapprove the entire sentence. However, the convening authority does not have discretion to increase the sentence. In addition, the convening authority may disapprove of any of the guilty findings. The accused is informed that she/he may submit certain information for the convening authority to consider when taking action on the case.

The convening authority may also consider submissions such as clemency recommendations from any court member, the military judge, or other person. The convening authority has the discretion to take action on the findings and sentence of a court-martial. The convening authority may consider (1) the record of the trial; (2) personal records of the accused; and (3) any matters that the convening authority judges important. The convening authority also considers all factors surrounding the sentence, such as rehabilitation possibilities, deterrent effects, and matters relating to clemency. When the accused is found not guilty, the convening authority may not dispute the finding or take action; however, when the accused is found not guilty only by reason of lack of mental responsibility, the convening authority may commit the accused to an appropriate facility after the necessary hearing is conducted.

As the discussion above indicates, a convening authority may take a variety of actions with regard to the findings of a case. They may choose to (1) take no action; (2) change a finding to a lesser-included offense; (3) dismiss a specification or charge; or (4) direct a rehearing. Interestingly, the convening authority may make these decisions "for any reason or no reason" and does not need to explain their reasoning for ordering or not ordering a rehearing.

APPELLATE REVIEW

All courts-martial are at least reviewed by a judge advocate after trial, but not all need to go through appellate review. The record of trial by general court-martial is reviewed by the Judge Advocate General if the case has not already become subject to appellate review. There are three types of appeals courts that a record may go through after trial: the Court of Criminal Appeals, the Court of Appeals for the Armed Forces, and the US Supreme Court. Each succeeding court has more authority and determination.

There are certain general and special courts-martial cases that must go through appellate review. It is mandatory that the Judge Advocate General refers the record of any case in which the sentence adjudged is death to a Court of Criminal Appeals, which includes at least one panel of at least three appellate military judges. Also, courts-martial cases with sentences that amount to dismissal, dishonorable or bad-conduct discharge, or confinement for 1 year or longer are referred to this Court of Criminal Appeals. The Court of Criminal

Appeals determines if the findings and sentence are correct based on the evidence and decides if the sentence is appropriate.

The Court of Appeals for the Armed Forces is the next court in the appellate process. This court is composed of five civilian judges who automatically review a case where death is included in the sentence. The Court of Appeals for the Armed Forces will also review a case if the Judge Advocate General deems necessary after review by the Court of Criminal Appeals or after petition by the accused. This court addresses only questions of law.

The final stage in the appellate process, and the highest court overall, is the US Supreme Court. Basically, there are certain cases in which the decision of the Court of Appeals for the Armed Forces "may be reviewed by the Supreme Court by writ of certiorari." Once this court has taken action, the Judge Advocate General forwards the case to the appropriate authority or has the convening authority take the determined action. Few military courts-martial cases have been reviewed by the Supreme Court.

FINAL THOUGHTS

The American military justice system has many similarities to civilian procedures used both in the United States and elsewhere. However, there are also a number of features that are either rare or nonexistent in other justice domains. Systematic research on juries generally is difficult, and focusing on military courts-martial involves many additional hurdles and complications. However, one of the purposes of the present volume is to bring a number of ideas concerning justice and the use of juries into a common focus. We think that military courts-martial, with their many idiosyncratic characteristics, may both help to inform future discussions on these issues and lead to many new and interesting avenues for research and evaluation.

ACKNOWLEDGMENTS

V.B.H. was supported by grants from the National Science Foundation (BNS 9905397), the Air Force Office of Scientific Research (F49620-02-1-0234) and the National Institute for Mental Health (1 R15 MH63734) and R.S.T. by National Science Foundation grant (SES 0136332).

We appreciate the contributions of Biff LeGrand and the book editors to this chapter.

REFERENCES

Apodaca et al. v. Oregon (1972). *United States Supreme Court Reports*, *406*, 404–415.

Ballew v. Georgia (1978). *United States Law Week*, *46*, 4217–4224.

Burger, J. M. (1981). Motivational biases in the attribution of responsibility for an accident: A meta-analysis of the defensive attribution hypothesis. *Psychological Bulletin*, *90*, 496–512.

Davis, J. H., Kerr, N. L., Atkin, R., Holt, R., & Meek, D. (1975). The decision processes of 6- and 12-person juries assigned unanimous and two-thirds majority rules. *Journal of Personality and Social Psychology*, *32*, 1–14.

Davis, J. H., Tindale, R. S., Nagao, D. H., Hinsz, V. B., & Robertson, B. A. (1984). Order effects in multiple decisions by groups: A demonstration with mock juries and trial procedures. *Journal of Personality and Social Psychology*, *47*, 1003–1012.

Filkins, J., Smith, C. M., & Tindale, R. S. (1998). The fairness of death qualified juries: A meta-analytic/Simulation approach. In R. S. Tindale, J. E. Edwards, L. Heath, E. J. Posavac, F. B. Bryant, E. Henderson-King, Y. Suarez-Balcazar, & J. Myers (Eds.), *Social psychological applications to social issues: Applications of theory and research on small groups* (Vol. 4, pp. 153–176). New York: Plenum Press.

Hans, V. P., & Vidmar, N. J. (1982). Jury selection. In N. Kerr & R. Bray (Eds.), *The psychology of the courtroom* (pp. 39–81). New York: Academic Press.

Hastie, R., Penrod, S. D., & Pennington, N. (1983). *Inside the jury*. Cambridge, MA: Harvard University Press.

Horowitz, I. A. (1980). Juror selection: A comparison of two methods in several criminal cases. *Journal of Applied Social Psychology*, *10*, 86–99.

Janis, I. (1982). *Groupthink*. Boston: Houghton-Mifflin.

Kameda, T. (1996). Procedural influence in consensus formation: Evaluating group decision making from a social choice perspective. In E. Witte & J. H. Davis (Eds.), *Understanding group behavior: Consensual action by small groups* (Vol. 1, pp. 137–161). Mahwah, NJ: Lawrence Erlbaum Associates.

Kaplan, M. F., & Krupa, S. (1986). Severe penalties under the control of others can reduce guilt verdicts. *Law and Psychology Review*, *10*, 1–18.

Kaplan, M. F., & Miller, C. E. (1987). Group decision making and normative versus informational influence: Effects of type of issue and assigned decision rule. *Journal of Personality and Social Psychology*, *53*, 306–313.

Kassin, S. M., & Sommers, S. R. (1997). Inadmissible testimony, instructions to disregard, and the jury: Substantive versus procedural considerations. *Personality and Social Psychology Bulletin*, *23*, 1046–1054.

Kassin, S. M., & Studebaker, C. A. (1998). Instructions to disregard and the jury: Curative and paradoxical effects. In J. M. Golding & C. M. MacLeod (Eds.), *Intentional forgetting: Interdisciplinary approaches* (pp. 155–171). Mahwah, NJ: Lawrence Erlbaum Associates.

Keltner, D., Gruenfeld, D. H., & Anderson, C. (2003). Power, approach, and inhibition. *Psychological Review*, *110*, 265–284.

Kerr, N. L., MacCoun, R. J., & Kramer, G. P. (1996). Bias in judgment: Comparing individuals and groups. *Psychological Review*, *103*, 687–719.

Kerr, N. L., Niedermeier, K. E., & Kaplan, M. F. (1999). Bias in jurors vs. bias in juries: New evidence from the SDS perspective. *Organizational Behavior and Human Decision Processes*, *80*, 70–86.

Kerwin, J., & Shaffer, D. R. (1994). Mock jurors versus mock juries: The role of deliberations in reactions to inadmissible testimony. *Personality and Social Psychology Bulletin*, *20*, 153–162.

Lombardero, D. A. (1996). Do special verdicts improve the structure of jury decision-making? *Jurimetrics Journal*, *36*, 275–324.

Manual for Courts-Martial United States (2002). Washington, DC: U.S. Government Printing Office.

Martin, L. L., & Tesser, A. (1992). *The construction of social judgments*. Hillsdale, NJ: Lawrence Erlbaum Associates.

McGuire, W. J. (1969). The nature of attitudes and attitude change. In G. Lindsey & E. Aronson (Eds.), *The handbook of social psychology* (2nd ed., Vol. 3, pp. 136–314). Reading, MA: Addison-Wesley.

Military Justice Overview (2003). Obtained from the Office of the Navy Judge Advocate General, Washington Navy Yard, DC, USA.

Nagao, D. H., & Davis, J. H. (1980). Some implications of temporal drift in social parameters. *Journal of Experimental Social Psychology, 16*, 479–496.

Olczak, P. V., Kaplan, M. F., & Penrod, S. D. (1991). Attorneys' lay psychology and its effectiveness in selecting jurors: Three empirical studies. *Journal of Social Behavior and Personality, 6*, 1–21.

Penrod, S. D., & Heuer, L. (1998). Improving group performance: The case of the jury. In R. S. Tindale, J. E. Edwards, L. Heath, E. J. Posavac, F. B. Bryant, E. Henderson-King, Y. Suarez-Balcazar, & J. Myers (Eds.), *Social psychological applications to social issues: Theory and research on small groups* (Vol. 4, pp. 127–152). New York: Plenum Press.

Ridgeway, C. L. (2001). Social status and group structure. In M. H. Hogg & R. S. Tindale (Eds.), *Blackwell handbook of social psychology: Group processes* (pp. 352–375). Oxford, UK: Blackwell Publishers.

Roan, J. B., & Buxton, C. (2002). The American military justice system in the new millennium. *The Air Force Law Review, 52*, 185.

Saks, M. J. (1976). The limits of scientific jury selection: Ethical and empirical. *Jurimetrics Journal, 17*, 3–22.

Saks, M. J., & Marti, M. W. (1997). A meta-analysis of the effects of jury size. *Law and Human Behavior, 21*, 451–467.

Sawyer, J. E. (1997, November). *Information sharing and integration in multifunctional decision-making groups.* Paper presented at the Society of Judgment and Decision Making Annual Meeting, Philadelphia, PA.

Schlueter, D. (1999). *Military Criminal Justice Practice and Procedure* (5th ed.). Charlottesville, VA: LEXIS Law.

Sheffey, S., Tindale, R. S., & Scott, L. A. (1989, May). *Information sharing and group decision making.* Paper presented at the Midwestern Psychological Association Annual Convention, Chicago, IL.

Strodtbeck, F. L., James, R. M., & Hawkins, C. (1957). Social status in jury deliberations. *American Sociological Review, 22*, 713–718.

Sue, S., Smith, R. E., & Caldwell, C. (1973). Effects of inadmissible evidence on the decisions of simulated juror: A moral dilemma. *Journal of Applied Social Psychology, 3*, 345–350.

Thibaut, J. W., & Walker, L. (1975). *Procedural justice.* Hillsdale, NJ: Lawrence Erlbaum Associates.

Tindale, R. S., & Davis, J. H. (1983). Group decision making and jury verdicts. In H. H. Blumberg, A. P. Hare, V. Kent, & M. F. Davies (Eds.), *Small groups and social interaction* (Vol. 2, pp. 9–38). Chichester, UK: Wiley.

Tindale, R. S., & Nagao, D. H. (1986). An assessment of the potential utility of "Scientific Jury Selection": A "thought experiment" approach. *Organizational Behavior and Human Decision Processes, 37*, 409–425.

Tindale, R. S., & Vollrath, D. A. (1992). "Thought experiments" in applied social research. In F. B. Bryant, J. E. Edwards, R. S. Tindale, E. J. Posavac, L. Heath, E. Henderson, & Y. Suarez-Balcazar (Eds.), *Social psychological applications to social issues: Methodological issues in applied social research* (Vol. 2, pp. 219–238). New York: Plenum Press.

Tversky, A., & Kahneman, D. (1974). Judgment under uncertainty: Heuristics and biases. *Science*, *185*, 1124–1130.
Uniform Code of Military Justice (UCMJ). Retrieved November 11, 2004 from http://www.military-network.com/main_ucmj/main_ucmj.htm
Vollrath, D. A., & Davis, J. H. (1979). Evaluating proposals for social change with minimal data: An example from grand jury reform proposals. *Law and Human Behavior*, *3*, 121–134.
Williams v. Florida, 90 S. Ct. 1893 (1970).

Part II

Mixed (Lay and Professional) Juries

7

Issues and Prospects in European Juries: An Overview

MARTIN F. KAPLAN, ANA M. MARTÍN, and JANINE HERTEL

European juries differ importantly in form and function from North American juries, and from one another, evoking social-psychological principles not normally applied to the latter. The vast majority of social-psychological research has been conducted on the processes and their consequence in North American juries; this chapter is intended to stimulate research that will address characteristics unique to European trial juries. We first survey the core characteristics of European juries, highlighting differences and similarities among several national systems. In limited space, we do not attempt to exhaustively describe all national juries (see Vidmar, 2000, for a thorough review; see also the chapters on individual systems in this volume) but we do touch on the essential systemic characteristics found in Europe as a whole. We then discuss the social-psychological concepts and research evoked by issues uniquely raised by European juries. Relevant implications and research will be cited, and suggestions for future applied and comparative research will be offered.

In the first section we identify features that differentiate between European national systems. These include (1) "mixed" or *Escabinado* juries composed of lay and professional jurors versus "pure" juries of laypersons alone; (2) degree of limitations on jury discretion and power; (3) variations in evidentiary rules; and (4) rules for reaching and justifying verdicts. These features invite applications from social-psychological research and theory, which are discussed in the second section. Applications include: (1) intragroup influence; (2) group member roles and status; (3) group discussion of information that is initially unshared by all members; (4) order and sequence of polling; (5) effects of decision rule; (6) minority and majority power and processing differences; and (7) selectivity and depth of information processing.

CORE CHARACTERISTICS OF EUROPEAN JURIES

Mixed Versus Pure Juries: General Characteristics

Perhaps the most critical difference between European and North American juries lies in their composition. In some (though not all) of the former, mixed juries of laypersons and professional judges are the rule. Moreover, from one nation to the other, the layperson faction is selected differently, has a different charge, and serves for different terms, all being important variations.

Pure juries are composed entirely of laypersons. England and Scotland have had such juries for much of their history, as detailed elsewhere in this volume. On the other hand, the pure juries of Spain and Russia are of more recent vintage, having been developed in the past decade following major political changes in their governments. Interestingly, the forces that produced pure juries had to reconcile the movement toward democracy in their nations with a long-standing distrust of the laity. Hence, we will see in a later section that the restraints placed on Spanish and Russian pure juries are quite unlike those found in Anglo-American juries.

Mixed juries, containing both laypersons and judges (or "professional jurors") are more common in continental Europe. In most instances, the jury panel contains a preponderance of the former, though the exact number of each varies with the nation and the type of crime. In Germany and Poland, for example, a court of two laypersons and one professional judge tries civil and most criminal cases, whereas serious crimes are heard by two laypersons and three judges in Germany and the reverse proportion in Poland. Mixed juries in Italy contain eight jurors, six of whom are laypersons, and France has nine laypersons among its 12 jurors. Perhaps reflecting a greater trust in juries that contain at least one professional judge, nations with pure juries have larger panels: nine in Spain, 12 in Russia and England, and 15 in Scotland (though the Scottish jury size is due to the complexity of the decision structure—see the chapter in this volume). Also owing to the presence of professional judges in mixed juries, they are entrusted with deciding penalties as well as verdicts in criminal cases.

Another characteristic accruing to mixed juries is their presence at several levels of the judicial process. That is, in pure jury systems, lay jurors participate only in courts of original jurisdiction, not in appeal courts. In France and Italy, however, laypersons serve in both original and appeal mixed courts, whereas in Poland and Germany, mixed juries are limited to the original trial. Common to mixed but not pure juries, jurors may ask questions of witnesses during the trial, though this prerogative is rarely exercised (see the chapters on France and Germany in this volume).

Within mixed juries, formal steps are taken to reduce the difference in status between laypersons and professional judges. The former are informed of the importance of their participation (though, as repeatedly shown in this volume, the instructions are impotent), and in at least one country (Poland) both factions wear the same outfits (though in another, Italy, they wear "different" regalia!). More importantly, rules govern the voting order during deliberation, so that in all instances, lay jurors vote before judges, as a gesture to lessen the undue influence of the latter. However, in all countries, the senior judge chairs the panel, and in at least one country (Germany) the senior professional judge summarizes the case before deliberation.

LAY JUROR SELECTION

Initial selection of citizens to jury pools is either by random selection from voter lists (e.g., England, France, Russia, Scotland, and Spain) or by the "key man" method (e.g., Germany, Italy, and Poland) whereby important officers in the community, such as mayors, assessors, and municipal commissioners, select potential jurors. Whether the different methods result in demographically different populations with different judicial attitudes remains to be seen. Certainly, the appearance of fairness and objectivity is questionable in the "key man" method of identifying lay jurors, but in at least two nations, Italy and Germany, the lists are posted and citizens who were not chosen may add their names if they meet qualifications. This safeguard adds another empirical question yet unaddressed: Is there a qualitative difference in demographics and attitudes between jurors who were selected and those who volunteered for service?

Once the jury pool is identified, and the few eligible for exclusion have been removed, assignment to trials is typically random. Few requests for avoiding service are accepted; in all countries jury service is officially considered both an honor and a requirement. Service, however, varies greatly in length. In some countries (e.g., France, Russia, and Spain), laypersons serve for the length of the trial for which one was selected. In Italy, a layperson serves for three months, regardless of the number of trials. In Germany and Poland, though, one is on call for four years, with a maximum of 12 days of service per year, and 12 trials during the four-year term in Germany. Thus, the term and frequency of trial service vary considerably not only between pure and mixed juries among European nations, but also within such juries, raising the possibility of experience effects.

When jurors are randomly selected for a particular trial, there is minimal vetting for being placed on that jury, certainly compared to the voir dire practices of North American jury selection. In most jurisdictions, dismissing jurors by challenge is not practiced.

JURY DECISION MAKING

It is evident from the preceding that a major distinctive characteristic of many European juries is that they are composed of a mixture of lay and professional judges. This composition is the basis for considerable analysis in the chapters in this volume, but each chapter looks at different potential consequences, and from different vantages within social psychology. However, all treatments come back to one central issue: Do the status and experience differences between jury factions matter? And if so, how do they play out? This will be the central concern in the second half of this chapter.

In the deliberation process, we find a second major distinction in European juries: There is formal and systematic pressure for pure juries to justify their decisions. In both Spain and Russia, where pure juries are a recent phenomenon (after decades of absence from the system), juries are provided with a list of questions, both specific and unique to the trial, which must be answered to justify not only the verdict, but also the reasoning behind the verdict. Juries give not only a verdict, but also a response to each question of fact, giving them considerably more issues for which to attain consensus than in other pure juries. The burden may indeed be quite large: In the chapter on Spanish and Russian juries in this volume, cases are documented in which hundreds of questions were provided. In the highly publicized political trial of businessman Mikhail Khodorkovsky in Russia, judges repeated 1200 pages of evidence and testimony in court that had been "proven" before reporting their verdict ("Trial proves a top snooze-maker," 2005).

Before leaving this brief overview of European juries, it is worthwhile to note that the division between mixed and pure juries is also reflected in the prescribed decision rule. In the mixed jury countries, a guilt verdict requires a two-thirds (France, Germany), or majority (Italy, Poland) vote. In pure juries, the requirement is more stringent; Spain requires seven out of nine to vote guilty, both overall and on each proposition in the question list, and England requires a 10 to two vote. Russia requires unanimity unless a decision is not reached within a reasonable amount of time, then it accepts a vote of seven to five for guilt. Scotland requires only eight of 15 to vote guilty, but it also has a third alternative of "not proven" (see the chapter on England and Scotland in this volume). If pure juries are considered less reliable than mixed juries, it follows that a more overwhelming vote is needed to find for guilt in the former.

We identify, then, three distinctive characteristics of European juries for social-psychological analysis. The major characteristics are *jury composition* (mixed vs. pure), and *verdict justification* or detailed questions lists that are required of some juries. But we first examine *juror selection*, as integral to composition issues.

SOCIAL-PSYCHOLOGICAL ISSUES RAISED BY VARIATIONS IN EUROPEAN JURIES

Juror Selection

Who Serves on Juries? Laypersons serve on pure or mixed juries, depending on the national system. Beyond this distinction, there are marked differences in how they are selected and how long they serve. As detailed earlier, and in other chapters in this volume, inclusion in juror pools ranges from identification by community officials to random selection from voter lists. In some countries, particularly those in which jurors were selected by officials, additional jurors may volunteer for service, producing a distinction between "drafted" and volunteer jurors. Finally, juror service ranges from short-term (e.g., one trial) to long-term (e.g., on-call for four years). Common to all nations are the few statutory excuses for avoiding service, and the minimal juror examination and use of challenges prior to trial, compared to North American juries.

The consequences of variations in juror selection and length of service provoke social-psychological questions. Immediately obvious is the question of whether persons selected by the "key man" system (that is, by community leaders) differ from those selected from more public and general sources, e.g., voter lists, and whether these sets of drafted jurors differ from volunteer jurors in demographic attributes and social and legal attitudes. This would appear to be a rather straightforward subject for studies, though none have been reported. More subtly, are there differences between these groups with regard to their social identity vis-à-vis the community? In most European nations, jury rules are explicit in naming lay jurors as the representatives of the community in legal proceedings. Is this sense of identity enhanced by selection by political leaders versus random selection versus volunteering? In turn, enhanced sense of identity would strengthen the cohesion of lay factions in mixed juries and facilitate their ability to withstand the influence of professional factions.

Other issues emerge, too, with the variations in juror selection. Does the method of selection affect reactance? It is conceivable that drafted jurors, particularly those chosen randomly (and therefore those who had least power over their inclusion), would experience more reactance. Those having less motivation to serve (i.e., randomly selected jurors) could potentially suffer in requisite cognitive skills such as attention and recall during trial, compared to volunteers.

Aside from issues regarding the jurors themselves, there are other questions that arise. How representative of the community is a jury pool that was selected by community leaders, or that contains volunteers? Does the method of selecting jurors affect community perceptions of the courts and justice system? Selection by community leaders could conceivably enhance the stature of selectees, but does this improve attitudes toward the courts?

Length of Service European juries vary greatly in length of service for the individual juror. One potential consequence is that jurors with longer terms of service may assume an aura of professionalism, identifying more with professional judges in mixed tribunals. Another consequence is that jurors who have served for extended periods on the same panel may be liable to adopt a "group set" (Thibaut & Strickland, 1956) whereby maintenance of group harmony becomes a more important goal than adherence to task demands. With an increase in cohesiveness comes greater effort to produce agreement (Back, 1951) to maintain cohesion. Though this normative conformity could well be a problem in professional judge factions of mixed juries, due to greater length of conjunctive service, it may also appear in lay juries that coact over a greater length of time.

Jury Composition

The most critical distinction in the structure of European juries is the use of pure, or strictly lay juries, versus mixed, or *Escabinado* juries. We will concentrate on the issues raised by the latter type of juries since virtually all applied jury research, particularly on North American juries, has focused on lay juries. Fortunately, social-psychological research on small group behavior is plentiful regarding the interaction of minority and majority factions (whether status is defined by power or size) and many implications can be drawn for the European mixed jury.

Structurally, mixed juries have two factions: lay and professional judges. In all nations having such juries, their composition, rationale, and duties are more or less clearly defined (see the relevant chapters in this volume for details). However, from a decision-making standpoint, it remains to be seen whether they do indeed constitute separate factions. That is, they are factions only if they differ in preferred outcomes in each case. Empirical evidence on this score is sparse, but generally paints lay judges as being more conviction-prone and punitive than professional judges (see, e.g., Bliesener; Catellani & Milesi, this volume), although perceptions by professional judges offer an opposite view (see, e.g., Parlak, this volume). As Ginet, Guimond, and Greffeuille (this volume) point out, whether the factions differ in initial verdict preferences probably depends on the interaction of case specifics and issues with lay and professional legal philosophies; therefore, empirical research is needed to uncover distinctive attitudes and their effect on verdict proclivities of factions.

Owing to variations in training and personal determinants, mixed jury factions likely differ in legal philosophies. Research is needed to identify faction differences (if any) in punitiveness, goals of punishment, and strict interpretation of the law versus social justice as goals of legal proceedings. Several of the chapters in this volume report promising research beginnings with regard to a number of attitude variables. In this chapter, it is not necessary to assume that factions possess different goals, attitudes, or initial verdict preferences; instead, we examine whether the factions differ in "processes" of group decision-making, and how such differences can affect decisions.

Role Differentiation and Status In coacting groups, especially those with formalized duties such as juries, members are likely to assume differentiated roles (Bales & Slater, 1955), often delineated by status differences (Adams, 1965). As demonstrated elsewhere in this volume, status differences in mixed juries are unavoidable. However, the issue is whether role differentiation via status matters for group process and decision outcomes. Lee and Ofshe (1981) found in a non-jury decision setting that it is not the status per se of professional members that enhances their dominance, but their authoritative behavior. Thus, in studying the interaction of mixed jury factions, it would be fruitful to look at their behavior during deliberation.

But lay and professional jurors are differentiated in two, opposing ways. One is in status (or more to the point, expertise and authoritative behavior) and the other is in numbers. While laypersons have less authority, they have numerical superiority in nearly all instances (except for particular crimes in Germany). In drawing a parallel with the literature on minority and majority factions, do we consider lay jurors as a minority or majority? For present purpose, we suggest that the lay faction may be considered a "functional" minority, both because they generally exert less influence in juries (Kaplan & Martín, 1999; Martín,

Kaplan, & Álamo, 2003; see also Bliesener; Catellani & Milesi; Ginet et al., and Parlak, this volume), and they are perceived by the professional judge faction as less relevant and efficacious (Parlak, this volume). Moreover, though potential participants in groups predict that numerically larger factions will exert greater influence during discussion, in reality size does not affect the number of arguments generated by individuals (Kerr & Watts, 1982). It remains to be seen whether number of arguments generated is unaffected by foreknowledge of status/expertise, though Kaplan and Martín (1999) found the "type," but not the "amount" of argumentation to be affected by faction status in mock juries.

At the outset we noted that role differentiation in mixed juries is codified by court practice. However, an interesting question for future study is whether, and to what extent, members identify with their faction. Do lay jurors identify with their nominal faction? Or do they aspire to identification with professional judges? Where lay service is of lengthy duration, will this lead to stronger identification with the lay role, or to identification with professional, long-term judges? Does the strength of identification with one's faction enhance certain group identity effects, such as out-group homogeneity (Linville & Fischer, 1993) whereby the "other" group is seen as more homogeneous in its views than one's own group, and the "black sheep" effect (Marques, Yzerbyt, & Leyens, 1988) whereby a deviant member of one's faction is judged extremely? In research cited by Parlak (this volume) we already see evidence of one effect of group identity, wherein professional judges (who likely have strong in-group identity, developed over time and similar experiences) routinely derogate the layperson outgroup.

When the Minority Dissents The interesting case emerges in instances where the power minority—the lay faction—disagrees with the power majority. Such instances may be fairly common as they need not be limited to verdict preferences, but could occur in discussion of any facts that must be proven at trial. Evidence in nonjury settings suggests that minority dissent has a salutary effect on decision process and outcome. Exposure to minority dissent facilitates finding new solutions to a problem (Nemeth & Wachtler, 1983), and increases cognitive activity in the majority (Nemeth, 1995). Minority dissent stimulates divergent thought whereby the group thinks of the issues from multiple perspectives (Maass & Clark, 1983; Nemeth, 1995), and considers information not commonly shared by all members (Klauer, Wegener, & Ehrenberg, 2002). Thus, a viable minority can increase the breadth of ideas shared in discussion. But it is not so simple a matter for minority input to improve the tone of discussion. First, for minorities to be effective, it is important that they maintain consistency in their behavior (Moscovici & Lage, 1976), and that they provide social support within the faction (Allen & Levine, 1968). Given that lay jurors are from diverse backgrounds, might not serve together on multiple panels, and do not behave with the same authority as professional jurors, consistency and social support may not always be found. To illustrate potential behavioral differences between factions, persons low in self-esteem behave more defensively, justifying themselves by being compliant (Schuetz, 1998). Lay jurors are also less likely to express their feelings than professional jurors. Anderson and Berdahl (2002) found that persons higher in power are more likely to express their true attitudes, and less likely to perceive threat (see also anecdotal research reported in Parlak, this volume). Further working against the positive impact of the lay faction (again, considering laypersons as a power minority) is that minorities are more selective in acquiring information during trial, focusing on evidence they can use during deliberation to defend their views (Van Hiel & Franssen, 2003). This defensive posture accords with Schuetz's (1998) conclusion of defensiveness in self-presentation, and bodes poorly for a strong and consistent pattern of dissent by disagreeing lay factions.

It can be concluded that strong pressures work against consistent and unified dissent by the power minority (lay) faction. Where the laypersons in mixed juries disagree with the majority viewpoint "and" consistently express the disagreement, consideration of facts and "stories" about the case events is broadened, and conformity is lessened. With a vigorously presented dissent by minorities, the group as a whole is less likely to adopt a confirmatory bias in acquiring and weighing information (Schulz-Hardt, Jochims, & Frey, 2002). Thus, while much research shows that dissent improves the decision process, such research typically inserts the dissent into the discussion; it is unclear whether optimum conditions exist in mixed juries for the free communication of lay juror views.

Influence and Processing Styles We now consider the way in which lay and professional factions process information and engage in deliberative argumentation. We have already seen that by dissent, minorities can increase the breadth of information and variety of decisions considered by the group. It follows that groups entertaining a greater variety of options for understanding the case would be more likely to use a diagnostic strategy in acquiring and discussing information than a confirmatory strategy. That is, where there is a vocal minority, juries should consider a broader range of information and interpretation in order to solve the issues rather than consider only information that would confirm a preferred verdict. Indeed, Schulz-Hardt et al. (2002) confirm that dissent prevents the confirmation bias.

The dual-process model (Chaiken, 1980; Chaiken, Liberman, & Eagly, 1989) posits a continuum in reasoning about an issue ranging from heuristic to systematic processing. The former entails the use of judgmental rules that simplify decision-making. It is characterized by less in-depth processing as well as less breadth in information accessed and used—as, for example, focusing on one or a very few items for the decision. Systematic reasoning is more effortful, and represents a more comprehensive, inclusive, and integrative mode of thought. Should we expect differences between lay and professional jurors in their level of reasoning within this continuum? The answer is complicated by the tendency for both the theory and research on dual-process models to blur the distinction between how minority and majority factions reason, how they argue to the other faction, and how they respond to arguments from the other faction. Moscovici and Lage (1976) argued that numerical majorities would expend less effort (that is, would be more heuristic) because having the numerical superiority, they could meet the goal for sufficiency without difficulty. Minorities, on the other hand, do not have numbers on their side, and so must argue the facts thoroughly. This analysis may not apply to the mixed jury, where the power minority is the numerical majority. But the larger problem is whether one is looking at private reasoning, initial argument, and subsequent discussion. Majorities with greater decision power, whether by status or numbers, may put less effort into thinking about the issues, but as we have seen, introduction of minority dissent increases the diversity of thought in the group. So, while minorities might initially reason, and perhaps even argue more systematically, they may ultimately engender systematic thought in the majority. What is needed, in mixed juries or in any group context, is clear delineation between level of private thought, public argumentation, and response to argumentation (Kaplan & Wilke, 2001; Wilke & Kaplan, 2001). Further qualifying conclusions regarding reasoning levels of the factions, minorities reason more systematically when self-interest "is not" involved, and majorities reason more systematically when self-interest "is" involved (Martin & Hewstone, 2003).

Influence processes may also differ in whether they are predominantly normative or informational (Deutsch & Gerard, 1955). Normative influence is a social form of influence in which pressure is exerted to conform to the expectations and preferences of others. Informational influence is a more task-centered influence to accept information about the issues as evidence of reality. At first glance, it would be expected that minorities would favor an informational argument style and majorities a normative style since the within group norm favors the latter faction (e.g., Moscovici & Lage, 1976). But in European juries the professional faction should possess expert, as well as normative power by virtue of training and experience, and so should naturally wield informational influence. Or, might the sort of influence used, and most effective for each faction depend on the nature of the case issues? The type of influence used by group members is highly determined by whether the issue is predominantly intellective (a matter of determining facts) or judgmental (no factually correct solution, but solution is determined by preferences). Intellective issues elicit more informational, and judgmental issues elicit more normative influence (Kaplan, 1989; Kaplan & Miller, 1987; Rugs & Kaplan, 1993). In a mock jury experiment involving juries of three lay and two trained members, Kaplan and Martín (1999) found that trained jurors were more influential than lay jurors only when the cases presented a predominantly judgmental issue (e.g., harassment). The former also were more active than lay jurors in such cases, and exerted more normative influence. Lay jurors engaged in more informational influence. Thus, at least in a mock setting, naïve or lay jurors wield more informational and less normative influence than trained or professional jurors. In turn, the faction using the influence style most effective for the particular issue would likely be more influential in that instance. One may conclude that since professional judges were more influential using normative influence in judgmental cases, the type of power they possessed was, in French and Raven's (1959) terms, "social-normative" power.

We need content-based analyses of mixed jury deliberations that systematically measure information acquisition (e.g., a confirmatory vs. a diagnostic strategy), reasoning levels (e.g., systematic vs. heuristic), and influence processes (e.g., normative vs. informational), and then relate such differences between lay and professional jurors to their impact on the decisions. Following the lead of Kaplan and Martín (1999), it is important to recognize that acquisition strategies, processing, and influence styles of minority and majority factions could well interact with the nature of the issues being decided. The degree to which the underlying issue in a case is intellective or judgmental should be systematically taken into account in any real or mock jury research.

Verdict Justification and Questions Lists

In those European systems that employ pure juries, two nations (Russia and Spain) require formal justification of verdicts as a check on the competence of juries and as a record to facilitate future appeals (see Martín & Kaplan, in this volume). Juries are asked specific questions about the case, in the form of propositions, and must provide answers according to statutory decision rules. Questions are posed so that in order to justify the summary verdict, e.g., to prove guilt, consensus must be reached on each proposition. That is, the jury must formally demonstrate that certain elements have been, or have not been proven. In addition, in Spain, the jury must provide a brief rationale indicating the evidence for finding a particular proposition proved or not proved.

This is obviously quite a task for lay juries. Does this make them better decision makers? Framed in terms of dual-process theory, does it produce more systematic (compared to heuristic) reasoning? Are juries more likely to examine relevant and critical evidence in depth, eschewing irrelevant, superficial evidence and stereotypes? In terms of argumentation and influence processes, does provision of questions to be addressed and justified promote informational over normative influence? Similarly, does it facilitate evidence-driven over verdict-driven discussion? By focusing on the evidence, does it minimize the intrusion of biases? These are fertile grounds for social-psychological analysis, but as yet no direct research on these questions has been attempted in European lay juries, or in their mock-jury surrogates. However, some tentative, though conflicting answers may be gleaned from social-psychological research.

At first glance, one would think that specifying logical elements of the decision and forcing jurors to apply evidence toward consideration of these elements would foster a central route to persuasion (Cacioppo, Petty, Kao, & Rodriguez, 1986), systematic reasoning (Chaiken, 1987), and an evidence-driven style of deliberation (Hastie, Pennington, & Penrod, 1983). But recall that the question lists can be quite lengthy, and can introduce a plethora of items to consider. This can lead to a heavy cognitive load, which can interfere with systematic, in-depth reasoning. With overload, there is less integration and use of complex information unless one has an accessible schema to organize the information (Bargh & Thein, 1985). Where would jurors find such a pre-existing schema to simplify the information load imposed by the questions? Possibly from their biases and stereotypes! In a complex judgment situation that increases cognitive load, people organize the information to be consistent with their stereotypes, and neglect stereotype-inconsistent information (Bodenhausen & Lichtenstein, 1987). Thus, if the questions produce an overload, jurors may restrict their systematic reasoning to evidence consistent with their stereotype, ignoring relevant information that may prove them wrong. Under lower load, however, it has been shown that people have better recall for stereotype-inconsistent information (Macrae, Hewstone, & Griffiths, 1993). Thus, increasing load can lead to less diversity of information taken into account—an undesirable outcome. Though forcing decision makers to consider many factors narrows their focus to information most relevant to a decision (Tordesillas & Chaiken, 1999), the aforementioned studies suggest that processing could be directed to more salient and accessible evidence, that is, that evidence provided by the questions list, or worse, pre-existing stereotypes.

The question lists may also be suggestive regarding which evidence to favor. How the questions are phrased, and which evidence items are highlighted could be a cue to differential weight to be placed on certain evidence, and which verdicts are more probable. In decision-theoretic terms, the particular questions that are asked could make the likelihood of some events more probable, or at the least, would make some evidence more available to recall (Tversky & Kahneman, 1973, 1974). Thus, the very questions could invoke a major heuristic availability. Nor is the requirement to answer factual questions a safeguard against biases. It has been demonstrated that answers to individual questions are themselves differentially affected by biases (De la Fuente, García, & De la Fuente, 2003).

It is arguable that restricting deep consideration to evidence that is consistent with the emerging consensus verdict and dismissing contradictory evidence is a possible and negative consequence of the suggestiveness and overload-producing functions of long, involved questions.

CONCLUSION

The two most salient features of European juries—the provision of mixed juries in some nations and the requirement for formally justifying elements of decisions in those with pure juries—might serve as a safeguard against the potential incompetence, bias, and capriciousness of lay jurors. While either having professional jurors sit with laypersons on juries, or instituting direction on how lay juries are to reason about the case might appear to be strong safeguards against lay juror errors (compare to the US, where the possibility of juror error is controlled by judicial instructions and detailed rules of evidence and trial procedure), there is little direct evidence of their effectiveness in improving the quality of lay juror decision making. Reference to existing social-psychological theory and research provides mixed support for these innovations. The safeguards currently in place may indeed produce unintended negative consequences. Only research on existing and mock European juries, as systematically outlined in this chapter, can provide definitive answers on the outcomes of mixed juries, and stringent controls on lay juries.

REFERENCES

Adams, J. S. (1965). Inequity in social exchange. In L. Berkowitz (Ed.), *Advances in experimental social psychology* (Vol. 1, pp. 267–299). New York: Academic Press.

Allen, V. L., & Levine, J. M. (1968). Social support, dissent and conformity. *Sociometry*, *31*, 138–149.

Anderson, C., & Berdahl, J. L. (2002). The experience of power: Examining the effects of power on approach and inhibition tendencies. *Journal of Personality and Social Psychology*, *83*, 1362–1377.

Back, K. W. (1951). Influence through social communication. *Journal of Abnormal and Social Psychology*, *46*, 9–23.

Bales, R. F., & Slater, P. E. (1955). Role differentiation in small decision-making groups. In T. Parsons & R. F. Bales (Eds.), *Family socialization and interaction process* (pp. 259–306). New York: The Free Press of Glencoe.

Bargh, J. A., & Thein, R. D. (1985). Individual construct accessibility, person memory, and the recall-judgment link: The case of information overload. *Journal of Personality and Social Psychology*, *49*, 1129–1146.

Bodenhausen, G. V., & Lichtenstein, M. (1987). Social stereotypes and information-processing strategies: The impact of task complexity. *Journal of Personality and Social Psychology*, *52*, 871–880.

Cacioppo, J. T., Petty, R. E., Kao, C. F., & Rodriguez, R. (1986). Central and peripheral routes to persuasion: An individual difference perspective. *Journal of Personality and Social Psychology*, *51*, 1032–1043.

Chaiken, S. (1980). Heuristic versus systematic information processing and the use of source versus message cues in persuasion. *Journal of Personality and Social Psychology*, 39, 752–766.

Chaiken, S. (1987). The heuristic model of persuasion. In M. P. Zanna & J. M. Olson (Eds.), *Social influence: The Ontario symposium* (pp. 3–39). Hillsdale, NJ: Lawrence Erlbaum Associates, Inc.

Chaiken, S., Liberman, A., & Eagly, A. H. (1989). Heuristic and systematic information processing within and beyond the persuasion context. In J. S. Uleman & J. A. Bargh (Eds.), *Unintended thought* (pp. 212–252). New York: Guilford Press.

De la Fuente, S. L., García, J. G., & De la Fuente, S. E. I. (2003). Validez de la Escala de Sesgo del Jurado en relación con las decisiones grupales de jurados simulados [Validity of the Juror Bias Scale in relation to mock jury decisions.] *Psicothema*, *15*, 148–154.

Deutsch, M., & Gerard, H. B. (1955). A study of normative and informational social influence upon individual judgment. *Journal of Abnormal and Social Psychology*, *51*, 629–636.

French, J. P. R. Jr., & Raven, B. H. (1959). The bases of social power. In D. Cartwright (Ed.), *Studies in social power* (pp. 150–167). Oxford: University of Michigan.

Hastie, R., Pennington, N., & Penrod, S. D. (1983). *Inside the jury*. Cambridge, MA: Harvard University Press.

Kaplan, M. F. (1989). Task, situational, and personal determinants of influence processes in group decision making. In E. J. Lawler & B. Markovsky (Eds.), *Advances in group processes* (Vol. 6, pp. 87–105). Greenwich, CT: JAI Press.

Kaplan, M. F., & Martín, A. M. (1999). Effects of differential status of group members on process and outcome of deliberation. *Group Processes and Intergroup Relations*, 2, 347–364.

Kaplan, M. F., & Miller, C. E. (1987). Group decision making and normative versus informational influence: Effects of type of issue and assigned decision rule. *Journal of Personality and Social Psychology*, *33*, 306–313.

Kaplan, M. F., & Wilke, H. A. M. (2001). Cognitive and social motivation in group decision making. In J. P. Forgas & K. D. Williams (Eds.), *The social mind: Cognitive and motivational aspects of interpersonal behavior* (pp. 406–428). New York: Cambridge University Press.

Kerr, N. L., & Watts, B. L. (1982). After division, before decision: Group faction size and predeliberation thinking. *Social Psychology Quarterly*, *45*, 198–205.

Klauer, K. C., Wegener, I., & Ehrenberg, K. (2002). Perceiving minority members as individuals: The effects of relative group size in social categorization. *European Journal of Social Psychology*, *32*, 223–245.

Lee, T., & Ofshe, R. (1981). The impact of behavioural style and status characteristics on social influence: A test of two competing theories. *Social Psychology Quarterly*, *44*,73–82.

Linville, P. W., & Fischer, G. W. (1993). Exemplar and abstraction models of perceived group variability and stereotypicality. *Social Cognition*, *11*, 92–125.

Maass, A., & Clark, R. D. III. (1983). Internalization versus compliance: Differential processes underlying minority influence and conformity. *European Journal of Social Psychology*, *13*, 197–215.

Macrae, C. N., Hewstone, M., & Griffiths, R. J. (1993). Processing load and memory for stereotype-based information. *European Journal of Social Psychology*, *23*, 77–87.

Marques, J. M., Yzerbyt, V. Y., & Leyens, J.-P. (1988). The "Black Sheep Effect": Extremity of judgments towards ingroup members as a function of group identification. *European Journal of Social Psychology*, *18*, 1–16.

Martin, R., & Hewstone, M. (2003). Majority versus minority influence: When, not whether, source status instigates heuristic or systematic processing. *European Journal of Social Psychology*, *33*, 313–330.

Martín, A. M., Kaplan, M. F., & Álamo, J. M. (2003). Discussion content and perception of deliberation in Western European versus American juries. *Psychology, Crime & Law*, *9*, 247–263.

Moscovici, S., & Lage, E. (1976). *Social influence and social change.* London: Academic Press.

Nemeth, C. (1995). Dissent as driving cognition, attitudes and judgements. *Social Cognition*, *13*, 273–291.

Nemeth, C., & Wachtler, J. (1983). Creative problem solving as a result of majority versus minority influence. *European Journal of Social Psychology*, *13*, 45–55.

Rugs, D., & Kaplan, M. F. (1993). Effectiveness of informational and normative influences in group decision making depends on group interactive goal. *British Journal of Social Psychology*, *32*, 147–158.

Schuetz, A. (1998). Assertive, offensive, protective and defensive styles of self-presentation: A taxonomy. *Journal of Psychology*, *132*, 611–628.

Schulz-Hardt, S., Jochims, M., & Frey, D. (2002). Productive conflict in group decision making: Genuine and contrived dissent as strategies to counteract biased information seeking. *Organizational Behavior and Human Decision Processes*, *88*, 563–586.

Thibaut, J. W., & Strickland, L. H. (1956). Psychological set and social conformity. *Journal of Psychology*, *25*, 115–129.

Tordesillas, R. S., & Chaiken, S. (1999). Thinking too much of too little? The effects of introspection on the decision-making process. *Personality and Social Psychology Bulletin*, *25*, 623–629.

Trial proves a top snooze-maker (2005). *Los Angeles Times*, May 26, p. A3.

Tversky, A., & Kahneman, D. (1973). Availability: A heuristic for judging frequency and probability. *Cognitive Psychology*, 5, 207–232.

Tversky, A., & Kahneman, D. (1974). Judgment under uncertainty: Heuristics and biases. *Science*, *185*, 1124–1131.

Van Hiel, A., & Franssen, V. (2003). Information acquisition bias during the preparation of group discussion: A comparison of prospective minority and majority members. *Small Group Research*, *34*, 557–574.

Vidmar, N. J. (Ed.). (2000). *World jury systems*. Oxford, UK: Oxford University Press.

Wilke, H. A. M., & Kaplan, M. F. (2001). Task creativity and social creativity in decision-making groups. In C. M. Allwood, & M. Selart (Eds.), *Creative decision-making in the social world* (pp. 35–51). Stockholm, Sweden: Kluwer.

8

Juries in Italy: Legal and Extra-Legal Norms in Sentencing

PATRIZIA CATELLANI and PATRIZIA MILESI

INTRODUCTION

To reach a verdict, jurors are required to evaluate the judicial case they are faced with according to the legal norms and precedents of a given country. Ideally, confronted with the same case and having the same norms as reference standards, all jurors should come to the same decision. This is not likely to happen, however, because judicial decision-making rarely consists of an automatic application of a given norm to a given case. More often, it is the outcome of a more complex reasoning process, implying a reconstruction of the judicial case and the attribution of meaning to relevant norms and precedents in order to assess whether the law has been broken or not. For example, let us consider the case of a man who has been charged with having raped a girl who accepted a lift in his car. Based on the available evidence, jurors must reconstruct the whole sequence of facts highlighting what may be relevant for the legal qualification of the case. At the same time, they must devise a clear representation of the meaning of "rape" according to the extant norms and precedents. The whole task may turn out to be rather complex and may be influenced (or even biased) by jurors' reference to extra-legal norms, rooted in their previous experiences, beliefs, or worldviews (see Devine, Clayton, Dunford, Seying, & Pryce, 2001 for a review).

Extra-legal norms may concern behaviors or events perceived by jurors as "normal," having frequently happened in the past and being likely to happen in the future (e.g., "Usually people do not go around naked"). Extra-legal norms may also concern behaviors or events perceived by jurors as "normative" (e.g., "People should not go around shouting at night"). As psychosocial research has clearly shown (see Thibaut & Kelley, 1959), "normal" behaviors often become "normative." In other words, what is perceived as frequent within a given society (a routine-based norm) is likely to be transformed into something that is perceived as right and proper for that society (a social norm). For example, a routine-based norm such as "Usually women refuse lifts from strangers" may be easily transformed into the social norm "Women should refuse lifts from strangers."

In everyday life, we often compare real events or behaviors with "normal" or "normative" ones. Such a comparison is usually automatic and serves several functions, such as organizing social information in a simple and economic way, explaining and evaluating the world around us, or planning our own behavior. Routine-based and social norms are very likely to be evoked also when jurors are confronted with judicial cases. Under given circumstances, the evocation of an extra-legal norm may be useful in the reconstruction of the judicial case. For example, faced with a case of a husband going out naked on the road after having beaten his wife, a juror might evoke the routine-based/social norm according to which *a person usually does not/should not go out naked on the road*, and might therefore focus attention on the defendant's "abnormal" behavior. This focus might be useful in assessing the defendant's state of mind when he committed the crime. However, the evocation of an extra-legal norm may also be an obstacle to the pronunciation of a fair verdict. It may lead a juror to focus attention on facts that deviate from the "normal" or "normative" in everyday life, but are irrelevant for the legal qualification of the episode, and should therefore not be taken into account. For example, the above-mentioned rape case might evoke the gender-related norm that women should refuse lifts from strangers, enhancing attention to the victim's behavior, thereby reducing the responsibility attributed to the defendant (see Catellani, Alberici, & Milesi, 2004).

In this chapter, we examine how laypeople and professional judges refer to legal and extra-legal norms in reasoning about judicial cases, and we see how this may influence the final verdict. This is an especially crucial issue in a country, like Italy, where mixed juries are employed, that is, juries that are made up by both lay jurors and professional judges. First, we take into account the composition and functioning of mixed juries in Italy, highlighting a series of factors that contribute to create an imbalance in the role played in the jury by lay jurors and professional judges. Then, we examine how lay and professional judges may differ in referencing legal and extra-legal norms when reasoning about judicial cases. Such difference is especially highlighted by studies on counterfactual reasoning, a type of reasoning that consists of simulating alternatives to real events starting from the norms that are available to the person's mind. For example, faced with the above-mentioned rape case, a juror might invoke the gender-related norm according to which women should not accept lifts from strangers, and this might lead the juror to generate the counterfactual "*If the woman hadn't accepted the lift, she wouldn't have been raped.*" In turn, this might influence the juror's interpretation of the whole crime episode. Following on this, we offer suggestions on training that could enhance the quality of judicial decision-making in mixed juries.

ITALIAN MIXED JURIES

Unlike other criminal justice systems (e.g., the North American one), the Italian one does not include juries composed of laypeople only. On the contrary, in Italy, lay jurors are always supported by professional judges. More specifically, Italian criminal juries are composed of six lay jurors and two professional judges, of whom one is the president of the trial and the other one is the so-called *a latere* judge. In the legislator's mind, the aim of such a mixed composition is to ensure common people's participation in the administration of justice and to fulfill the defendant's right to be judged by one's peers. Professional judges' technical judgments are meant to be integrated with lay jurors' common feelings and opinions, and such complementarity is expected to enhance the quality of jury decision-making (law 10 April 1951, no. 287; see Lanza, 1997).

Italian mixed juries pass judgment only for offenses that are deemed of major importance, either because of the severity of the punishment (at least 24 years' imprisonment or life sentence) or because they have been committed against the State. Some examples of the latter are: genocide, terrorist association, complicity and business with the enemy at the time of war, subversive association, and an attempt to take the life of the President of the Republic (article 5 of the criminal procedure code). Less serious offenses appear at magistrates' courts.

Procedures for the selection of lay jurors are quite complex. In each municipality, the mayor along with two assessors makes up two lists of all jury eligible residents: one for the jury of the first-degree trial and the other for the jury of the appeal. Jury eligible people are Italian citizens, in full possession of their civil and political rights, showing a "good moral conduct," aged between 30 and 65 years, and with at least a secondary school diploma for the first trial and a high school diploma for the appeal. Magistrates and officers employed in the administration of justice, members of the army and the police, and ministers of religion may not serve on a jury. The mayor sends the lists of all prospective jurors to the president of the law court. The lists are then shown in public places to allow for complaints about the omission or illegitimate inclusion of names; the president of the court revises the lists accordingly. Fifteen days before the first hearing of the trial, the president of the court, along with another magistrate and the prosecution, draws from each list 50 names in order to fill the jury panels for the next 2 years. Only people who claim legitimate and proven impediments to serve on the jury may be excused. For each court, the president draws at random the names of the six jurors who will compose the jury, and a number (usually two or three) of reserve jurors. This complex procedure aims at ensuring the absolute fairness of selection and at preventing any interference from outside.

Each court holds four sessions a year, each 3 months long. Thus, lay jurors serve on a jury for one session only. However, if the trial has not ended after 3 months, they keep serving on the jury until the end of the trial. Lay jurors who have served on a jury may not serve again for the following 2 years.

Before trial, lay jurors must swear that they will carry out their duty conscientiously, with awareness of the "supreme moral and civil importance" of their office, that they will listen carefully to both the prosecution and the defense, they will form an impartial opinion, without hostility or favor, and they will keep secrecy. In Italy, unlike the US, neither the prosecution nor the defense can challenge jury selection. A juror may be challenged and rejected only when he/she is shown to have serious personal enmity against the defendant, or to have openly voiced an opinion about the case before trial.

In the courtroom, some outward signs distinguish lay jurors from professional judges. Lay jurors are invited to wear a dark suit and they are given a silk sash with the three-colored stripes of the Italian flag, which they wear knotted on their left side. Professional judges wear the black gown typical of magistrates, embellished with golden ornaments. Furthermore, at the hearings, the first judge to enter the courtroom is the president, immediately followed by the other professional judge, and finally by lay jurors. During the trial, lay jurors may not ask questions directly but only through the mediation of the president, who is the only one who asks questions to the witnesses and the parties.

While law regulates recruitment of lay jurors, article 527 of the code of criminal procedure only broadly describes jury deliberation. According to that article, the jury, under the lead of the president, makes the first and separate decision about preliminary issues regarding procedure. After that, the jury deliberates about the verdict (i.e., whether the defendant is guilty or not) and about the extent of the punishment and/or other legal measures to be applied. This procedure is very different from, for example, the US procedure, where lay jurors only decide the verdict, and consequent sanction is decided upon by the court magistrates. Article 527 of the Italian code of criminal procedure prescribes a precise order for jurors' voting. The first to vote must be lay jurors, starting with the youngest. After all the lay jurors have voted, the second judge votes, and then the President. This procedure for voting order clearly seeks to avoid undue influence by jurors with more expertise and/or personal influence.

Three different decision rules are to be distinguished: unanimity, actual majority, and fictitious majority. If there are two alternatives for the final sanction, the actual majority is computed (five against three, six against two, or seven against one). If there are more than two alternatives for the final sanction, article 527 prescribes a procedure aimed at reducing the number of alternatives to two. On the one hand, votes supporting the most severe sanction are combined with votes supporting the immediately less severe sanction; on the other, votes supporting the least severe sanction are combined with the immediately more severe sanction. The two resulting positions are compared and the rule of the actual majority is then applied. In the case of votes being evenly distributed (four against four), the rule of the so-called fictitious majority is applied instead, that is, the decision favoring the defendant prevails.

The law no. 287, 10 April 1951, establishes that professional judges and lay jurors must have the same function and decisional process regarding both determining facts and applying the law. However, the process of jury deliberation brings the seeds of power disparities between lay jurors and professional judges. As said above, the jury must decide on both preliminary and factual issues (article 527 of the criminal procedure code). This entails the possibility that differences between lay jurors and professional judges emerge from the very beginning of their interaction. This difference deals in the first place with the legal ignorance of lay jurors as compared with professional judges. For example, in a case in which the crucial piece of evidence that proves the defendant's guilt was collected in an illegitimate way, professional judges are likely to object to its admissibility, while lay jurors lack specific juridical instruments to rebut the professional judges' objections.

The difference between lay jurors and professional judges has also to do with their mastery of judicial language. Professional judges are advised to simplify their technical language when they interact with lay jurors in order to overcome this difference (Lanza, 1997). This implies that juridical concepts will be translated into common ones and are inevitably delivered to lay jurors through the mediation of professional judges. Thus, there is the risk that the frame of reference of professional judges will be the only working frame within the jury, enhancing further the already powerful position of professional judges in Italian criminal juries.

A further asymmetry comes in when article 527 prescribes that the president, who is always a professional judge, must direct the discussion within the deliberation room. The president usually tries to avoid contrasts among jurors and aims at reaching a verdict by unanimous consensus (Lanza, 1997). Given the clear "superiority" of the president, this is likely to be quite an easy task. Thus, inconsistent with the original aim of combining juridical technicality with common people's feelings, actual procedures for deliberating in criminal juries give much weight to professional judges, above all the president.

The Italian jury system also employs a mixed jury in the juvenile courts. Italian juvenile mixed juries are composed of two professional judges and two "honorary judges," that is, professionals who are competent in juvenile deviance (i.e., psychologists, sociologists, and social workers). Honorary judges are not selected at random but they are chosen among professionals of the relevant domains. They serve on the court for 3 years and can be reappointed in their office. Thus, in juvenile courts, professional and honorary judges interact with each other for quite a long period. This is likely to make their respective reasoning more similar and decision-making processes smoother than the ones observed in criminal mixed juries (Lanza, 1994).

COUNTERFACTUALS IN THE JUDICIAL CONTEXT: CONTRASTING REALITY WITH ITS ALTERNATIVES

To come to a common decision regarding a judicial case, a jury must agree on those legal and extra-legal norms that are relevant to the case and should be referenced in the decision. This is a difficult task, however, because different jurors may (spontaneously or deliberately) evoke different norms. The task may become even more difficult in a mixed jury, where jurors' different familiarity with the justice system may favor differential reference to norms. Evidence of how lay jurors and professional judges refer to norms when reasoning about a judicial case may be found in studies on counterfactual reasoning in the judicial context.

As mentioned in the introduction, counterfactual reasoning involves comparing a real event with one or more hypothetical events in which the mutation of an antecedent ("*If the woman hadn't accepted the lift…*") determines the mutation of the consequence ("…*she wouldn't have been raped*"). Recourse to counterfactual reasoning is recommended in criminal and civil codes in order to establish whether a defendant's conduct caused a negative outcome and consequently to evaluate the defendant's responsibility in the event. In all legal systems, the assessment of a causal link between the defendant's conduct and the negative outcome is a crucial issue. Most explicitly, the Italian criminal code establishes that "nobody can be punished for a fact that is considered a crime by law, if the damage or the danger, upon which the existence of the crime depends, is not a consequence of his/her action or omission. Not preventing an event that one is obliged to prevent is equal to causing it" (article 40). By a cause is meant each antecedent *without* which the event itself would not have occurred. In Italian legal literature, the use of counterfactual reasoning is strongly implicated under the so-called double formula: (1) an action is a necessary condition of the event if, once that action is mentally canceled from the number of occurred facts, the event would not have happened; and (2) an action is *not* a necessary condition of the event if, once it is mentally canceled from the number of occurred facts, the event would have happened all the same. The defendant's conduct is likely to be deemed causal when it represents a necessary condition that, among others, has concurred to produce the event (Cadoppi, 1999; Stella, 2003). Therefore, according to code prescriptions, counterfactual reasoning should be focused on the defendant's conduct and should be used to evaluate whether this conduct was a necessary condition for the negative outcome to occur. Consequently, the social psychological study of counterfactual reasoning is quite relevant to understanding the core implication of this code.

Professional judges are much more likely to be familiar with the above recommendations than lay jurors. As a matter of fact, counterfactual research has shown that jurors may use counterfactual reasoning in an implicit and uncontrolled way, which may be inconsistent with the one prescribed by codes of legal procedure. As an example, we may take into account a study by Bothwell and Duhon (1994) in which mock jurors were asked to generate counterfactuals regarding the case of the owner of a golf course tried for the death of a golfer who had been struck by lightning. Some of them thought that the accident would not have occurred if the golf course had had a better warning system. Many of them, however, were more inclined to think that the accident would not have occurred if the golfer had been more careful and had sought shelter in the clubhouse. This means that some jurors generated counterfactuals about the event according to legal prescriptions about warning and safety systems in golf courses, while others generated counterfactuals according to the imagined behavior of other golfers under the same circumstances. The behavior of the second group of jurors differs from the one suggested by the above-mentioned Italian code of criminal procedure in two respects. First, their counterfactuals focused on the victim (i.e., the golfer) rather than the defendant (i.e., the owner of the golf club). Second, their counterfactuals focused on preventive behavior not enacted (i.e., "*If the golfer had gone to the clubhouse, things would have been different*") rather than negating a necessary event that did in fact occur (i.e., "*If the golf course hadn't had a bad warning system, things would have been different*"), as judicially prescribed (see the Judgment Dissociation Theory, Mandel, 2003; see also Mandel &

Lehman, 1996). One might wonder whether professional judges would have generated counterfactuals more in line with code prescriptions and whether these counterfactuals would have prevailed over the ones of lay jurors in a mixed jury.

Thus, spontaneous counterfactual reasoning may surreptitiously provoke a change in the locus and definition of causality. Focusing on the conduct of actors other than the defendant as potential preventors of the negative outcome may lead the jurors not to consider (or consider to a lesser extent) whether the defendant's conduct was a necessary cause for the negative outcome to occur. This may have relevant consequences on responsibility evaluation, and the correspondent definition of sanction and compensation. For example, in Bothwell and Duhon's study mock jurors who focused on the victim awarded the plaintiffs (relatives of the deceased) lower compensation than mock jurors who focused on the defendant in their counterfactuals (see also Wells & Gavanski, 1989). Similarly, in rape cases counterfactuals focused on the victim's preventive behavior (e.g., "*If the victim had cried for help, things would have been different*") increase the blame assigned to the victim and decrease the blame assigned to the assailant (Branscombe, Owen, Gartska, & Coleman, 1996; see also Nario-Redmond & Branscombe, 1996). Studies in a judicial context have indeed observed that the amount of blame assigned to an actor is linked to the counterfactuals focused on that actor, and in turn, defendant punishment and victim compensation are established accordingly (inter alia rape and car accident cases, Branscombe et al., 1996; Nario-Redmond & Branscombe, 1996; burglary cases, Branscombe, Crosby, & Weir, 1993; negligence cases, Wiener, Gaborit, Pritchard, & McDonough, 1994). Understanding what counterfactuals may be more available to the juror's mind, that is, more likely to be spontaneously generated, is therefore of special relevance.

According to the Norm Theory (Kahneman & Miller, 1986), hypothetical events that are consistent with norms are most likely to come to the person's mind at that very moment. Much research has focused on people's reference to routine-based norms (see above) in the generation of counterfactuals. It has been shown that when people are faced with an actor's behavior that is unusual or exceptional for that actor, they are likely to generate counterfactuals in which the actor's behavior is set against its norm (the routine behavior). Consequently, counterfactuals are more likely to focus on exceptional rather than routine behaviors (*exceptional–routine effect*, inter alia Klauer, Jacobsen, & Migulla, 1995; Wells, Taylor, & Turtle, 1987). Several studies carried out in a judicial context have shown that the exceptional–routine effect may have relevant, though paradoxical, consequences in the evaluation of a judicial case. An example may be found in a study by Miller and McFarland (1986). A man who was shot on a robbery occurring in a convenience store and lost the use of his right arm was awarded higher compensation by mock jurors who were told that he rarely shopped at that convenience store than by mock jurors who were told that he was a regular customer. Sanction of the perpetrator follows a complementary pattern. In the case of a man who was mugged while walking home, Macrae, Milne, and Griffiths (1993, Study 2) found that participants recommended harsher punishment for the perpetrator, rated the crime as more serious, and felt greater sympathy for the victim when the incident was preceded by exceptional circumstances (i.e., the victim had taken a new route home) than by routine circumstances (i.e., the victim had taken his regular route home). Similar results were reported for a rape charge in which the victim was attacked in a routine (library) compared to unusual (deserted alleyway) setting, though results interacted with the identification of mock jurors with the victim or perpetrator (Kaplan & Miller, 1978).

Perceived normality of a given behavior involves more than simply its usualness. Perceived normality of an actor's behavior may also deal with the conformity versus nonconformity of the behavior to a social norm inherent in the event's context or to the social category to which the actor belongs. For example, let us consider the case of a woman who usually goes to work by train but decides to go by car for a change. Her car has a breakdown and she accepts a lift from a male stranger who afterwards rapes her. Consistent with the exceptionality effect, a juror should be likely to compare the victim's behavior with her routine behavior (i.e., "*If only she had taken the train, things might have been different*"). However, a juror might also compare the victim's behavior with the perceived standard behavior of a (nonraped) woman, which implies not accepting a lift from a stranger (i.e., "*If only she had not accepted a lift from a stranger, things might have been different*"). In this second case, a behavior that does not conform to a relevant social norm is perceived as "abnormal" and is contrasted with the "normal" behavior that does conform to that norm. Besides the above-mentioned exceptionality effect, a *nonconformity effect* (Catellani et al., 2004; Catellani & Milesi, 2005) may therefore be envisaged, according to which behaviors that do not conform to a social norm may be especially likely to be counterfactually mutated. This is likely to be the case especially for jurors who are characterized by a high endorsement of the relevant social norm.

We will now consider three categories of social norms that have been shown to influence jurors' judgment. Some social norms are rather specific. This is the case for *stereotype-based norms*, related to specific social categories or specific contexts. Other social norms are instead more general. This is the case for *culture-based norms* or *ideology-based norms*, which often apply to different social categories and/or different contexts. In any case, the degree of endorsement of a given social norm (be it specific or general) may vary from a person to another. Therefore, there will be a range of variation in the likelihood of a juror referring to a given social norm in evaluating a judicial case. In examining this issue, we will now focus our attention on how reference to social norms becomes part of the reasoning process that *precedes* jurors' verdict. In particular, we will show how norm evocation may lead jurors to the generation of "normal" counterfactuals, thus influencing their evaluation of the case at hand.

The likelihood of jurors referring to these extra-legal norms while reasoning upon a case depends not only on how much they endorse them, but also on the degree of control jurors are able to exert over their reasoning process. A controlled (instead of automatic) use of counterfactual reasoning may improve the quality of the juror's decision, by reducing reference to legally nonrelevant norms. We will see that such controlled use of counterfactual reasoning is observed in professional judges more than in lay judges.

REFERENCE TO STEREOTYPE-BASED NORMS

When jurors are confronted with a criminal case, they are likely to compare it with a *crime script* including the actors and the events that characterize the "normal" occurrence of that kind of crime (Finkel & Groscup, 1997; Krahè, 1991; Wiener, Richmond, Seib, Rauch, & Hackney, 2002). According to this perspective, the script of a given crime provides jurors with a standard for evaluating a specific judicial case. Although both professional judges and lay jurors are likely to compare the case at hand to its correspondent script, research data collected so far are mainly focused on lay jurors and cannot be extended to professional judges until pertinent studies have been carried out.

Lay jurors seem to be more likely to convict when the facts closely match with their script for the crime. On the contrary, they become more cautious when the case under evaluation contains features that deviate from the script (Howard, 1984; Krahè, 1991; Smith, 1991, 1993; Smith & Studebaker, 1996). For example, a woman who deviates from the profile of the typical victim in a rape case simply by working in a nontraditional occupation (e.g., a gas station attendant working at night) is more likely to be blamed for being raped as compared to a woman who works in a traditional occupation (Acock & Ireland, 1983). Consistently, responsibility attributed to the rapist may be lower. Similarly, mock jurors are less confident that a rape defendant is guilty, and they recommend a less severe sentence, when the victim's behavior deviates from the behavior expected from a woman who is involved in a rape, for example when the victim resisted too much or too little compared to the level of resistance implied by the rape script (Branscombe & Weir, 1992), or when the victim was in a situation not likely to invoke thoughts of rape (Kaplan & Miller, 1978). The evocation of a crime script depends on how knowledge is organized in the jurors' mind, but also on how the judicial case is labeled by the prosecution or the defense during the trial. For example, a homicide occurring during a bar fight may be labeled as manslaughter or an intentional murder, and a different script may therefore be evoked in the juror's mind.

Scripts regarding certain crimes may include expectancies regarding the identity of typical perpetrators. For example, Blacks are perceived as the typical defendants for a car theft (Jones & Kaplan, 2003; see also Gordon, 1990), while drug addicts are perceived as typical defendants for burglary (van Knippenberg, Dijksterhuis, & Vermeulen, 1999). Typical perpetrators of crimes often belong to stereotyped social categories. Accordingly, social psychological research has demonstrated the relevant effects of stereotypes, mainly ethnic stereotypes, on lay jurors' judgments. Creditable explanations for the stereotype effect assume that stereotypes work as a judgmental heuristic. They simplify case information processing by increasing the amount of attention focused on stereotyped case protagonists (inter alia Bodenhausen, 1988; Gordon & Anderson, 1995; Jones & Kaplan, 2003; van Knippenberg et al., 1999). Thus, when the defendant belongs to a stereotyped social category, crime explanations are very likely to focus on the defendant's stereotypic characteristics, that is, on internal factors rather than on external, situational ones. This kind of focus makes judgments more severe, and this means that a Black defendant will probably be judged more severely than a White defendant for certain racial-stereotypical crimes.

A demonstration of the role played by stereotypes in lay jurors' reasoning comes from research showing that jurors with different endorsement of given stereotypes tend to generate different counterfactuals on the same judicial case. For example, many well-established stereotype-based norms describe the appropriate behavior for women in order to avoid rape. According to such norms, a woman should not engage in a host of risky behaviors, such as accepting lifts from strangers (Acock & Ireland, 1983), walking late at night (Pallak & Davies, 1982), or drinking on her own in a pub (Krahè, 1988). At the same time, a woman is expected to assume a number of preventive behaviors, such as trying to escape and opposing appropriate dissent and resistance (e.g., saying "no" to unwanted advances and fighting back, Howard, 1984). In two studies, Catellani et al. (2004) presented Italian mock jurors with a rape report in which the victim's behaviors were balanced as regards their conformity versus nonconformity to stereotype-based norms. For example, it was stated that the victim "*got frightened when the man took off the gun and laid it aside*" (conforming behavior), but also that the victim "*was pleasant with the man*" (nonconforming behavior). The victim's behaviors were also balanced as regards their being actions (e.g., "*she talked freely to the man*") or inactions (e.g., "*she did not cry out for help*"). After reading the report, participants were asked to complete counterfactual stems starting with "*The outcome might have been better, if only … .*" Participants' endorsement of the rape victim stereotype was also measured, using a scale developed by Lonsway and Fitzgerald (1995). Results of both studies confirmed the presence of a nonconformity effect in counterfactual reasoning; jurors with higher endorsement of the rape victim stereotype were especially inclined to focus counterfactuals on the victim's nonconforming behaviors. The effect was greatest with respect to the victim's nonconforming *inactions*, with those highest in rape stereotyping focusing on what the victim could have done (but did not) to prevent the crime from occurring, and generating counterfactuals like "*… if only she had cried out for help*" or "*… if only she had said 'no' more strongly.*" Their accent on the victim's inactions shows that the nonconformity effect may be so strong that they overcome the more general tendency observed in past research to focus counterfactuals on actions more than on inactions (*action–inaction effect*; inter alia Catellani & Milesi, 2001; Kahneman & Miller, 1986).

In another study (Catellani & Milesi, 2004), mock jurors were presented with the report of a rape case in which counterfactuals based on the victim's nonconforming behaviors were implicitly conveyed through linguistic indicators like *even* or *without*. For example, a sentence like "*She accepted the kiss without any resistance*" implicitly hints at the counterfactual hypothesis that "*If she had put up some resistance, things might have ended differently.*" Half of the participants were told that the report had been made by the police, while the other half were told that the report had been made by the defendant. As in the previous study, participants were asked to generate counterfactuals regarding the case and to evaluate both the defendant's and the victim's responsibility. Participants' endorsement of the rape victim stereotype was also measured. Results showed that when stereotype-consistent counterfactuals are implicitly suggested by the defendant, that is, by a supposedly unreliable source, all participants are less inclined to reproduce the same counterfactuals in their own reconstruction of the facts. Interestingly, however, in the same condition those high in stereotyping are especially inclined to generate "original" counterfactuals, that is, counterfactuals that are still consistent with the rape victim stereotype but that were not suggested by the defendant. This result suggests that being exposed to stereotype-consistent counterfactuals by a source that is likely to be unreliable may have created a situation of cognitive dissonance in participants with higher stereotype endorsement. They find themselves in the position of endorsing stereotypic beliefs that are also endorsed by an unreliable source. In order to overcome cognitive dissonance, highly stereotyped persons avoid reproducing counterfactuals suggested by a suspected source, but at the same time engage in a systematic cognitive activity that leads them to generate further stereotype-consistent counterfactuals. Thus, the tendency to stick to one's own stereotypes may be so strong that a challenge to them may paradoxically end up with an increase, rather than a reduction, of counterfactual thoughts supporting these stereotypes.

As with research on crime scripts, research on stereotype reference in judicial reasoning should be usefully extended to professional judges. This would assess whether stereotypes influence professional judges' reasoning similarly to lay jurors' reasoning, or whether such influence is moderated by the higher control professional judges exert over their reasoning processes (see paragraph on jurors' expertise below).

REFERENCE TO CULTURE-BASED NORMS

Social norms may vary a great deal from one society, or culture, to the other. As an example, we may go back to the host of stereotyped expectancies regarding a rape victim (see above). These expectancies are related to other, more general, expectancies regarding "proper" behaviors of men and women in sexual interactions and dating relationships. These behaviors are well rooted in and specific of each culture, so that behaviors that are considered neutral in one culture may have sexual implications in another. For example, in Asian and Arab cultures if a woman smiles at a man to whom she has not been introduced, the smile is considered sexual; on the contrary, in many western cultures this is considered just a friendly behavior (Barna, 1985). Consistently, the rape victim stereotype is also likely to vary from one culture to another. Confirmation has been found in a study by Milesi and Alberici (2001), investigating differences in the rape scripts of Italian and Moroccan people. Italians focus their attention on the rape victim's behavior during the interaction with the assailant more than on her status (e.g., not being married or living alone). They expect her to evidence strong physical resistance, to try strongly to dissuade the assailant from his violence, and to make repeated attempts to escape. These results are consistent with previous findings in studies carried out in western cultures, stressing the relevance of the resistance offered by the victim for the evaluation of responsibility of both the victim and the assailant in rape cases (see above Branscombe & Weir, 1992; see also Estrich, 1987; Krahè, 1991). Unlike Italians, Moroccans focus their attention on the victim's status more than on the victim's actions aimed at avoiding rape, consistent with gender role prescriptions in traditional Moroccan culture, which assign women a passive role in social interactions. Cross-cultural differences in the rape script are likely to lead to different evaluations of rape cases (see also Heaven, Connors, & Pretorius, 1998). As already mentioned, jurors are less likely to convict the defendant and more likely to distrust the victim's allegations of rape, if the rape case departs from the commonly accepted script of the "typical rape" situation. Thus, if one considers the cross-cultural differences described above, the Italian jurors are likely to be more lenient if the victim did not adequately resist the assailant, whereas the same may not be true for Moroccans.

A further cultural source of variation in jurors' reasoning and judgment has to do with the individualism–collectivism dimension, although empirical data in this regard are still missing. Individualist cultures stress the priority of individual needs over group needs, prefer loosely knit social relationships, and value self-discipline, self-sufficiency, personal accountability, and autonomy. On the contrary, collectivist cultures stress the priority of group over individual needs, prefer tightly knit social relationships, value conformity, and integration within the group (inter alia Triandis, 1989; Markus & Kitayama, 1991). Jurors belonging to individualist versus collectivist cultures are likely to evoke different norms when they interpret and evaluate judicial cases. For example, research on attribution processes has shown that collectivists are more attentive to how situational factors may influence actors' behavior than individualists are (Choi & Nisbett, 1998; Miller, 1984). It is hence conceivable that a collectivist juror might be much more likely to wonder whether things might have been different if the actor had been in a different situation than an individualist juror would. In turn, this might influence the juror's decision.

The examination of cross-cultural differences among jurors surely deserves further attention, as society is becoming more and more ethnically differentiated, and juries are therefore more and more likely to be a mix of different cultures.

REFERENCE TO IDEOLOGY-BASED NORMS

Ideological orientation is a further source of reference norms that may be available to a juror's mind when evaluating a judicial case. In the present context, by ideological orientation we mean a set of organized general attitudes toward crime and principles of justice.

Many studies have investigated the relationship between lay jurors' authoritarianism and dogmatism on the one hand, and jury verdicts on the other (see Devine et al., 2001 for a review). There is strong evidence for the existence of a relationship between the number of authoritarian/dogmatic jurors in a jury and jury decisions. Juries containing a high proportion of authoritarian/dogmatic jurors tend to convict more often and inflict harsher sentences than juries with a low proportion of such individuals. However, high authoritarians are less punitive than low authoritarians when the defendant is a person in authority (Mitchell, 1973), or when the crime is the consequence of obedience to or the exercise of authority (García & Griffitt, 1978; Hamilton, 1976).

A number of studies have focused on how professional judges' ideological orientation may influence the verdict and the subsequent sanction (Carroll, Perkowitz, Lurigio, & Weaver, 1987; Giner-Sorolla, Chaiken, & Lutz, 2002; Tetlock, Bernzweig, & Gallant, 1985). In another study (Catellani & Milesi, 2006), we investigated how the criminal philosophy of professional judges and honorary judges in Italian juvenile mixed juries (see description above) may influence their judicial reasoning and their imposed sanction. In 1988, the Italian juvenile criminal code was reformed to favor the promotion and rehabilitation of minors involved in criminal episodes. More punitive legal positions were abandoned, and a variety of alternatives to imprisonment were made available in order to support the reintegration of deviant minors into society. These alternatives include detention centers, home confinement, and community service. Their implementation is closely dependent on the intervention of social services. Our study involved professional judges and honorary judges (psychologists, sociologists, and criminologists) enrolled in various Italian juvenile courts (see the chapter on German courts for a full discussion of this type of jury composition in juvenile courts). We investigated whether counterfactual thinking and the final verdict would vary as a function of the judges' area of expertise and their endorsement of the promotion-oriented philosophy underlying the reformed juvenile code. Judges were presented with a report of an armed robbery perpetrated by a minor and were invited to complete open-ended counterfactual stems, starting with "*The outcome might have been different, if only* … ." They were then asked to rate their agreement with two different sanctions: imprisonment and detention center. Finally, their endorsement of the promotion-oriented philosophy was assessed, through rating the relevance attributed to three articles of the juvenile criminal code stressing juveniles' promotion. Results showed significant differences between judges largely due to their promotion-oriented philosophy, and only secondarily to their area of expertise. Compared with lower promotion-oriented judges, higher promotion-oriented judges generated a significantly higher number of counterfactuals, and were more inclined to focus part of these counterfactuals on actors other than the deviant minor, especially social services (e.g., "*The outcome might have been better, if only territorial social services had taken charge of the defendant's family*" or "… *if only social services had intervened in advance, considering that the defendant's brother had been already involved in illegal activities*"). In addition, higher promotion-oriented judges were generally more favorable to detention centers than imprisonment, while lower promotion-oriented judges favored detention centers only when they thought that the juvenile defendant would be unlikely to commit further crimes.

Interestingly, in the Catellani and Milesi (2006) study, no significant difference as a function of the judges' area of expertise was observed. In fact, one might have expected professional judges to be more oriented toward prevention and honorary judges to be more oriented toward promotion. It should be noted, however, that professional and honorary judges have been cooperating in Italian juvenile courts for many years now. Such cooperation is likely to have softened differences owing to the area of expertise and led to the creation of a common frame of mind, having a positive influence on the working of the juvenile criminal system (Lanza, 1994).

JURORS' EPISTEMOLOGICAL APPROACH

Jurors' reference to extra-legal norms in judicial reasoning is likely to depend not only on the mental availability of these norms, but also on the degree of sophistication of their reasoning. Weinstock and Flaton (2004) investigated how epistemological orientation may influence lay jurors' reasoning and, consequently, judgment. Participants serving jury duty heard reenactments of two murder cases and were asked a number of open questions regarding their verdict, how they justified it, and how certain they were of it. They were also presented with alternative verdicts (i.e., verdicts they did not pronounce) and asked to explain why they did not choose them. Analyses of jurors' accounts showed that the relationship between the amount of evidence used and certainty regarding verdict is not direct. Jurors who claim to be *fairly* certain use more evidence than those who claim to be *absolutely* certain. A different epistemological approach is likely to characterize these two groups of jurors, and the difference concerns the degree of certainty one requires in order to state something.

According to Weinstock and Flaton (2004), absolutely certain jurors become certain quite early and consequently they stop seeking evidence rather soon. In turn, such a limited search for evidence leads to a limited consideration of plausible alternatives, thus further increasing these jurors' certainty in the chosen explanation (see the notion of "need for closure"; Kruglanski & Webster, 1996). On the contrary, fairly certain jurors believe that one cannot reach a point of absolute certainty. Consequently, they search for more evidence and use it to examine and compare several alternatives, in order to choose the most plausible one. These people are also more ready to counterargue, discount, and anticipate the arguments for other possible verdicts. This view accords with the finding that people with strong hypotheses of defendant guilt owing to race-crime contiguity seek less information, and information that is likely to confirm rather than test their hypothesis (Jones & Kaplan, 2003). Different jurors may have different criteria for certainty and the sufficiency of evidence coverage, regardless of the standard jury instruction of the "reasonable doubt." Actually, research on juror reasoning has found a significant number of lay jurors characterized by an "absolutist" epistemology, that is, by the tendency to settle on the first possible solution without giving a full consideration of alternative explanations and discrepant evidence (Kuhn, Weinstock, & Flaton, 1994). Further studies on the jurors' epistemological orientation are needed. For example, it is still a matter of debate whether a "critical" (instead of "absolutist") epistemological orientation is related to expertise in a given domain, to general reasoning ability, or to a tendency toward systematic, rather than heuristic reasoning.

JURORS' EXPERTISE

Investigation on how judicial expertise may influence juries' reasoning and sentencing is of crucial relevance especially in countries like Italy (and others described in this volume) where juries are mixed.

A study carried out by one of us (Catellani, 1992) suggests that judicial expertise may indeed favor the adoption of a "critical" epistemological approach when reasoning about a judicial case. Expert and novice judges were required to think aloud about a case, and reach a verdict and a sanction. Analysis of the thinking aloud protocols revealed several differences between the groups, two of which are especially worth mentioning here. First, while reflecting upon the case expert judges use counterfactual thinking more often than novice judges. They compare and evaluate several alternative versions of the facts in order to achieve the most plausible reconstruction of the case at hand. This use of counterfactual thinking is consistent with the adoption of the "critical" epistemological approach described above. Second, expert judges are more likely to focus on the elements of the judicial case that are relevant for the case's legal qualification. On the contrary, they are less likely to focus their attention on elements that are not legally relevant. Taken together, these two differences suggest that, as compared to novices, experts have a higher control over their reasoning, evaluate and compare the plausibility of more alternative interpretations of the case, and are more likely to exclude, at least at a conscious level, those based on extra-legal norms. Note that the two differences, considering more alternatives, and focusing on relevant information, are the hallmarks of systematic reasoning (Chaiken & Trope, 1999).

If expert and novice judges appear to reason differently, the difference between expert judges and lay jurors is likely to be even more marked. Mixed juries may therefore be characterized by an imbalance in the reasoning abilities of the participants (Martín, Kaplan, & Álamo, 2003). Apart from such imbalance, the simple label of "expert" attributed to the judge (or the judges) in a mixed jury may have an influence on the entire decision-making process. Previous research has shown that people who are identified as the "experts" in a group involved in a reasoning task are more influential than the other group members (Bonner, Baumann, & Dalal, 2002; Stevenson & Over, 2001; see also Chaiken, 1980). For example, in a study on deductive reasoning, Stevenson and Over (2001) have found that people make inferences about the likelihood of a premise based on the expertise of the person producing it. On the one hand, when a premise is uttered by a novice and an alternative premise by an expert, people tend to infer that the expert is correcting the novice's error. On the other, when the premise is uttered by an expert and the alternative by a novice, people are inclined to think that the novice is wrong in disagreeing with the expert.

These results suggest that the decision-making process of a mixed jury may be characterized by a strong asymmetry in the influence of professional judges and lay jurors. In Italy, such an asymmetry is likely to be further enhanced by the fact that mixed juries deliberate not only on crime commission but also on procedural aspects and on the sanction. The last two issues often require complex reasoning processes that rely heavily on specific judicial knowledge. Consistently, an

Italian judge who has been serving for many years in mixed juries has highlighted that professional judges often intervene to solve disagreements among lay jurors and their interventions are given much weight (Lanza, 1997).

SUGGESTIONS FOR TRAINING JURORS (AND IMPROVING JURY DECISIONS)

Our discussion of how lay jurors and professional judges refer to extra-legal norms in judicial reasoning allows us to make some speculations about what conditions might improve decision quality in mixed juries.

We have seen that extra-legal norms are easily available to the jurors' minds and their evocation is likely to be automatic, that is, outside the person's conscious control, and may lead to biased judgments. One may therefore wonder about the possibility of increasing jurors' control over their reasoning process, thus reducing reference to extra-legal norms that may be easily available to the jurors' mind but not relevant (if not misleading) in the evaluation of the judicial case. Some researchers do indeed suggest that jurors may try to control their reference to stereotype-based norms. For example, they may do so in order to appear unprejudiced (Sommers & Ellsworth, 2000), but this effort may simply lead to a different type of bias, namely, an over correction effect. Foley and Pigott (2002) presented a judicial case involving either a Black or a White defendant to different juries, having either a White or a Black foreperson. Results showed that jurors attributed less responsibility to a Black defendant than a White one when the foreperson was Black, thus falling prey to reversed discrimination. No race-based difference was observed when the foreperson was White. Thus, a Black foreperson in a jury is likely to make the race issue salient in the context, and to induce jurors to diminish the responsibility of a Black defendant in order to appear unprejudiced.

Considering these limitations in jurors' reasoning, recent research has tried to highlight what conditions may improve decision quality and reduce biases (see Devine et al., 2001). The basic assumption of these studies is that the quality of jury decision-making would improve, if jurors systematically analyzed different alternatives before making a consensual reconstruction of the case, its legal definition, and the final verdict. One might imagine that in a jury such a comparative evaluation of different alternatives would be easier if jury is composed of diverse members, with different points of view. This does not seem to be the case, however. The presence of more people reasoning on the same issue does not necessarily lead to the expression and comparative evaluation of different points of view. On the contrary, some research results suggest that juries may be even more biased than single jurors (inter alia Kerr, Niedermeier, & Kaplan, 1999; Kerr, MacCoun, & Kramer, 1996). Consistently, recent research has shown that the "confirmation bias," that is, the tendency of individuals to seek more information supporting one's preferred alternative than information conflicting with this alternative, may also be found in group decision-making (Frey & Schulz-Hardt, 2001).

Useful suggestions on how to improve control on judicial reasoning may be found in the reasoning process we have previously described as typical of jurors with a "critical" epistemological approach and of expert judges. As we have seen, these people tend to compare and evaluate different possible reconstructions and interpretations of the judicial event, not limiting themselves to the most available ones. A controlled and systematic use of counterfactual reasoning (such as the one that is observed in expert judges) may be especially useful in this regard. It may allow a useful confrontation of different interpretations, reducing the risk of sticking to the one that is most available to the juror's mind, or most accepted by a majority. One might train jury members to make them aware of the potentials of counterfactual thinking in the judicial context. This might improve the quality of jurors' reasoning, reduce the asymmetry between lay jurors and professional judges, and be helpful in preparing lay jurors to resist attorneys' persuasive techniques, which very often rely on counterfactuals. However, a training program for both professional judges and lay jurors might not be easily implemented, especially if one considers that Italian lay jurors serve on a jury only for a 3-month session. Alternatively, a similar training program might be implemented for professional judges only, and this alone might lead to an improvement in the quality of juries' decisions, at least in countries where mixed juries are employed. As we have seen, suggestions coming from an expert member of a decision-making group are likely to have a powerful influence on the other members of the group. In a specific case, the influence might consist in the trained judge (or judges) evoking a counterfactual mind-set in the rest of the jury, thus reducing the likelihood for the jury to stick to the most easily available, and possibly biased, interpretation of the case at hand (see also Kray & Galinsky, 2003). In a sense, the expert judges would play the role of the "devil's advocate" described in studies on group decision-making (see Frey & Schulz-Hardt, 2001). In these studies, one or more members of the group are assigned the task of challenging other group members' ideas, and the consequence is often an improvement in the overall quality of the final decision.

CONCLUSION

In this chapter, we have focused on how lay jurors and professional judges refer to legal and extra-legal norms while reasoning about judicial cases. We have made special reference to studies on counterfactual reasoning in the judicial context. In these studies, jurors are shown to mentally compare the actual case at hand with what they perceive as "normal" or "normative" according to their previous experiences, focusing on aspects that are often irrelevant for the legal evaluation of the case. While such a spontaneous use of counterfactual thinking may produce a biased decision, more controlled use of counterfactual thinking may improve decision quality. This is confirmed by studies on jurors characterized by a critical epistemological approach and/or by higher judicial expertise. When reconstructing a judicial case, these jurors do not stop at the most easily available interpretation, but instead generate and compare several possible interpretations in order to choose the most plausible. Such a strategic use of counterfactual reasoning is likely to reduce reference to legally irrelevant norms. Even when only a minority of the jury can count on this kind of competence (e.g., trained judges in mixed juries), the whole jury is likely to benefit from it. In order to improve the quality of the juries' final decisions, instructions and training programs aimed at fostering the generation and comparison of different counterfactual alternatives would therefore seem highly recommended.

REFERENCES

Acock, A. C., & Ireland, N. K. (1983). Attribution of blame in rape cases: The impact of norm violation, gender, and sex role attitude. *Sex Roles*, *9*, 179–193.

Barna, L. M. (1985). Difficulties in communicating among people of different cultures. In L. Samovar & P. Porter (Eds.), *Intercultural Communication: A Reader* (pp. 330–338). Belmont, CA: Wadsworth.

Bodenhausen, G. V. (1988). Stereotypic biases in social decision-making: Testing process models of stereotype use. *Journal of Personality and Social Psychology*, *55*, 726–737.

Bonner, B. L., Baumann, M. R., & Dalal, R. S. (2002). The effects of member expertise on group decision-making and performance. *Organizational Behavior and Human Decision Processes*, *88*, 719–736.

Bothwell, R. K., & Duhon, K. W. (1994). Counterfactual thinking and plaintiff compensation. *Journal of Social Psychology*, *134*, 705–706.

Branscombe, N. R., & Weir J. A. (1992). Resistance as stereotype-inconsistency: Consequences for judgments of rape victims. *Journal of Social and Clinical Psychology*, *11*, 80–102.

Branscombe, N. R., Crosby, P., & Weir, J. A. (1993). Social inferences concerning male and female homeowners who use a gun to shoot an intruder. *Aggressive Behavior*, *19*, 113–124.

Branscombe, N. R., Owen, S., Gartska, T., & Coleman, J. (1996). Rape and accident counterfactuals: Who might have done otherwise and would it have changed the outcome? *Journal of Applied Social Psychology*, *26*, 1042–1067.

Cadoppi, A. (1999). *Il valore del precedente nel diritto penale: uno studio sulla dimensione in action della legalità*. [The value of the precedent in the criminal trial: A study on the action dimension of legality]. Torino: Giappichelli.

Carroll, J. S., Perkowitz, W. T., Lurigio, A. J., & Weaver, F. M. (1987). Sentencing goals, causal attributions, ideology and personality. *Journal of Personality and Social Psychology*, *52*, 107–118.

Catellani, P. (1992). *Il giudice esperto. Psicologia cognitiva e ragionamento giudiziario*. [The expert judge. Cognitive psychology and judicial reasoning]. Bologna: Il Mulino.

Catellani, P., Alberici, A. I., & Milesi, P. (2004). Counterfactual thinking and stereotypes: The nonconformity effect. *European Journal of Social Psychology*, *34*, 421–436.

Catellani, P., & Milesi, P. (2001). Counterfactuals and roles: Mock victims' and perpetrators' accounts of judicial cases. *European Journal of Social Psychology*, *31*, 247–264.

Catellani, P., & Milesi, P. (2004). Does your counterfactual become my counterfactual? Stereotyped expectations and suspicion. Manuscript submitted for publication.

Catellani, P., & Milesi, P. (2005). When the social context frames the case: Counterfactuals in the courtroom. In D. Mandel, D. J. Hilton, & P. Catellani (Eds.), *The psychology of counterfactual thinking*. London: Routledge.

Catellani, P., & Milesi, P. (2006). Counterfactuals and orientation to defendants' promotion in juvenile juries. Manuscript submitted for publication.

Chaiken, S. (1980). Heuristic versus systematic information processing and the use of source versus message cues in persuasion. *Journal of Personality and Social Psychology*, *39*, 752–766.

Chaiken, S., & Trope, Y. (1999). *Dual-processes theories in social psychology*. New York: Guilford.

Choi, I., & Nisbett, R. E. (1998). Situational salience and cultural differences in the correspondence bias and in the actor-observer bias. *Personality and Social Psychology Bulletin*, *24*, 949–960.

Devine, D. J., Clayton, L. D., Dunford B. B., Seying, R., & Pryce J. (2001). Jury decision making: 45 years of empirical research on deliberating groups. *Psychology, Public Policy and Law*, *7*, 622–727.

Estrich, S. (1987). *Real rape*. Cambridge, MA: Harvard University Press.

Finkel, N. J., & Groscup, J. L. (1997). Crime prototypes, objective versus subjective culpability, and a commonsense balance. *Law and Human Behavior*, *21*, 209–230.

Foley, L. A., & Pigott, M. A. (2002). Race, self-presentation and reverse discrimination in jury decisions. *American Journal of Forensic Psychology*, *20*, 37–52.

Frey, D., & Schulz-Hardt, S. (2001). Confirmation bias in group information seeking and its implications for decision making in administration, business and politics. In F. Butera & G. Mugny (Eds.), *Social influence in social reality. Promoting individual and social change* (pp. 53–73). Bern: Hogrefe & Huber Publishers.

García, L. T., & Griffitt, W. (1978). Authoritarianism-situation interactions in the determination of punitiveness: Engaging authoritarian ideology. *Journal of Research in Personality*, *12*, 469–478.

Giner-Sorolla, R., Chaiken, S., & Lutz, S. (2002). Validity beliefs and ideology can influence legal case judgments differently. *Law & Human Behavior*, *26*, 507–526.

Gordon, R. A. (1990). Attributions for blue-collar and white-collar crime: The effect of subjects and defendant race on simulated juror decisions. *Journal of Applied Social Psychology*, *128*, 971–983.

Gordon, R. A., & Anderson, K. S. (1995). Perceptions of race-stereotypic and race-nonstereotypic crimes: The impact of response-time instructions on attributions and judgments. *Basic & Applied Social Psychology*, *16*, 455–470.

Hamilton, V. L. (1976). Individual differences in ascriptions of responsibility, guilt, and appropriate punishment. In G. Bermant, C. Nemeth, & N. J. Vidmar (Eds.), *Psychology and the Law*. Lexington, MA: Heath.

Heaven, P. C. L., Connors, J., & Pretorius, A. (1998). Victim characteristics and attribution of rape blame in Australia and South Africa. *Journal of Social Psychology*, *138*, 131–133.

Howard, J. A. (1984). The "normal" victim: The effects of gender stereotypes on reactions to victims. *Social Psychology Quarterly*, *47*, 270–281.

Jones, C. S., & Kaplan, M. F. (2003). The effects of racially stereotypical crimes on juror decision-making and information-processing strategies. *Basic and Applied Social Psychology*, *25*, 1–13.

Kahneman, D., & Miller, D. T. (1986). Norm theory: Comparing reality to its alternatives. *Psychological Review*, *93*, 136–153.

Kaplan, M. F., & Miller, L. E. (1978). Effects of juror identification with the victim depend on likelihood of victimization. *Law and Human Behavior*, *2*, 353–363.

Kerr, N. L., MacCoun, R., & Kramer, G. P. (1996). Bias in judgment: Comparing individuals and groups. *Psychological Review*, *103*, 687–719.

Kerr, N. L., Niedermeier, K. E., & Kaplan, M. F. (1999). Bias in jurors vs. bias in juries: New evidence from the SDS perspective. *Organizational Behaviour and Human Decision Processes*, *80*, 70–86.

Klauer, K. C., Jacobsen, T., & Migulla, G. (1995). Counterfactual processing: Test of a hierarchical correspondence model. *European Journal of Social Psychology*, *25*, 577–595.

Krahè, B. (1988). Victim and observer characteristics as determinants of responsibility attribution to victims of rape. *Journal of Applied Social Psychology*, *18*, 50–8.

Krahè, B. (1991). Social psychological issues in the study of rape. *European Review of Social Psychology*, *2*, 279–309.

Kray, L. J., & Galinsky, A. D. (2003). The debiasing effect of counterfactual mind-sets: Increasing the search for disconfirmatory information in group decisions. *Organizational Behavior and Human Decision Processes*, *91*, 69–81.

Kruglanski, A. W., & Webster, D. M. (1996). Motivated closing of the mind: "Seizing" and "freezing". *Psychological Review*, *103*, 263–283.

Kuhn, D., Weinstock, M. P., & Flaton, R. A. (1994). How well do jurors reason? Competence dimensions of individual variation in a juror reasoning task. *Psychological Science*, 5, 289–296.

Lanza, L. (1994). *Gli omicidi in famiglia. Le dinamiche della decisione in Corte d'assise con l'analisi di trenta casi di omicidio domestico*[Homicides within the family. Decision processes in court: Analysis of thirty cases of domestic homicide]. Milano: Giuffrè.

Lanza, L. (1997). Il percorso della decisione [Decision percourse]. In A. Forza (Ed.), *Il processo invisibile. Le dinamiche psicologiche nel processo penale* (pp. 39–71). Venezia: Marsilio.

Lonsway, K. A., & Fitzgerald, L. F. (1995). Attitudinal antecedents of rape myth acceptance: A theoretical and empirical reexamination. *Journal of Personality and Social Psychology*, *68*, 704–711.

Macrae, C. N., Milne, A. B., & Griffiths, R. J. (1993). Counterfactual thinking and the perception of criminal behaviour. *British Journal of Social Psychology*, *84*, 221–226.

Mandel, D. (2003). Judgment dissociation theory: An analysis of differences in causal, counterfactual, and covariational reasoning. *Journal of Experimental Psychology: General*, *132*, 419–434.

Mandel, D. R., & Lehman, D. R. (1996). Counterfactual thinking and ascriptions of cause and preventability. *Journal of Personality and Social Psychology*, *71*, 450–463.

Markus, H. R., & Kitayama, S. (1991). Culture and the self: Implications for cognition, emotion, and motivation. *Psychological Review*, 98, 224–253.

Martín, A. M., Kaplan, M. F., & Álamo, J. M. (2003). Discussion content and perception of deliberation in western European versus American juries. *Psychology, Crime & Law*, 9, 247–263.

Milesi, P., & Alberici, A. I. (2001). Differenze interculturali nella definizione del reato di stupro. [Crosscultural differences in the definition of the rape crime]. *Psicologia & Giustizia. La Rivista Italiana On Line di Psicologia Giuridica*, *2*, 1. Retrieved January, 10, 2005, from http://www.psicologiagiuridica.com/GENERALE/ARCHIVIO.htm.

Miller, D. T., & McFarland, C. (1986). Counterfactual thinking and victim compensation: A test of norm theory. *Personality and Social Psychology Bulletin*, *12*, 513–519.

Miller, J. G. (1984). Culture and the development of everyday social explanation. *Journal of Personality and Social Psychology*, *46*, 961–978.

Mitchell, H. E. (1973). *Authoritarian punitiveness in simulated juror decision making: The good guys don't always wear white hats*. Paper presented at the Annual Meeting of Midwestern Psychological Association, Chicago.

Nario-Redmond, M. R., & Branscombe, N. R. (1996). It could have been better or it might have been worse: Implications for blame assignment in rape cases. *Basic and Applied Social Psychology*, *18*, 347–366.

Pallak, S. R., & Davies, J. M. (1982). Finding fault versus attributing responsibility: Using facts differently. *Personality and Social Psychology Bulletin*, *8*, 454–459.

Smith, V. L. (1991). Prototypes in the courtroom: Lay representations of legal concepts. *Journal of Personality and Social Psychology*, *61*, 857–872.

Smith, V. L. (1993). When prior knowledge and law collide: Helping jurors to use the law. *Law and Human Behavior*, *17*, 507–536.

Smith, V. L., & Studebaker, C. A. (1996). What do you expect? The influence of people's prior knowledge of crime categories on fact-finding. *Law and Human Behavior*, *20*, 517–532.

Sommers, S. R., & Ellsworth, P. C. (2000). Race in the courtroom: Perceptions of guilt and dispositional attributions. *Personality and Social Psychology Bulletin*, *26*, 1367–1379.

Stella, F. (2003). *Giustizia e modernità. La protezione dell'innocente e la tutela delle vittime* [Justice and modernity. Protection of the innocents and of the victims]. Milano: Giuffrè Editore.

Stevenson, R. J., & Over, D. E. (2001). Reasoning from uncertain premises: Effects of expertise and conversational context. *Thinking & Reasoning*, *7*, 367–390.

Tetlock, P. E., Bernzweig, J., & Gallant, J. L. (1985). Supreme court decision-making: Cognitive style as a predictor of ideological consistency voting. *Journal of Personality and Social Psychology*, *48*, 1227–1239.

Thibaut, J. W., & Kelley, H. H. (1959). *The social psychology of groups*. Oxford, England: Wiley.

Triandis, H. C. (1989). The self and social behaviour in differing cultural contexts. *Psychological Review*, *96*, 506–520.

Van Knippenberg, A., Dijksterhuis, A., & Vermeulen D. (1999). Judgement and memory of a criminal act: The effects of stereotypes and cognitive load. *European Journal of Social Psychology*, *29*, 191–201.

Weinstock, M. P., & Flaton, R. A. (2004). Evidence coverage and argument skills: Cognitive factors in a juror's verdict choice. *Journal of Behavioral Decision Making*, *17*, 191–212.

Wells, G. L., & Gavanski, I. (1989). Mental simulation of causality. *Journal of Personality and Social Psychology*, *56*, 161–169.

Wells, G. L., Taylor, B. R., & Turtle, J. W. (1987). The undoing of scenarios. *Journal of Personality and Social Psychology*, *53*, 421–430.

Wiener, R. L., Gaborit, M., Pritchard, C. C., & McDonough, E. M. (1994). Counterfactual thinking in mock jurors' assessments of negligence: A preliminary investigation. *Behavioral Sciences and the Law*, *12*, 89–102.

Wiener, R. L., Richmond, T. L., Seib, H. M., Rauch, S. M., & Hackney, A. A. (2002). The psychology of telling murder stories: do we think in scripts, exemplars, or prototypes? *Behavioral Sciences and the Law*, *20*, 119–139.

9

Human Justice or Injustice? The Jury System in France

MAGALI GINET, SERGE GUIMOND, and CATHERINE GREFFEUILLE

INTRODUCTION

Psychologists in France have had a longstanding interest in the justice system (Finkelstein, 2004). As early as 1905, Binet identified a number of problems and advocated the development of a "science of testimony" to solve them. Building on this and more recent research by social psychologists, this chapter presents an overview of some of the typical features of the French jury system followed by an analysis focusing on witness psychology. Every system of justice, and the jury system in particular, can be studied at the micro-level by considering the characteristics of individuals involved in such a system. For example, one basic feature of the jury system in France is that jurors are instructed to pay attention first and foremost to oral evidence. From a psychological point of view, important theoretical and empirical questions can be raised in relation to this emphasis on oral evidence and testimony. Indeed, a significant part of contemporary research in France focuses on issues surrounding the role of eyewitnesses. Many studies discussed below concern psychological processes that may explain when and why witnesses give more, or less reliable testimony. However, systems of justice are closely linked to the social fabric as a whole and must also be examined at a macro-level. We will briefly point to some studies raising these larger issues relating the functioning of the justice system to inter-group relations, stereotyping, and prejudice. But before considering the social psychological research, let us first examine the main features of the jury system in France.

THE JUSTICE SYSTEM AND THE JURY IN FRANCE

In France, there are three different courts of law, each with specific penal jurisdictions. But only one calls for a jury: the Criminal Court (Cour d'assise), which generally decides the most serious offenses (e.g., murder, manslaughter, etc). As a rule, the Criminal Court sits every 3 months. A somewhat heterogeneous body comprises the Court itself: Three magistrates, including a presiding judge and two assessors, a barrister representing the State, and a clerk, employed by the State and in charge of the minutes of the criminal proceedings. Finally, a jury made up of nine citizens (12 in the case of an appeal) randomly selected within the population completes the court. Thus, with three magistrates and nine lay jurors, the French criminal court can be considered a mixed jury in the same sense as several other European tribunals studied in this volume.

Selecting Lay Jurors in France

Consistent with the ideal of justice for the people and by the people, no special knowledge or expertise is required to be appointed a juror in France. The main criteria are that a lay juror is a French citizen and at least 23 years old, is able to read and write, and is duly registered on the electoral rolls. Jurors are randomly selected from electoral rolls so as to ensure that the jury is as representative of the population as possible.

Random selection is closely monitored and follows a specific procedure. In a nutshell, the law requires that a series of lists be drawn up which are narrowed down until a final list of potential jurors is set up. First, an annual list is drawn up in each "département" (i.e., the administrative division in France), and the mayor of each village or town draws by a lot from this list three times more names than was initially decreed for each village or town. The names of those who, for any reason (see below), are deemed ineligible, are withdrawn from this initial list. Thirty-five names are drawn by a lot from the annual listing. Of these 35, in the end nine will be selected as possible jurors.

Before the final list is reached, provisions are made for replacements should one or more jurors be unable to fulfill the duties. Lastly, during the random selection of names to be included on the final list, either the defendant or the prosecution can challenge the selection of a juror deemed inappropriate or ineligible. For example, a person can be considered unacceptable for a given case because of his/her age, gender, occupation, or place of residence. However, only up to five names can be challenged in the first instance, and up to six in the case of an appeal (which would involve a jury of 12 people as mentioned above).

The law also states that certain conditions may render a person ineligible to carry out jury service. Thus, people found guilty of a felony or misdemeanor and sentenced for more than 6 months in prison are rejected. Also excluded from the final selection are those who have already served as a lay juror in the "département" over the last 5 years and those whose occupation entails jury ineligibility such as government members, members of the bar, magistrates in office, and so on. Finally, family members of the defendant, of other members of the jury or of the court, or of witnesses in the case are automatically excluded.

Lay jurors have rights and duties that they accept under oath. Their contribution to the exercise of justice is twofold. They must examine the charges brought against the accused, and understand the personality of the accused. Jurors have three distinct duties. First is a duty of complete attention and concentration with respect to the debates between the charges brought against the accused, and the arguments in his/her favor or dedicated to the defense. A juror's obvious inattentiveness (i.e., sleeping or reading a newspaper) may lead the Court to have him/her replaced by an extra juror. Failing that, it may cause the decision of the Criminal Court to be nullified. Jurors also have a duty of impartiality and must refrain from expressing their opinion on the guilt of the accused, the credibility of a witness, or the value of a piece of evidence prior to deliberation. Indeed, presumption of innocence is a fundamental principle of criminal law.

Finally, jurors are forbidden to communicate about the matter. They pledge not to talk about the matter with anyone except the other jurors and the magistrates. They cannot speak with the parties involved in the trial (barristers, counsels for the prosecution, victim, or accused) or to journalists. A breach of this rule could also entail suspension of the case. Jurors are also bound by the secrecy of deliberations.

Lay jurors have duties, but they also have rights. Jurors are entitled to information about their rights and duties as stipulated in the 1981 circular of the French Ministry of Justice. They have the right to put questions to the accused, to witnesses, and to experts, provided they have requested permission from the presiding judge. Jurors must be careful not to express their opinion in the wording of the question. If they prefer they may pass on a note to the presiding judge requesting him/her to put the question in their place. Finally, jurors are allowed to take notes, and to use these notes during the deliberations.

Lay Jurors during a Trial in Criminal Court

The Hearing During the hearing, all evidence must be presented orally; this represents one of the fundamental rules of the French Criminal Court. This rule requires that the Criminal Court may come to a decision only upon elements debated orally and after the hearing of all parties involved. This is the reason why neither the magistrates nor the lay jurors are allowed to refer to the case file during the deliberation, unless debates are reopened and all parties are heard again. It is also by virtue of this rule that the magistrates or the lay jurors are not allowed to read the written statements of the witnesses before the oral testimonies take place. The witness must be heard during the trial, the case file being secondary. The second fundamental element is that the hearing, once begun, may not be interrupted and must continue until the case is ended by the Court, that is to say by the mixed jury.

Stages of the Hearing The clerk reads aloud the charges brought against the accused in order to prove that the charges are serious enough to justify trial before a Criminal Court. This also enables the accused to know the exact charges and to prepare his/her defense. Witnesses and experts are heard following which barristers and the State present their observations. The order of presentation is always the same. Prosecution is the first to speak regarding the facts and the guilt of the accused, but not on the sentence. After trial, the prosecuting attorney will make his/her closing speech, presenting all the arguments proving that the accused is guilty and asking the jury to pronounce a sentence in accordance with the best interest of society. The defending counsel, representing the rights and the best interest of the accused, speaks after the counsel for the prosecution and endeavors to show either that there is not enough evidence proving that the accused is indeed guilty, or that the counsel for the prosecution is requiring too harsh a sentence. He/she also may contest the regularity of the trial debates or of the investigation (for instance, he/she may be asked to give a formal report of events that occurred during the debates), he/she may request that special questions be put to the jurors, etc. Following the defending counsel's closing remarks, the accused is traditionally asked if he/she has anything to add for his/her defense.

After the accused's statement, the presiding judge declares the hearing closed. The judge reads the questions (main, subsidiary, special) that the Court (including the jurors) must answer. The main question or verdict is treated first, and, depending on the verdict, follow-up questions addressing possible causes of penal irresponsibility, aggravating circumstances, the subsidiary questions, and each fact constituting a legal cause of exemption or reduction in the sentence are introduced. Before the Court withdraws, the presiding judge reads the instruction from article 353 of the code of criminal procedure reminding the jurors of their essential task.

Deliberation The magistrates and lay jurors deliberate and vote together on both the facts and the application of the law. They deliberate over the materiality of the facts, the verdict, and the appropriate sentence to be applied. The presiding judge invites each juror to speak and to express and justify his/her opinion.

Deliberation is divided in two phases. In the first phase, the Court and the jury deliberate and come to a decision about the verdict. The Court and the jury vote in writing and by separate ballots, treating each question successively. The first vote concerns the main fact, and if necessary the reasons for finding for innocence. It also concerns each of the aggravating circumstances, the subsidiary questions, and each fact that may represent a legal cause for exemption or sentence reduction.

The president counts the votes in the presence of the members of the jury who may check the ballots. He/she announces the result of the vote immediately and the ballots are burned. A qualified majority of eight votes (10 in case of an appeal) is required for a decision unfavorable to the accused. Blank or spoiled ballots are counted in favor of the accused. Therefore, the accused is acquitted if only seven votes (nine in case of an appeal) deem him/her guilty even if there are void or blank ballots. If the accused is declared not guilty, the Criminal Court immediately pronounces the acquittal. If he/she is declared guilty, the Criminal Court must immediately deliberate over the sentence. The vote is carried out by secret ballot and separately for each person accused. Decisions concerning the sentence require a simple majority of voters. At least seven votes (nine in case of an appeal) must concur on the same length of a sentence. However, at least eight votes (10 in case of an appeal) are required for the maximum sentence to be pronounced. Should no sentence be agreed upon by a majority of seven votes (eight in case of an appeal) after two rounds, a third round is carried out in which the strictest sentence proposed during the preceding round is excluded. If the majority is not reached during this third round, another round is carried out once again ruling out the strictest sentence, and so on, until a sentence is agreed upon with seven votes. Ballots are destroyed after the vote.

Following the deliberation, the public hearing is reconvened. The Presiding judge reads the answers to the questions and pronounces the guilty sentence, the acquittal, or the pardon. Once the decision has been announced, the service of the lay jurors ends. Issues concerning damages follow, but the lay jurors do not take part in this discussion. The jury system in France always follows these guidelines and procedures for all cases with the exception of the Criminal Court for minors, which is composed of a presiding judge, two assessors, and a lay jury. Minors are judged by this Court only if the minor was over 16 years old when the criminal acts were committed. If the minor was not yet 16, he/she is judged by a juvenile court. The main difference between the Criminal Court for minors and the Criminal Court proper pertains to the fact that, should a minor be declared guilty, it is required that the Criminal Court for minors come to a decision as to the type of sentence that should apply: either educational measures or, depending on the circumstances and the personality of the minor, a full sentence. Finally, terrorist acts are judged by a special Criminal Court, without a lay jury.

THE CONTRIBUTION OF SOCIAL PSYCHOLOGICAL RESEARCH IN FRANCE

The Testimony

One of the main characteristics of the French legal system is the importance given to oral communication. Indeed, during a trial, the judgment phase relies for the most part on verbal testimony given over a relatively short period of time. In this context, a single convincing item of testimony may have a substantial impact on the jurors' final decision. This impact is strengthened by the fact that, as mentioned earlier, French criminal law grants the juror much latitude in assessment of the evidence put forth ("*principe de l'intime conviction*": article 427 of the code of criminal procedure). Among the evidence available to him/her (statement of the suspected or convicted person, testimony, pieces of evidence collected either through a search or expertise), the juror has full freedom to place more value on one particular element rather than another. It is therefore quite obvious that a single piece of testimony may bend judgment in a given direction, the more so because the juror owes no explanation as to why he/she placed more value on one piece of testimony rather than on another piece of evidence.

Several studies in social psychology are relevant to understanding how a single piece of testimony can influence the juror's decision. For instance, some studies have shown the importance of the *form* of the message conveyed during the testimony. Brewer and Burke (2002) have demonstrated that witness confidence has a strong influence on mock-jurors' judgments. In other respects, another approach examined the importance of the *content* of the testimony per se. Many studies, specifically those done by Loftus (1979), showed that the content of testimony can be influenced by an external source arising after the criminal event, such as discussions, questions asked by police officers, etc. Other studies concern influence arising during the criminal event itself. Such is the case of studies on the influence of a witness' attitude on the quality of his/her account. The very first studies on this particular topic (Boon & Davies, 1988) showed that a witness who is prejudiced or who has certain specific attitudes can distort his/her testimony to his/her advantage compared to a witness who would not have prior attitudes. In France, Greffeuille, Ginet, and Guimond (in press) carried out a set of studies inspired by the paradigm devised by Boon and Davies (1988). The authors used a complex movie on a rape that would be difficult to remember, with the aim of being as close as possible to the ecological conditions of testimony. A recognition test, inspired by the one used by Boon and Davies (1988), allowed them to evaluate eyewitnesses' distortions from the original scenes. They found that when witnesses have categorical information concerning the protagonists of the event about to be recalled, they distort their testimony in accordance with this categorical information. Thus, prior expectations of witnesses can have an influence on the way the information will be selected, and hence on the content of the testimony itself.

Stereotyping, Prejudice, and the Criminal Justice System

Group processes occurring during deliberation can have a strong impact on jurors' decisions (Myers & Kaplan, 1976; Nemeth, 1984). Given that in the French system jurors deliberate with professionals having expert status, questions can be raised about the effects of this differential status on the decision (Kaplan & Martín, 1999). Recent research carried out in France does confirm the important influence that status and expertise can exert on mock juries (Bordel, Vernier, Dumas, Guingouain, & Somat, 2004; Guingouain, Manchec, & Testé, 2002; Mazé, Finkelstein, & Quentin, 2004). Furthermore, we know that mock jurors are likely to judge in- and outgroup members differently (Bagby & Rector, 1992; Bottoms, Davis, & Epstein, 2004). Together, these results suggest that extra-legal factors (Kaplan, 1989) and even socio-structural factors may have a significant influence on jury deliberations. One recent theory of inter-group relations having important implications for understanding these results is social dominance theory (SDT) (Sidanius & Pratto, 1999).

According to SDT, the criminal justice system more often than not functions to insure that the rights and privileges of dominant groups are protected. Indeed, Sidanius and Pratto (1999) have documented in detail the considerable and varied evidence that supports such a claim not only with regards to the United States but also across a wide variety of cultures and nations. For example, they find that members of low status groups (i.e., Blacks) face more severe sanctions than members of dominant groups (i.e., Whites) and that these differences are observed at all stages of the criminal justice process from the likelihood of arrest to the likelihood of conviction. Thus, in drug-related crimes, they point out that in the Unites States "While only about 13 percent of monthly drug users are African-Americans, African-Americans are targeted in 35 percent of drug possession arrests, 55 percent of drug possession convictions, and 74 percent of prison sentences for drug possession" (Sidanius & Pratto, 1999, p. 208). Similar findings are reported for a large number of countries including Canada, Australia, the Netherlands, and even in a relatively egalitarian society such as Sweden. However, given the general fact that members of low status groups are more likely to have higher rates of criminality than members of dominant groups, should we not expect to find these sorts of discrepancies? SDT argues that the law does, in part, function in the interest of the common good but that the evidence is clear that it does also, in part, function to protect and maintain the status, privileges, and power of dominants. The fact that members of stigmatized social groups may indeed commit more crimes is seen as both cause and consequence of the group-based social hierarchy that structures societies around the world. Rather than regarding these various facts as independent, the theory argues that they are dynamically interconnected.

To start looking at these interconnections and understanding their psychological basis, SDT proposed a new variable called “social dominance orientation” (SDO). This is an individual difference variable representing the predisposition to support social hierarchy and group-based dominance. It represents an individual’s preference or general attitude toward group-based dominance and inequality. A scale was developed by Pratto, Sidanius, Stallworth, and Malle (1994) to measure this orientation. It is composed of eight items reflecting a positive attitude toward group dominance and inequality (e.g., “Some groups are simply inferior to other groups”) and eight items indicating a favorable orientation toward social equality (reverse coded, e.g., “Group equality should be our ideal”). The reliability and validity of this scale has been documented in extensive research (see Sidanius & Pratto, 1999).

How is this variable relevant for an understanding of the French jury system? There are no definitive answers to that question as the social dominance perspective has only begun to be applied in this area. But there are reasons to believe that it may prove to be extremely important. First, SDO is currently the single most powerful psychological variable known to predict prejudice against low status outgroups (Altemeyer, 1998). Many studies have found that of all possible individual difference variables that can be reliably measured, only two predict prejudice: right-wing authoritarianism (RWA) and SDO (Altemeyer, 1998; Duckitt, 2001), with SDO usually being the most powerful predictor. Indeed, there is clear evidence that RWA and SDO are distinct constructs. The correlation between these two variables is typically weak and often not statistically significant (Altemeyer, 1998; Sidanius & Pratto, 1999). Using the SDO scale, then, may be useful in any setting where stereotyping and prejudice may lead to unfair judgments. Furthermore, as we outline below, there is evidence that SDO levels vary among members of various groups and organizations.

In this regard, SDT distinguishes between institutions and social roles in terms of their general effects on group-based hierarchy. Some institutions and social roles are defined as hierarchy-enhancing (HE) because they tend to work for the interests of the powerful against the powerless (e.g., FBI, KGB). Other institutions and social roles are defined as hierarchy-attenuating (HA) because they tend to work in the opposite direction, trying to favor subordinate groups and reduce inequality (e.g., Amnesty International). For the reasons outlined above, the criminal justice system is considered as a good example of an HE institution. To function effectively as such, SDT suggests that the criminal justice system will tend to recruit people having particularly high levels of SDO. Police officers and prison guards, as examples of HE social roles, are thus expected to show high levels of SDO. However, to the extent that a component of the criminal justice system functions in an HA fashion, it should recruit personnel suited for their roles and having, among other things, relatively low levels of SDO. These predictions were borne out in a study comparing undergraduate students from UCLA, adults called to jury duty in Los Angeles County, street officers from the Los Angeles Police Department, and public defenders from Los Angeles County (see Sidanius, Liu, Shaw, & Pratto, 1994). Even after controlling for major demographic differences between the groups, the results showed, as predicted, that police officers have higher SDO scores than students or jurors. It also showed that public defenders, as an HA social role, have significantly lower SDO scores compared to students and jurors.

Studies carried out in France generally support the social dominance perspective. SDO is a significant predictor of prejudice and discrimination against people of North African origins in France (Dambrun & Guimond, 2001; Dambrun, Guimond, & Duarte, 2002; Michinov, Dambrun, Guimond, & Meot, 2005). It also predicts a favorable attitude toward the "National Front," an extreme right-wing political party advocating discriminatory policies against North Africans in France (Dambrun, Maisonneuve, Duarte, & Guimond, 2002). Furthermore, consistent with the idea that a career in law can be defined as a social role that is more HE than a career in psychology, Guimond, Dambrun, Michinov, and Duarte (2003) found that first-year university students in France score significantly higher on SDO when their major field of study is law rather than psychology. This is consistent with similar findings obtained in the United States (see Pratto et al., 1994). However, Guimond et al. (2003) also obtained cross-sectional evidence suggesting that being socialized in the field of law (HE) may increase SDO scores whereas being socialized in the field of psychology (HA) may have the opposite effect. More specifically, they found that third-year university students in law have higher SDO scores compared to their first-year counterparts whereas the reverse occurs in psychology. Indeed, it was predicted, and found, that third-year students in law would display more prejudice against North Africans than third-year psychology students and that this difference would be mediated by SDO (see Guimond et al., 2003 for more details).

It appears then that in France, where White French people are the dominant group and people of North African background the main subordinate group, SDT offers a powerful way of understanding who will be prejudiced and why. But more concretely, in terms of the operation of the justice system, the fact that law students display higher levels of SDO and prejudice against North Africans than psychology students raises serious questions. If justice is to be served well, prejudiced attitudes and discriminatory behaviors against members of a particular group need to be controlled. Otherwise, one can expect members of those groups to be recipients of an unfair system of justice. SDT suggests that one should not be too hopeful that a person who receives legal training would be more able to guard against these biases since legal institutions are themselves agents of social dominance. Further research is needed to document whether there are enough opposing forces (high and low SDO in this case) within the justice system to insure a balance.

Given these potentially troubling possibilities, what can be done to try to correct them? Obviously, any reasonable answer to this question will require the concerted efforts of large numbers of people and institutions over an extended period of time. Nevertheless, we provide below some modest but concrete examples of the ways in which social psychologists in France have tried to improve the day to day workings of the justice system by focusing on means of improving the reliability of testimony and preventing biases in the identification of suspects.

The Cognitive Interview: Improving the Quality of Testimony

Given the typical features of the French jury system, in which all evidence has to be presented orally during the trial, the form and content of testimony can exert a strong influence on the decisions of Justice. Consequently, any effort to improve the quality of testimony becomes crucial. Several tools have been developed with this in mind. One main example is the "cognitive interview," which aims to help witnesses have better access to their memories and to facilitate communication between all involved. The theoretical bases of this technique are found in Tulving's model of memory (1983). It consists of four instructions given to the witness before testimony. The witness is asked to (1) return mentally to the context surrounding the facts; (2) report everything, including uncertain or unimportant information; (3) describe the scene in a different chronological order; (4) describe the scene from a variety of perspectives. This technique was successfully tested through various studies carried out either in the laboratory (Aschermann, Mantwill, & Köhnken, 1991; Fisher, Geiselman, Raymond, Jurkevich, & Warhaftig, 1987; Py, Ginet, Desperies, & Cathey, 1997) or in the field with legal professionals (Fisher, Geiselman, & Amador, 1989; Ginet & Py, 2001; Memon, Holley, Milne, Köhnken, & Bull, 1994). These studies show that the cognitive interview improves accuracy of testimony without significantly increasing the number of incorrect (see, however, Köhnken, Milne, Memon, & Bull, 1999, for a meta-analysis) or confabulated details.

In France, the cognitive interview proved to be a worthwhile tool especially since French police officers receive very little interviewer training and do not rely on specific hearing techniques. However, one constraint linked to the French criminal law procedure calls for an adaptation and assessment of the protocol for the Anglo-Saxon cognitive interview (see Figure 9.1). Indeed, police officers must draw up a written statement during the hearing. This report is the only retained trace of the witness' statement. Based on this report the examining magistrate decides whether or not to continue the investigation. As the cognitive interview is profitable in terms of the wealth of information collected, it is important to ensure that this advantage is applied to the written statement provided by the police officer. A study carried out by Ginet and Py (2001) with French police officers addresses this matter. The protocol for the cognitive interview used in this study included a phase of three free recalls, followed by specific questions. The four instructions were systematically dissociated (cf. Figure 9.1). At first, 15 students watched a crime on tape (either a burglary, a purse theft, or an assault) at the university. A week later, they were summoned to the police station and were

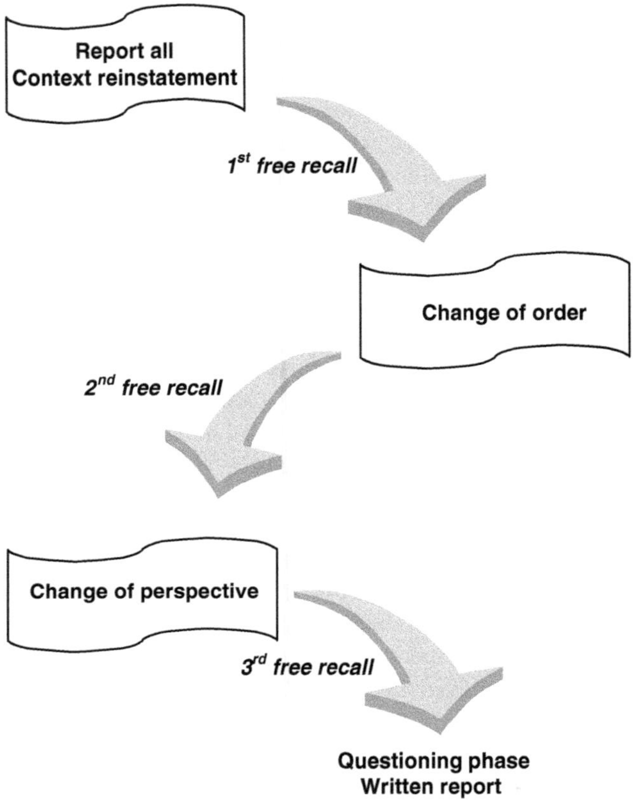

FIGURE 9.1 Cognitive interview (French protocol).

interviewed by one of the eight police officers who had agreed to take part in the study. The police officers were only instructed to carry out the interview in their usual manner and to draw up a written statement. This group was labeled "standard police interview." In a second phase, the eight police officers were randomly divided into two groups of four. The first group was trained in the technique of structured interview. This training consisted in making the police officers aware of certain basic principles for the carrying out of interviews: Using free recall, refraining from asking leading questions or negative questions, the question sequence should go from the general to the specific, etc. The second group received training in the technique of cognitive interview. The training modules comprised both theory and practice. In a final phase, 29 new students were interviewed by the trained police officers. The interviews were all taped on audiocassettes, entirely transcribed and rated on a grid. Results show that cognitive interviews are more fruitful compared to either standard interviews or structured interviews in terms of the number of accurate information items collected during the interview. More relevant for the validation of the French protocol for the cognitive interview, this advantage was generalized to the written statement, that is, the transcription by the police officer of the oral witness statement. No difference was observed between the cognitive interview and the two other types of interviews with respect to the generation of incorrect details.

However, there was an unexpected effect of the cognitive interview on the number of confabulated details generated: witnesses interviewed following this technique generated fewer confabulated details that those who went through standard witness interviews. This decrease was also observed following transcription on the written statements. This effect may be due to the fact that the free recalls obtained through the cognitive interview were so thorough that it permitted limiting the number of questions asked. Among the questions asked spontaneously by the police officers, some had been misleading (30 percent according to the analyses carried out on the written statements). By decreasing the number of questions asked, the number of misleading questions was also lowered, thus in turn lowering the risk of contaminating the witness' statement. In conclusion, the results of this study confirmed the effectiveness of the cognitive interview for French police officers. The study also verified the advantage of a statement written after the witness hearing and upon which the examining magistrate will base judgment. In addition, the study demonstrates that the cognitive interview improves not only the thoroughness of the statements but also their quality, owing to the reduced risk of fabrication.

Although this first study represents an important step toward validating the French protocol for cognitive interview, it remained important to verify that the technique was as efficient when the witnessed event generates strong emotions. Indeed, actual testimony situations are often associated with significant levels of emotion (Christianson, 1992). However, the events used in studies of the cognitive interview are not very emotional (e.g., films, disruption during a class at the university). The issue of the interaction between the cognitive interview technique and the level of emotion triggered by the crucial scene has not been thoroughly examined (Ginet, 2003; Py & Ginet, 2001). Yet, it is important to know whether the advantage of the cognitive interview is maintained even when the eyewitness experiences strong emotions. Several studies concerning eyewitness testimonies examine the link between negative emotions and memory accuracy. The results are inconsistent. Indeed, some studies report harmful effects of emotion on testimony (Clifford & Scott, 1978; Kramer, Buckhout, Fox, Widman, & Tusche, 1991) while others showed positive effects (Christianson & Loftus, 1987; Heuer & Reisberg, 1990; Libkuman, Stabler, & Otani, 2004). The explanations offered to make sense of these inconsistencies (Christianson, 1992) take into account one of the main characteristics of emotions: their intensity. It appears that either too little or too much emotion may harm the functioning of the memory, whereas optimum mnemonic performance is found between the extremes (Yerkes & Dodson, 1908). These effects seem to stem from an attention narrowing on the central elements of the scene (Christianson & Loftus, 1987; Easterbrook, 1959). With this in mind, a moderate or strong level of emotion should lead witnesses to focus on the central events of the crime scene, which would improve their mnemonic performance for important detail. Furthermore, we assumed that the cognitive interview would make available an increased amount of information, namely through contextual indices cued by putting themselves into the original context.

In a study conducted with the French protocol for the cognitive interview, 68 first-year psychology students watched a film about a pedestrian being hit by a car. Electrodes on the arms of the participants were linked to a bogus measuring instrument and to a computer. Half the participants were told that they would be subjected to painful electric shocks during the film, while the other half was informed that physiological measures would be collected. In actual fact, no electric shocks were given. The purpose of this device was to induce stress in the participants. A week later, the students were summoned to recount, individually and orally, the content of the film. The cognitive interview technique was used with half of them, while the other half was interviewed following a structured protocol (same general context for the interview, without the instructions). Results show a clear advantage of the cognitive interview on the amount of accurate information recollected but without a substantial increase in the number of confabulated details generated. On the other hand, this advantage was accompanied by an increase in the number of incorrect details. This confirms the trend observed in the literature and highlighted by Köhnken et al.'s (1999) meta-analysis. More interestingly, a positive effect of emotion was observed. This positive effect was observed on the quality rather than on the quantity of information generated (no effect on the amount of accurate information recounted). Indeed, the participants under stress generated fewer incorrect and confabulated details than those who did not have such expectations. Lastly, no significant interaction was observed between the type of interview and the level of stress of the participants on any of the measures used. Therefore, the cognitive interview does not increase the positive effects of emotions. In conclusion, this study demonstrates once more the effectiveness of the cognitive interview. Moreover, it shows that the advantage extends to a stressful situation. It also shows that emotions have a facilitating effect on the recall process with respect to the quality of the information recalled. If we refer to the attention-narrowing hypothesis, we may suppose that higher levels of stress would be likely to induce opposite effects. In that case, only a limited amount of information would draw the attention of the witness. Studies carried out in an ecological context would be definitive.

Improving the Accurate Identification of Suspects

Although the cognitive interview is an effective tool to collect oral information about facts, free recall generated by a witness is not the sole significant witness element. Composite pictures can also be important in the context of an investigation. In 2000 in France, 731 composite pictures were produced (Somat & Vazel, 2004), showing how important the police deem this type of element in their investigation. However, some authors have shown that it may be difficult for eyewitnesses to identify a suspect on the basis of a composite picture (Shepherd & Ellis, 1996; Vazel, 2002). This bears on the problem of the frequently mediocre quality of composite pictures. The problem may in part stem from a lack of systematic methodology of French police officers while assisting witnesses in producing composite pictures (Somat & Vazel, 2004). Indeed, police practices are highly heterogeneous. Moreover, interviews are mainly geared toward specific questions leading the witness to process features in an analytical way. These practices do not produce optimum results with respect to witness memory (Somat & Vazel, 2004) since, by asking specific questions, the officer in charge of the investigation is likely to influence the responses of eyewitnesses (Geiselman, Fisher, Cohen, Holland, & Surtes, 1986). Moreover, the processing of facial features involves a holistic rather than an analytical approach (Tanaka & Farah, 1993).

With this in mind, Somat and Vazel (2004) came up with the novel idea of adapting the cognitive interview to constructing composite pictures. The authors added a fifth instruction to the four original instructions in the protocol, which was termed the holistic processing instruction. The witness is asked to give a general description of the offender's face. She/he must think of the features one after the other and recall the general impression of this particular face. This adapted protocol was assessed in the context of a series of field studies. A man barged into a classroom and left after a few seconds. Several minutes later, detectives entered the classroom and told the students that they were looking for a suspect that looked like the one they had seen a few minutes earlier. The police then called for volunteer witnesses who were interviewed in order to produce a composite picture of the suspect. Some witnesses were interviewed with an adapted version of the cognitive interview while others were interviewed by standard procedure followed by police in the field. The composite pictures were produced using computer software. Each picture was evaluated twice. First, judges evaluated the similarity of the composite picture produced by witnesses to a photo of the target-face. Then, different judges identified the suspect among a series of photos on the basis of the composite pictures. There was a clear advantage for the structured cognitive interview on both measures; the technique substantially improved the quality of the composite pictures produced.

Collecting evidence relating to the physical appearance of an offender is a fundamental aspect in the interview of a witness (Demarchi, Ginet, & Py, 2004). Physical description of the offender represents 30 percent of the total volume of information contained in written witness statements (Yuille & Cutshall, 1986). However, several studies show that such descriptions contain little useful information (Tollestrup, Turtle, & Yuille, 1994). The majority of the facial components reported are limited to the upper half of the face. Moreover, these descriptions are unreliable, as one description out of five collected is wrong (Koppen & Lochun, 1997; Py, Demarchi, & Reynes, 2004). With this in mind, Py and Demarchi (2004) devised an original interview protocol specifically adapted to the description of offenders and geared toward optimizing both the thoroughness and the quality of the information collected. These authors started by evaluating the strategies spontaneously adopted by individuals to describe people. They were able to show that 80 percent of people interviewed mention general elements such as gender, height, age, ethnic group, and physique before adding more specific details such as hair-length or color of eyes. In addition, these specific details are reported following a sequence moving from the upper half of the face (hair) to the lower half (chin). Details concerning the lower half of the face are very seldom mentioned, however. Following this observation, the authors suggested a specific instruction to systematize the strategies spontaneously used by individuals.

The witness was asked to describe the offender starting with more general elements such as gender, age, etc., and moving to more specific details. The results from several studies show that this particular instruction leads to a significant increase in the number of accurate physical descriptions of an offender compared to a condition where no instruction is given. Even more encouraging is the fact that it leads to an improvement in the accuracy rate (+11 percent). However, this instruction fails to increase the number of details concerning the lower part of the face. Taking into account the observation that most individuals describe faces from top to bottom, the authors suggested a second instruction designed to reverse this strategy and to make the elements of the lower part of the face more salient. Witnesses are thus encouraged to describe the offender's face starting with the lower part of the face moving to the upper part. This type of instruction increases the total volume of overall information collected. Thus, according to Py and Demarchi (2004), in order to have a witness accurately describe an offender, it is recommended to use the first instruction (description from the general to the specific) during the first free recall session, and the second instruction (description from bottom to top) during the second recall. More specific questions should be asked subsequently.

The cognitive interview, the cognitive interview adapted to the drawing up of composite pictures, or the interview adapted to the description of individuals, all share the same purpose of optimizing witness recall. However, witnesses may sometimes be asked to recognize rather than recall the features of a suspect, for instance in the case of an identification lineup in which the suspect is embedded in an array of other people (distractors). To be considered a convincing piece of evidence for the justice system, identification via a lineup should be properly carried out. However, researchers in social psychology have highlighted several problems at this level. Two categories of problems are typically identified.

First are procedural problems, especially with respect to the instruction given to the eyewitness during the lineup. Indeed this instruction can be crucial and should therefore be unbiased. A bias appears when it is hinted that the suspect is present in the lineup (Do you recognize the suspect?) and when the police officer does not accept "I don't know" for an answer. Furthermore, the suspect must not be readily distinguished from the distractors (handcuffs, shackles, unique appearance, etc.).

The second category of factors pertains to structural biases, in other words biases linked to the selection of distractors surrounding the suspect. Generally, distractors are selected according to the physical features they have in common with the suspect. The identification parade can therefore be considered biased as the suspect represents a prototype and is bound to stand out compared to the rest of the lineup. This bias is likely to increase the probability of generating false recognitions (Wells, Rydell, & Seelau, 1993; Wogalter, Marwitz, & Leonard, 1992). In this context, Demarchi and Py (2004) conducted an evaluative study of the proportion of biased lineups carried out by various investigation services in France. Twelve pictures of lineups in investigations of felony cases were independently evaluated by students. The students were given a single instruction: "Find the suspect." No other information was provided. Seven out of the twelve lineups were considered to be biased. Indeed, in those cases, the suspect was identified with a probability unaccountable by chance only. If outsiders are able to spot the suspect based on the structure of the lineup (nonplausible distractors, salient implication), but without having actually witnessed the suspect, it is obvious that an actual eyewitness or victim will be subjected to the same influences. There do exist, however, procedures to limit this type of bias in the choice of distractors. One efficient method consists of selecting distractors according to the description provided by the eyewitness or victim rather than according to his/her similarity to the suspect (Demarchi & Py, 2004; Wells et al., 1993).

CONCLUSION

In this chapter, we have discussed some of the typical features of the jury system in France and outlined a number of studies carried out from a social psychological perspective. We have emphasized research on testimony because the jury system in France relies heavily on the testimony of witnesses. Our finding that stereotypes can shape the memory of witnesses is consistent with a large number of studies in social psychology documenting the sometimes-subtle role that stereotyping and prejudice can play in social life. After raising these issues of prejudice and discrimination, which are certainly no more typical of the French system than other national systems, we presented some original lines of work seeking to improve the fairness of the justice system in France. Grounded in established psychological principles, this research suggests that there are a number of ways to improve the accuracy of testimony and decrease the biased identification of suspects. These efforts are modest and more research is vitally needed. But the initial results are encouraging. They provide some concrete examples of the ways in which psychological research on the criminal justice system can offer not only a theoretical but a practical contribution as well.

REFERENCES

Altemeyer, B. (1998). The other authoritarian personality. In M. P. Zanna (Ed.), *Advances in experimental social psychology* (Vol. 30, pp. 47–92). New York: Academic Press.

Aschermann, E., Mantwill, M., & Köhnken, G. (1991). An independent replication of the effectiveness of the cognitive interview. *Applied Cognitive Psychology*, *5*, 489–495.

Bagby, R. M., & Rector, N. A. (1992). Prejudice in a simulated legal context: A further application of social identity theory. *European Journal of Social Psychology*, *22*, 397–406.

Binet, A. (1905). La Science du Témoignage [The science of testimony]. *L'Année Psychologique*, *11*, 128–136.

Boon, J. C. W., & Davies, G. (1988). Attitudinal influences on witness memory: Fact and fiction. In M. Gruneberg, P. Morris, & R. Sykes (Eds.), *Practical Aspects of Memory: Current Research and Issues. 1. Memory in Everyday Life* (pp. 53–58). Chichester: Wiley.

Bordel, S., Vernier, C., Dumas, R., Guingouain, G., & Somat, A. (2004). L'expertise psychologique, élément de preuve du jugement judiciaire? [Is expert testimony treated as an actual piece of evidence in judiciary decisions?]. *Psychologie Française*, *49*, 389–408.

Bottoms, B. L., Davis, S. L., & Epstein, M. A. (2004). Effects of victim and defendant race on jurors' decisions in child sexual abuse cases. *Journal of Applied Social Psychology*, *34*, 1–33.

Brewer, N., & Burke, A. (2002). Effects of testimonial inconsistencies and eyewitness confidence on mock-juror judgments. *Law and Human Behavior*, *26*, 353–364.

Christianson, S. Ä. (1992). Emotional stress and eyewitness memory: A critical review. *Psychological Bulletin*, *112*, 284–309.

Christianson, S. Ä., & Loftus, E. F. (1987). Memory for traumatic events. *Applied Cognitive Psychology*, *1*, 225–239.

Clifford, B. R., & Scott, J. (1978). Individual and situational factors in eyewitness testimony. *Journal of Applied Psychology*, *63*, 352–359.

Dambrun, M., & Guimond, S. (2001). La théorie de la privation relative et l'hostilité envers les Nord-Africains [Relative deprivation theory and hostility toward North Africans]. *International Review of Social Psychology*, *14*, 57–89.

Dambrun, M., Guimond, S., & Duarte, S. (2002). The impact of hierarchy-enhancing vs. attenuating academic major on stereotyping: The mediating role of perceived social norm. *Current Research in Social Psychology*, *7*, 114–136.

Dambrun, M., Maisonneuve, C., Duarte, S., & Guimond, S. (2002). Modélisation de quelques déterminants psychosociaux de l'attitude envers l'extrême droite [Modeling the social-psychological determinants of support for extreme right-wing movements]. Cahiers Internationaux de Psychologie Sociale, 55, 49–63.

Demarchi, S., & Py, J. (2004). *Les biais structuraux dans les parades d'identification: une étude évaluative en France* [Bias in identification lineups: An evaluation study in France]. Unpublished manuscript, Université de Paris 8.

Demarchi, S., Ginet, M., & Py, J. (2004). Les outils pour le recueil et l'évaluation des témoignages judiciaires. In P. Pansu & C. Louche (Eds.), *La psychologie appliquée à l'analyse des problèmes sociaux* [Psychology applied to the analysis of social problems]. Paris: Presses Universitaires de France.

Duckitt, J. (2001). A dual-process cognitive-motivational theory of ideology and prejudice. In M. P. Zanna (Ed.), *Advances in experimental social psychology* (Vol. 33, pp. 41–112). San Diego, CA: Academic Press.

Easterbrook, J. A. (1959). The effect of emotion on cue utilization and the organization of behavior. *Psychological Review*, *66*, 183–201.

Finkelstein, R. (2004). Des applications de la psychologie sociale dans le domaine judiciaire: Nouvelles perspectives [Applying social psychology to the justice system: New perspectives]. *Psychologie Française*, *49*, 353–355.

Fisher, R. P., Geiselman, R. E., & Amador, M. (1989). Field test of the cognitive interview: Enhancing the recollection of actual victims and witness of crime. *Journal of Applied Psychology*, *74*, 722–727.

Fisher, R. P., Geiselman, R. E., Raymond, D. S., Jurkevich, L. M., & Warhaftig, M. L. (1987). Enhancing enhanced eyewitness memory: Refining the Cognitive Interview. *Journal of Police Science and Administration*, *15*, 291–297.

Geiselman, R. E., Fisher, R. P., Cohen, G., Holland, H., & Surtes, L. (1986). Eyewitness responses to leading and misleading questions under cognitive interview. *Journal of Police Science and Administration*, *14*, 31–39.

Ginet, M. (2003). *Les clés de l'entretien avec le témoin ou la victime* [The keys to interviewing witnesses or victims]. Paris: La documentation Française, Collection la Sécurité Aujourd'hui.

Ginet, M., & Py, J. (2001). A technique for enhancing memory in eyewitness testimonies for use by police officers and judicial officials: the cognitive interview. *Le Travail Humain*, *64*, 173–191.

Greffeuille, C., Ginet, M., & Guimond, S. (2004). Memory accuracy of eyewitnesses in case of rape: Effects of stereotypes and gender. *Current Psychology of Cognition*, *22*, 479–496.

Guimond, S., Dambrun, M., Michinov, N., & Duarte, S. (2003). Does social dominance generate prejudice? Integrating individual and contextual determinants of intergroup cognitions. *Journal of Personality and Social Psychology*, *84*, 697–721.

Guingouain, G., Manchec, K., & Testé, B. (2002). Insertion sociale et jugements judiciaires: Influences de l'anticipation de délibération en jury en fonction de l'origine ethnique endo- ou exogroupe de l'accusé [Social positions and judiciary decisions: Effects of anticipated jury deliberation as a function of the ingroup or outgroup membership of the suspect]. *Cahiers Internationaux de Psychologie Sociale*, *54*, 113–124.

Heuer, F., & Reisberg, D. (1990). Vivid memories of emotional events: The accuracy of remembered minutiae. *Memory and Cognition*, *18*, 496–506.

Kaplan, M. F. (1989). Judgements of murder mysteries as a means of studying juror cognition. *Basic and Applied Social Psychology*, *10*, 299–310.

Kaplan, M. F., & Martín, A. M. (1999). Effects of differential status of members on process and outcome of deliberation. *Group Processes and Intergroup Relations*, *2*, 347–364.

Köhnken, G., Milne, R., Memon, A., & Bull, R. (1999). The cognitive interview: A meta-analysis. *Psychology, Crime and Law*, *5*, 3–28.

Koppen, P. J., & Lochun, S. (1997). Portraying perpetrators: The validity of offender descriptions by witnesses. *Applied Law and Human Behavior, 21,* 661–685.

Kramer, T. H., Buckhout, R., Fox, P., Widman, E., & Tusche, B. (1991). Effects of stress on recall. *Applied Cognitive Psychology*, *5*, 483–488.

Libkuman, T. M., Stabler, C. L., & Otani, H. (2004). Arousal, valence and memory for detail. *Memory*, *12*, 237–247.

Loftus, E. F. (1979). *Eyewitness testimony.* London: Harvard University Press.

Mazé, C., Finkelstein, R., & Quentin, M. (2004). Un jury sous influence: L'impact des affects, du type d'expertise et des circonstances aggravantes sur l'activité décisionnelles des jurés [Juries under influence: The impact of affect, expert testimony and mitigating circumstances on the outcome of deliberation]. *Psychologie Française*, *49*, 357–372.

Memon, A., Holley, A., Milne, R., Köhnken, G., & Bull, R. (1994). Towards understanding the effects of interviewer training in evaluating the cognitive interview. *Applied Cognitive Psychology*, *8*, 641–659.

Michinov, N., Dambrun, M., Guimond, S., & Meot, A. (2005). Social dominance orientation, prejudice and discrimination. *Behavior Research Methods & Instruments*, 37, 91–98.

Myers, D. G., & Kaplan, M. F. (1976). Group-induced polarization in simulated juries. *Personality and Social Psychology Bulletin*, *2*, 63–66.

Nemeth, C. (1984). Processus de groupe et jurys: les Etats-Unis et la France [Group processes and the jury: The United States and France]. In S. Moscovici (Ed.), *Psychologie Sociale* (pp. 229–251). Paris: Presses Universitaires de France.

Pratto, F., Sidanius, J., Stallworth, L. M., & Malle, B. F. (1994). Social dominance orientation: A personality variable predicting social and political attitudes. *Journal of Personality and Social Psychology*, *67*, 741–763.

Py, J., & Demarchi, S. (2004). *A la recherche d'un protocole optimal pour la description des criminels* [Searching for the right method of describing suspects in criminal cases]. Unpublished manuscript, Université de Paris 8.

Py, J., & Ginet, M. (2001). Evaluer l'efficacité de techniques pour améliorer les souvenirs de témoins ou victimes à l'usage des professionnels de la justice [Evaluating the effectiveness of methods designed to improve memories of witness or victims]. *Revue Européenne de Psychologie Appliquée*, *51*, 121–132.

Py, J., Demarchi, S., & Reynes, S. (2004). *Une stratégie cognitive comme aide à l'investigation judiciaire: description des personnes et parades d'identification* [A cognitive strategy to assist criminal investigations: describing and identifying suspects]. Unpublished manuscript, Université de Provence.

Py, J., Ginet, M., Desperies, C., & Cathey C. (1997). Cognitive encoding and cognitive interviewing in eyewitness testimony. *Swiss Journal of Psychology*, *56*, 33–41.

Shepherd, J. W., & Ellis, H. D. (1996). Face-recall methods and problems. In S. L. Sporer, R. S. Malpass, & G. Köhnken (Eds.), *Psychological issues in eyewitness identification* (pp. 87–115). Mahwah, NJ: Lawrence Erlbaum Associates.

Sidanius, J., & Pratto, F. (1999). *Social dominance: An intergroup theory of social hierarchy and oppression.* New York: Cambridge University Press.

Sidanius, J., Liu, J. H., Shaw, J. S., & Pratto, F. (1994). Social dominance orientation, hierarchy attenuators and hierarchy enhancers: Social dominance theory and the criminal justice system. *Journal of Applied Social Psychology*, *24*, 338–366.

Somat, A., & Vazel, M. A. (2004). L'identification par portrait-robot peut-elle être améliorée? [Can we improve composite pictures?] In P. Pansu & C. Louche (Eds.), *La psychologie appliquée à l'analyse des problèmes sociaux*. Paris: Presses Universitaires de France.

Tanaka, J. W., & Farah, M. J. (1993). Parts and wholes in face recognition. *Quarterly Journal of Experimental Psychology*, *46*, 225–245.

Tollestrup, P. A., Turtle, J. W., & Yuille, J. C. (1994). Actual victims and witnesses to robbery and fraud: an archival analysis. In D. F. Ross, J. D. Read, & M. P. Toglia (Eds.), *Adult Eyewitness Testimony: Current Trends and Development* (pp. 144–160). Cambridge: Cambridge University Press.

Tulving, E. (1983). *Elements of episodic memory.* New York: Oxford University Press.

Vazel, M. A. (2002). *Proposition d'une méthodologie d'élaboration des portraits-robots* [Methodological proposals for the creation of composite pictures]. Unpublished doctoral dissertation, Université de Haute-Bretagne, Rennes 2 (France).

Wells, G. L., Rydell, S. M., & Seelau, M. P. (1993). On the selection of distractors for eyewitness line ups. *Journal of Applied Psychology*, *78*, 835–844.

Wogalter, M. S., Marwitz, D. B., & Leonard, D. C. (1992). Suggestiveness in photospread lineups: similarity induces distinctiveness. *Applied Cognitive Psychology*, *6*, 443-453.

Yerkes, R. M., & Dodson, J. D. (1908). The relation of strength of stimulus to rapidity of habit formation. *Journal of Comparative Neurology and Psychology*, *18*, 459–482.

Yuille, J. C., & Cutshall, J. L. (1986). A case study of eyewitness memory of a crime. *Journal of Applied Psychology*, *71*, 291–301.

10

Social-Psychological Implications of the Mixed Jury in Poland

DANUTA PARLAK

This chapter is devoted to understanding the nature and mechanisms of the Polish mixed jury in the context of social-psychological knowledge. The first section gives a brief description of the mixed jury in the light of legal regulations while the remaining sections reference social-psychological aspects of mixed jury activity. Thus, the second section deals with the negative stereotype of lay judges in the professional milieu and its impact on collaboration between mixed jury members. The third section reveals the lack of a clear-cut role of the lay judges in the Polish jurisdiction and its consequences for mixed jury functioning. The fourth section discusses the mechanisms of reaching a joint decision by a mixed jury and tackles the problem of sociocentrism that consists of the difficulty in adapting a point of view differing from one's own group. Lastly, the fifth section summarizes the main problems and indicates the need for future research.

THE POLISH MIXED JURY SYSTEM—LEGAL BASES

The Sphere of Mixed Jury Activity

The mixed jury (professional and lay judges adjudicating together) is the form of jury that has been employed in Poland for over 50 years. The inclusion of lay judges puts into practice a general constitutional principle of citizen participation in the jurisdiction.

The Polish legal system comprises common courts, administrative courts, military courts, and the Supreme Court. Common courts include district courts, regional courts, and courts of appeal. Legal proceedings function within the system of two instances: first instance (original trial) and appeal instance. Mixed juries deliberate exclusively in main trials in district and regional common[1] courts of the first instance, adjudicating guilt and punishment both in criminal and civil cases. They do not participate in appeal proceedings.

The mixed jury bench functions in two forms. The first is a regular bench consisting of one professional judge acting as a presiding judge, and two lay judges. This is typical of most civil and penal cases. The second is an enlarged bench consisting of two professional judges, and three lay judges. This bench functions only in regional court when punishments of 25-year imprisonment or life imprisonment are options. These are the most stringent punishments in Polish law and usually relate to cases of murder, or rape with extraordinary cruelty.

Generally, each case in the court of first instance should be deliberated by the mixed jury. Legislation, however, allows for a situation when certain penal cases and civil suits are tried by one professional judge or, when the case is particularly difficult, by three professional judges. In fact, the Penal and Civil Proceeding Codes of 1997 considerably increased the number of such "special" cases adjudicated without the participation of lay judges in courts of first instance.

As far as criminal cases are concerned, the mixed jury can be replaced by one professional judge in at least four situations: (1) simplified proceedings; (2) civil actions (with the exception of action for libel, which always requires participation of two lay judges and the professional judges); (3) petty criminal cases; and (4) proceedings by writ of payment.

Additionally, as mentioned above, the mixed jury can be replaced by a bench of three professional judges if the case is regarded as extremely complicated. The final decision concerning the choice of bench (strictly professional or mixed jury) is made by the President of the Court.

It is worth pointing out that there exists a special situation where trial by mixed jury is obligatory. This applies to cases in which decisions concerning petition for pardon are taken. Petition for pardon should be considered by the same bench that gave the original verdict. However, when the verdict was meted out by one professional judge, the petition for pardon must be considered by a mixed jury.

Lay judges also participate in civil cases. They take part in labor and social insurance cases, and also in family and guardianship cases (excepting alimony cases). Participation of a mixed jury bench is also obligatory in four nonlitigious proceedings: (1) deprivation or restriction of parental care; (2) granting permission on the parent's capability of managing the child's property; (3) adoption; and (4) resolution of conflict between employees of a company and its manager.

This brief discussion shows that despite the fact that legislation has established the participation of mixed jury in courts of first instance as a general rule, there are so many exceptions permitted by law that in practice most cases are tried exclusively by benches of one or three professional judges (Artymiak, 1996; Waltoś, 2002). This may be due to the influence of the professional legal community, whose estimation of lay judges' functioning is prevailingly negative, and who favor reducing lay judges' role in jurisdiction. This problem is treated below.

Recruitment of Lay Judges

The lay judge is elected by the local council in a secret ballot for a 4-year term on two levels: district and regional. Lay judges can be re-elected for an unlimited number of terms. Candidates are nominated by the President of the local courts, as well as by companies, associations, organizations, and trade unions. They can also be nominated by a group of at least 25 citizens of the given area who are on the voting rolls.

Lay judge candidates must be Polish citizens between 30 and 65 years old. The candidate should be of "impeccable character" and should have been living or working in the locality for at least one year. The lay judge, as a representative of society, is expected to know the local society to represent it well, hence the requirement of living for at least one year in a given area. Finally, a candidate who is to serve in labor or social insurance cases is expected to be competent in these matters.

There are other legal restrictions on selection of lay judges. In particular, people whose profession is related to the law are excluded. It concerns those employed in courts or in the prosecutor's office, police officers, advocates, attorneys, articled clerks, professional army officers,[2] prison officers, and the clergy.

When candidate selection has been completed, the President of the Court swears in lay judges in accordance with the oath administered to professional judges but suitably altered for lay judges. This procedure emphasizes the equality of lay and professional judges.

The Court President assigns lay judges individually according to the previously prepared list of order to a particular case. However, for cases in district court involving the maximum punishment, both professional and lay judges are appointed by lot.

Lay judges serve as a social duty. Although they are nominally not paid for their service, working laypersons receive a sum equivalent to their regular earnings, and those who do not work receive recompense for the time spent in court. Lay judges who live far from the seat of the court additionally receive travel and accommodation expenses equivalent to those given to professional judges.

Rights and Duties of Lay Judges

All members of the mixed jury have equal rights and duties in judicial proceedings except that a lay judge cannot preside over the trial. Lay judges have the same rights as professional judges in matters of hearing, deliberating, and voting. For example, they have full access to the case file before and during the trial, they have the right to question litigants during the trial, and their vote carries the same weight as that of a professional judge.

To underscore the procedural equality of lay and professional judges, they sit together at the judges' table at trial. All jury members wear the same outfit—a black gown with a violet jabot and violet edgings on the collar. The prosecutor and defense attorney wear different trim colors. The presiding judge wears a gold chain around his/her neck with a stylized image of the eagle, which is the symbol of Poland. This emphasizes the institutional power of the presiding judge as the State's representative.

Decisions concerning both guilt and punishment are reached by a simple majority. So, it is possible for lay judges to outvote the professional judge(s) to reach a verdict. An outvoted judge, professional or lay, has the right (but not the duty) to mark his/her *votum separatum*. However, the dissenting judge must give the justification of his/her decision. When the *votum separatum* has been put forward by one of the lay judges, the presiding judge is obliged to include this differing opinion in the grounds for sentencing.

Furthermore, to avoid undue influence by professional judges, regulations prescribe a specific order of voting. In both regular and enlarged mixed juries, votes are first taken by lay judges beginning with the youngest one, then by the professional judges, beginning with the one with the shorter service. The presiding judge votes last.

Lay judges of each court have their own Board, chosen from and by their peers. The Board's function is to represent lay judges in relationships with the President of the Court or the court's administration and to monitor the quality of lay judges' performance.

Lay judges are dismissed before term's end if they have been deprived of their civil rights. They may be also removed by the local council which elected them in the following cases: (1) being convicted of a crime; (2) neglecting court duties; (3) inability to perform their duties; or (4) highly disrespectful behavior undermining the court authority. In addition, lay judges may resign from their service before term's end when they have important reasons.

Lay judges may participate in court deliberations for a period of time not longer than 12 days a year, unless the Court President decides the situation requires special measures.

STEREOTYPED PERCEPTION OF LAY JUDGES IN THE LEGAL MILIEU

Negative Stereotypes of Lay Judges

As the mixed jury is an encounter of representatives of two different social groups, the question of their mutual perception is an important social issue. Particularly striking is the negative stereotype of the lay judge found in the legal community, not only among professional judges but also among prosecutors, attorneys, and other professional representatives of the legal system. This stereotype refers to both the behavior and the motivation of lay judges.

The stereotypical beliefs regarding lay judge behavior is that they are undisciplined, have little interest in court cases, do not participate actively in trial proceedings, are over-influenced by emotions, and tend to be unjustifiably lenient in sentencing (Siemaszko, 1994; Zawadzki & Kubicki, 1970). The lay judges' role is perceived to be window-dressing with no practical application. Research (Zawadzki & Kubicki, 1970) shows that 46 percent of professional judges thought that the participation of the lay judges had no impact on professional judges' decisions.

The second element in the negative stereotype held by legal professionals refers to lay judges' motivation to perform their duties (Siemaszko, 1994). According to professional judges, lay judges are motivated by personal rather than public interest. Their willingness to serve is attributed to need to fill their free time (64.8 percent), opportunity to meet interesting people (38.9 percent), and willingness to take part in public life (45.7 percent). Lay judges are also perceived as frequently motivated by personal benefit, for example, the potential to form relationships that will be personally advantageous (10 percent), or additional income for retired and unemployed people (29.2 percent).[3] Few professional judges attribute lay judges' motivation to such laudable reasons as willingness to participate in the court as a representative of the community (8.3 percent) or pure interest in legal matters (13.3 percent).

Generally, professional judges are highly skeptical of the involvement of lay judges. Sixty-eight percent of interrogated judges claimed that lay judge participation should be reduced, while 17.7 percent of professional judges stated that the institution of the mixed jury should be abolished altogether (Siemaszko, 1994).

Research (Siemaszko, 1994) also reveals a discouraging trend: the younger the professional judges, the more negative stereotype of lay judges they tend to have. Furthermore, the young generation of professional judges is seldom inclined to cooperate with lay judges in the court. Given three options—to adjudicate in cooperation with a professional bench, with a mixed jury, or by themselves only—young judges least frequently choose cooperation with lay judges (Jankowski & Wołowicz, 1987).

It is noteworthy that the negative stereotype of lay judges is commonly found even among recent law graduates, who have not even had any direct professional experience with lay judges. So it seems that a negative cognitive scheme of lay judges is passed from generation to generation in the legal milieu rather than based on direct personal experience.

Language in the Stereotyping of Lay Judges

A crucial role in lay judge stereotyping is played by language. As Maass and Arcuri (1996) point out, language has at least four functions in the process of stereotyping social groups: (1) conveying stereotypes; (2) organizing cognition; (3) maintaining stereotypes; and (4) expressing stereotyped identity.

Social groups can use different categories in describing members of other groups. A given feature or behavior can be described in a neutral or a negative way. Consequently, perception of this feature or behavior will differ depending on whether the expression is neutral or negatively loaded. Negative labels can automatically prime negative associations, evaluations, and emotions toward the referent group, even among individuals who do not overtly accept the stereotype. The language one chooses to define the group influences the way in which the group is perceived (Devine, 1989).

When describing lay judges, professional judges often use very strong language, negatively loaded with ironic or even patronizing nuances (Goszczyński, 2003; Siemaszko, 1994; Zawadzki & Kubicki, 1970). Some striking examples of such emotionally loaded phrases, which function in the Polish legal milieu nearly as proverbial expressions, will be quoted.

Professional lawyers, while describing what they perceive as excessive leniency in lay judges, use the expression "lay judge philanthropy." Here, the neutral word "leniency" is replaced with a phrase that evokes an ironic, patronizing and consequently disrespectful attitude toward lay judges. Complaining about the recruitment of lay judges who might be substandard often draws the expression "the manhunt for lay judges," while the expression "hauling the lay judges towards the sentence" refers to the perceived need to assist lay judges toward a verdict. They call their lay colleagues "drowsing pensioners," to both criticize their perceived lack of activity and the considerable number of elderly and retired persons in the lay judge pool. Lay judges are sarcastically called "professional judges' loudspeakers" to suggest that lay judges slavishly follow the professional judges' opinion instead of thinking on their own. The boldest summation of this specific attitude toward the institution of the lay judge is found in commonly used descriptions of lay judges as the "Muppets," or "decorations of the court bench." The use of these expressions stresses the facade function of lay judges in the opinion of the professional legal milieu.

Verbal labels, such as these quoted above, automatically activate the information associated with the label in the minds of lawyers. Even one who might not agree with the content conveyed by these verbal labels could be automatically influenced by the negative feelings and convictions induced by the label itself. When the label is activated there are very few possibilities of conscious control over the process of associations that the labels evoke (Devine, 1989).

Stereotyped information together with the specific expressions is assimilated by young generations of lawyers. Young lawyers, upon observing the language and behavior of their elder and more experienced colleagues, imitate both their vocabulary and behavior in their own attitude toward lay judges. Verbal labels, such as "lay judge philanthropy" or "drowsing pensioners" constitute a simple reference point upon which the stereotype of lay judge develops. Compared to carefully observing the performance of lay judges individually and collectively, and thinking about them in a more differentiated way, it takes little cognitive energy to evaluate them (and consequently treat them) in the categorically prescribed way.

THE LACK OF A CLEAR-CUT ROLE OF LAY JUDGES

There are very concise legislative regulations that could serve as the normative basis for clearly defining the lay judge's role. Most legal regulations treat the lay judge in relation to the professional judge's role. Although all members of a mixed jury have the same tasks in the process of adjudication, they perform these tasks from different standpoints, representing either formal legal institutions or the social sense of justice. Differences between the two roles may be intuitively evident, but the differences do not have a clear formal distinction in the legal charge to the factions. In practice, both professional and lay judges have difficulties in articulating the role of the lay judge (Borucka-Arctowa, 1970; Siemaszko, 1994). Is the lay judge a monitor of the professional judge in the name of society? Is he/she an equal partner or merely a professional judge's assistant? Doubts also attend the level of legal knowledge expected of lay judges. Should they be educated in legal matters via special courses? Or should they be unburdened by a legal point of view?

The lack of well-defined regulations concerning the lay judge role produces uncertainty and disorientation among lay judges as well as among professional judges. Individuals whose role is improperly formulated and who are members of a group with inferior status are prone to comply with the prestigious group's stereotyped expectations, even if they are negative (Jussim, 1986). Professional lawyers are a group of a high social status, hence their stereotyped opinions about lay judges are adopted by lay judges themselves.

Leniency is one of the most striking elements of lay judge stereotype in the legal milieu. As many as 80.6 percent of professional judges believe that lay judges are rather lenient or too lenient in sentencing. Also, 90 percent of prosecutors perceive that lay judges soften the verdict. This outlook is shared by 73.8 percent of advocates (Borucka-Arctowa, 1970). This stereotype, created by the professionals, may be treated by lay judges as a clue, which helps them to define their role in court as being a softening influence on the verdict, as findings proved (Borucka-Arctowa, 1970). This can be illustrated with the example of the statement of one of the interrogated lay judges: "A lay judge is lenient because he thinks that he ought to be lenient."

The stereotypes borrowed from the superior group are in the course of time internalized and eventually can become self-fulfilling prophecies (Jussim & Fleming, 1996), especially when they are sustained by the behavior of the dominant group. It is possible that professionals (especially prosecutors and judges), guided by this stereotype, are prone to more severe sentences to counterbalance the expected leniency of lay judges. Such severe sentences may then spur lay judges to soften them, which paradoxically gives credence to the stereotype and becomes part of the norm for lay judges through this vicious cycle.

MIXED JURY DECISIONS

Different Sentencing Strategies in a Mixed Jury

Mixed juries, by definition, reflect a clash of two different attitudes to justice: professional and social. Professional attitudes are based on specific education, thorough knowledge of legal regulations, and extensive legal experience. Social attitudes are based on commonsense and on values broadly accepted in society. Professional judges represent the official legal system, while lay judges represent the views and values actually prevailing in their groups. This inherent division takes for granted the existence of two different standpoints in an adjudicating team.

Research analyzing professional and lay judges' verdicts in both mock cases and real court records reveals the difference in sentencing strategies adopted by the members of the two groups (Turska, 1970). Professional judges focus on the offense itself more than on the perpetrator, which reflects the conviction that fair sentencing should incorporate the principle of equality before the law. Consequently, professional judges tend to give average penalties, with fewer variations, penalizing according to the crime, and not the defendant. Professional judges in their sentencing characteristically follow the principle of general prevention to protect society against further crime.

Lay judges, on the other hand, focus more on the offender, and take into account extenuating circumstances such as the offender's motivation, family situation and general life situation. Lay judges also center on the consequences of the sentence for the offender's relatives. Lay judges' dominating penal strategy is rehabilitation, that is, the corrective effect of punishment for the offender. What is more, contrary to the average penalty given by professional judges, lay judges' sentences tend to vary from lenient, when they positively evaluate the defendant's personality, to severe in such cases as brawls, assaults, and thefts of private property.

Therefore it can be inferred that both professional and lay judges take into consideration advantages to society in shaping sentences, but on a different social scale. Lay judges are apt to take into account interests of local groups encountered during the trial (e.g., defendants, victims, relatives), whereas professional judges are mindful of the interest of society as a whole.

The Problem of Understanding "the Other" Standpoint

Although sentencing strategies of lay and professional judges diverge, the mixed jury is obliged to reach a collaborative verdict. Ideally, both the principle of collective decision-making and the principle of citizen participation guarantee a fair verdict based on confrontation and coordination of lay and professional opinions. At its best, the mixed jury permits application of various points of view and eliminates the more one-sided view, which might occur in strictly professional benches. To reach an integrated decision from diverse views demands that members understand the reasoning of their partners.

As findings indicate, there are mutual suspicions in the mixed jury concerning the sentencing strategy of the other faction (Turska, 1970; Siemaszko, 1994). Professional judges allege that lay judges do not understand legal principles but are guided by emotion instead of rationality, and thus they are often social advocates for the defendant rather than being judges. In turn, lay judges accuse professional judges of adhering too strictly to the "letter of the law" without taking into account the defendant's present and future life context.

By criticizing rather than understanding and accepting the values of the other faction, both groups implicitly treat their own norms and strategies as valid and prescriptive. This process of nonacceptance of an alternative viewpoint can be considered in terms of sociocentric thought in the sense of Piagetian notions of ego centration and decentration (Flavell, 1963; Piaget & Inhelder, 1993). In the process of centration, a person focuses on a given aspect of a problem or on one point of view, usually one's own. In contrast, decentration is the ability to shift attention from one standpoint to another and consider all important aspects of a problem. Sociocentrism as a form of centration is defined as "a social actor subject's tendency to favor his own point of view with his own way of knowing. A sociocentric subject will tend to attribute his [sic] own categories of knowledge to other subjects' interpretation of social (and cognitive) practices" (Windisch, 1990, p. 34).

Applying this phenomenon to the mixed jury, we note some manifestations of sociocentric thinking (Parlak, 2004). Both professional and lay judges stick to their points of view, at the same time expecting the other side to fulfil the same functions as they do. Professional judges assume that lay judges will be governed by the same codified norms and values found in the legal regulations to which they adhere. Lay judges expect professional judges to be guided by social values and common sense interpretation of the law. Though aware that the other faction has different values and, consequently, sentencing strategies, both groups do not accept the values that drive their cojurists to a different idea of fairness, taking for granted that only their own values and norms are valid. Sociocentric persons, who treat their outlooks on fairness as indisputable, become prisoners to their perspective (Falk & Johnson, 1977; Flavell, 1968), thereby limiting their openness to others' idea of justice.

The Decision of the Mixed Jury

The ideal model of the mixed jury decision-making process assumes that different points of views (lay and professional) will be presented as equally valid, confronted and then coordinated from a wider perspective to reach a joint verdict. To satisfy this model, lay and professional judges should be ready to go beyond their viewpoints and enter deliberation with willingness to take into account their colleagues' standpoint rather than competitively enforce their own.

However, the reality is different. Research based on observation of the real court deliberation[4] reveals that the apparently common decision of the mixed jury often turns out to be one-sided. The research included 257 criminal cases adjudicated by the regular mixed jury bench (professional judge as a presiding judge and two lay judges) in the district court (Kubicki, 1970).

In 59.7 percent of deliberations, the presiding judge dominated the process of the decision-making, and thus the outcome. Domination, or one-sidedness of the deliberative process, was evidenced in three ways:

(1) Open domination of the presiding judge (20.6 percent). During the deliberation of this type, lay judges have no chance to present or discuss their points of view because the professional judge authoritatively makes the decision and merely announces it to the lay judges, expecting only their acceptance of the verdict.
(2) Allowance of pro forma lay judge participation but with the domination of the presiding judge (31.1 percent). This is a deliberation in which only formal appearance of lay judge equality is present. Although lay judges attempt to express their views, the presiding judge ignores or openly criticizes their arguments and enforces his/her own opinion from the beginning of the deliberation.
(3) Domination of presiding judge by means of passivity of lay judges (eight percent). Although the presiding judge inquires about the views of lay judges, they do not present their standpoints, either due to their lack of experience in court proceedings or the absence of views on the case. The professional judge then takes the initiative and makes the decision himself.

The remaining 40.3 percent of deliberations contained active participation from both lay and professional judges. However, it should be mentioned that, as findings prove, active participation in the deliberation process does not automatically guarantee that the decision really reflects the standpoints of all the disputants.

A truly common decision is reached by the mixed jury when the lay judges' and the professional judge's viewpoints on an adjudicated case overlap to a considerable extent. The lack of opposition makes the process of making common decision run smoothly.

The situation changes when factions diverge in their opinions. Analysis (Parlak, 2004) shows that during deliberation both professional and lay judges try to support their own position rather than taking into consideration the opposite perspective. Members of the mixed jury use different strategies to gain the greater influence over the final outcome:

(1) The power of persuasion. Lay and professional judges may attempt mutual persuasion. As they do not share the opposing viewpoint the acceptance of the decision is only formal, enforced by the stronger party. The greater power of persuasion of professional judges makes their point of view binding for all the members of the bench.
(2) The numerical majority. In other instances, lay and professional judges stand their ground so firmly that no party can be persuaded in the discussion. During the voting lay judges formally outvote the presiding judge. Here, the decision reflects the lay judges' perspective arising from their numerical majority.
(3) The compromise ("pure haggling"). In this lay and professional judges compromise by means of pure haggling, which means that each of the parties gives up on their conditions to some extent based on the principle "I will give in, if you give in." For example, lay judges accept a somewhat more severe sentence, while the presiding judge allows the sentence to be a bit more lenient than preferred. As there is no attempt at understanding the opponent's perspective on the adjudicated case, but mere yielding to the partner's conditions, one can hardly say that the verdict is a result of integration of lay and professional viewpoints.

To the general public, the verdict of a mixed jury is a common decision of professional lawyers and ordinary citizens unless the *votum separatum* is marked. In 257 of the observed cases of court deliberations, *votum separatum* was marked only four times, giving the initial appearance of integrated judgments. However, more extensive analysis, based on reports of observed deliberations, unveiled that the majority of the 253 apparently integrated decisions reflected only the professional or lay judge position. These two situations, domination of lay or professional standpoint, indicate two aspects of the same phenomenon: It is difficult for mixed jury members to decenter attention from their own to another viewpoint. Overly strong attachment to the norms and way of thinking valid in their own group does not allow members of the mixed jury to understand and legitimize the standpoint of the representatives of another social group. Such a sociocentric way of thinking hinders the process of reaching a truly common decision.

Domination by Professional Judges

It was found that professional judges were more influential in deciding verdicts. This power may arise from three sources: expert, legitimate, and normative power (Raven, 1993).

Expert power derives from perceived expertise and competence. This would be forthcoming from professional judges' expertise in legal matters, and their practical knowledge of the administration of justice. In the juries surveyed, lay judges frequently acknowledged the importance of judge experience in determining the verdict even when the lay judges initially preferred another verdict.

Legitimate power derives from the professional judge's formal role as presiding judge. By means of granting or withdrawing the right to speak, the professional judge can effectively limit the participation of lay judges and impose his/her own views, as often observed in deliberations with "single-handed" decisions.

Mock-jury research with mixed juries finds that professional judges wield social/normative influence by virtue of their social status (Kaplan & Martín, 1999). In the Polish sample of trials, it is not possible to separate the effects of expert, legitimate, and social bases of influence since differentiation requires either clear statements of influence during deliberation, or manipulation of case issues (as in Kaplan & Martín, 1999, see also the chapter by Kaplan, Martín & Hertel, in this volume) so that different cases will be responsive to different forms of influence.

However, in the Polish mixed jury there arises another important source of professional judges' domination—the negative stereotype of the lay judges prevalent in the legal milieu. Professional judges, guided by the image of lay judges as incompetent and ill-equipped, instantly turn down the lay judges' arguments, treating them as insignificant or downright erroneous. Consequently, instead of making an effort at understanding, they impose their own viewpoint as the only correct one.

CONCLUSIONS

There is incongruity between the mixed jury in principle and the Polish mixed jury in practice. In theory, equality of lay and professional judges is formal and legally guaranteed. They have equal rights in the adjudication process and equal status in the eyes of the law. In practice, professional judges exercise their superior status in dominance over both the process and outcome of decision-making. Domination may stem from their superiority in one or more bases of power: expertise, legitimacy, and social/normative status. Further weakening the role of lay judges are negative concepts of lay judges that are widespread in the legal milieu. In the absence of clear-cut descriptions of the lay judge's role, these stereotypes render them liable to their professional colleagues' influence. Instead of being the mutually decided, integrated decisions of professional judges and ordinary citizens, verdicts are often the result of domination of either the numerically superior or the more normatively powerful faction. In fact, lay and professional judges do not consider themselves as members of a mixed jury entity, but as representatives of two distinct, opposing groups, a view that facilitates sociocentric thinking.

In this context it is worth exploring how professional and lay judges perceive their joint responsibility for a verdict. Mindful of their power, and of stereotypes of lay judges, professional judges might adopt exclusive responsibility for decisions.

More generally, there is a need for future research to grasp the full impact of recent social and legal changes. First, new generations of professional judges have come to the bench. Next, Polish law reduced in 1997 the number of cases tried by mixed juries in favor of professional benches, which sends a negative message to the mixed jury institution. Might this serve to validate the negative stereotypes described here? Third, recent lay judge elections in 2003 considerably altered the structure of the lay judge pool (overrepresentation of the unemployed and poor interested in financial benefits rather than the public interest), which additionally undermined status of lay judges in the legal milieu and renewed the intense attack on the mixed jury institution. Finally, thought needs to be given to recategorization (Gaertner, Mann, Dovidio, Murrel, & Pomare, 1990) of the mixed jury in the minds of lay and professional judges. Cognitive representation of the mixed jury not as two separate factions (lay and professional judges) but as a superordinate group that has one common goal may encourage jury participants to cooperate rather than to compete. Consequently, they may be more willing to entertain the different point of view of cojurists as complementary to their own and equally important in achieving common decision. The effects of such modification of mixed jury representation on deliberation processes and outcomes need to be evaluated.

NOTES

1. Lay judges also sit in military courts, but taking into consideration the specific character of military court proceedings, this instance will not be included in this chapter, which is limited to lay judges in common courts. For considerations attending military courts in general, see Chapter (6) in this volume.
2. Military professionals can fulfill the lay judge's function in military courts, where there exists an additional requirement: The lay judge cannot be lower in military rank than the defendant.
3. The recent lay judge elections in 2003 created the specific situation that referred to this stereotype. After media widely announced that lay judges could expect to benefit financially from their service, there was great interest in the election among the unemployed, who wanted to serve as lay judges strictly for the compensation. Whether this validates a portion of professional judges' stereotypical beliefs, or is an instance of a self-fulfilling prophecy provoked by the media is arguable.
4. According to Polish law, deliberation is secret. However, the Minister of Justice, exclusively for scientific purposes, allowed the observation of the deliberation of real mixed juries.

REFERENCES

Artymiak, G. (1996). Udział czynnika społecznego w wymiarze sprawiedliwości w sprawach karnych i kolegialność orzekania—zasada czy wyjątek? [Social lay participation in administration of justice in criminal cases as well as collective adjudication—principle or exception?]. *Rzeszowskie Zeszyty Naukowe "Prawo-Ekonomia"*, *XIX*, 99–112.s

Borucka-Arctowa, M. (1970). Rola ławników w świetle poglądów samych ławników oraz przedstawicieliśrodowiska prawniczego. [The role played by the lay judges in the light of their opinions and in the light of opinions of the legal profession]. In S. Zawadzki & L. Kubicki (Eds.), *Udział ławników w postępowaniu karnym. Opinie a rzeczywistość* (pp. 29–67). Warszawa, Poland: Wydawnictwo Prawnicze.

Devine, P. (1989). Stereotypes and prejudice: Their automatic and controlled components. *Journal of Personality and Social Psychology*, *56*, 5–18.

Falk, D. R., & Johnson, D. W. (1977). The effects of perspective-taking and egocentrism on problem solving in heterogeneous and homogenous groups. *The Journal of Social Psychology*, *102*, 63–72.

Flavell, J. H. (1963). *The developmental psychology of Jean Piaget*. Princeton, NJ: D. Van Nostrand.

Flavell, J. H. (1968). *The development of role-taking and communication skills in the child*. New York: Wiley.

Gaertner, S. L., Mann, J., Dovidio, J. F., Murrel, A., & Pomare, M. (1990). How does cooperation reduce intergroup bias? *Journal of Personality and Social Psychology*, *59*, 692–704.

Goszczyński, A. (2003). Mapet sąd [The Muppets court]. *Polityka*, *38*, 3–11.

Jankowski, M., & Wołowicz, M. (1987). *Niezawisłość sędziowska w opinii samych sędziów* [Independence of the judiciary in the opinion of the judges]. Warszawa, Poland: Instytut Badania Prawa Sądowego.

Jussim, L. (1986). Self-fulfilling prophecies: A theoretical and integrative review. *Psychological Review*, *93*, 429–445.

Jussim, L., & Fleming, C. (1996). Self-fulfilling prophecies and the maintenance of social stereotypes: The role of dyadic interactions and social forces. In N. Macrae, M. Hewstone, & C. Stangor (Eds.), *The foundations of stereotypes and stereotyping* (pp. 161–192). New York: Guilford.

Kaplan, F. M., & Martín, A. (1999). Effects of differential status of group members on process and outcome of deliberation. *Group Processes & Intergroup Relations*, *2*, 347–364.

Kubicki, L. (1970). Udział ławników w orzekaniu [The part of lay judges in adjudicating]. In S. Zawadzki & L. Kubicki (Eds.), *Udział ławników w postępowaniu karnym. Opinie a rzeczywistość* (pp. 68–106). Warszawa, Poland: Wydawnictwo Prawnicze.

Maass, A., & Arcuri, L. (1996) Language and stereotyping. In C. N. Macrae, M. Hewstone, & C. Stangor (Eds.), *The foundations of stereotypes and stereotyping* (pp. 193–226). New York: Guilford.

Parlak, D. (2004). Cooperation or co-existence? A psychological analysis of Polish mixed jury decision-making. In A. Czerederecka, T. Jaśkiewicz-Obydzińska, R. Roesch, & J. Wójcikiewicz (Eds.), *Forensic psychology and law. Facing the challenges of a changing world* (pp. 276–286). Kraków, Poland: Institute of Forensic Research Publishers.

Piaget, J., & Inhelder, B. (1993). *Psychologia dziecka* [Child psychology]. Wrocław, Poland: Wydawnictwo Siedmioróg.

Raven, B. H. (1993). The bases of power: Origins and recent developments. *Journal of Social Issues*, *49*, 227–251.

Siemaszko, A. (Ed.). (1994). *Ławnicy. Rezultaty badań empirycznych* [The institution of lay judge. Results of empirical studies]. Warszawa, Poland: Oficyna Naukowa.

Turska, A. (1970). Analiza odrębności postaw ławnika i sędziego zawodowego w orzekaniu [The analysis of divergent attitudes of lay and professional judges on adjudicating]. In S. Zawadzki & L. Kubicki (Eds.), *Udział ławników w postópowaniu karnym. Opinie a rzeczywistość* (pp. 159–199). Warszawa, Poland: Wydawnictwo Prawnicze.

Waltoś, S. (2002). *Proces karny* [Penal proceedings]. Warszawa, Poland: Wydawnictwo Prawnicze Lexis Nexis.

Windisch, U. (1990). *Speech and reasoning in everyday life*. New York: Cambridge University Press.

Zawadzki, S., & Kubicki, L. (Ed.). (1970). *Udział ławników w postópowaniu karnym. Opinie a rzeczywistość* [The participation of lay judges in penal proceedings—opinions and real facts]. Warszawa, Poland: Wydawnictwo Prawnicze.

11

Lay Judges in the German Criminal Court: Social-Psychological Aspects of the German Criminal Justice System

THOMAS BLIESENER

INTRODUCTION

The German code of criminal procedure originally had two kinds of lay judges: those who compose the jury ("*Geschworene*"), and the honorary lay judges ("*Schöffen*"). With respect to the jury, whose procedures were similar to Anglo-American legal procedures for handling capital crimes, there was a division of responsibility between the jurors and the professional judges. The division was such that the 12-jury members made judgments solely about the question of guilt and the three professional judges about legal proceedings and sentencing. However, the lay judges had the same function and the same rights as professional judges in the ruling council (Roxin, 1979). In 1924, the German judiciary system changed form. This was initiated by the so-called Emminger reform. The jury courts were replaced by mixed courts although the old name "*Schwurgericht*" was retained.

In the court of original jurisdiction, the current German code of criminal procedure recognizes the involvement of lay judges in the "*Schöffengericht*" (two lay judges and a presiding professional judge), which is responsible for moderate offenses. They are also involved in the criminal division of a district court (two lay judges and three professional judges), which deals with serious and capital offenses (see Figure 11.1). According to statistical data on the justice system, nearly one-fourth of all criminal trials are finally dealt with by mixed tribunals. However, at least at the level of the county courts, lay participation is quite varied. Oswald and Langer (1989) analyzed the data of the 17 departments in a large city county court in the Central Federal Register. According to these data, 47–67 percent of the trials were concluded by penalty order without a main hearing. The rate of verdicts that were pronounced without lay participation ranged from 3 to 10 percent:

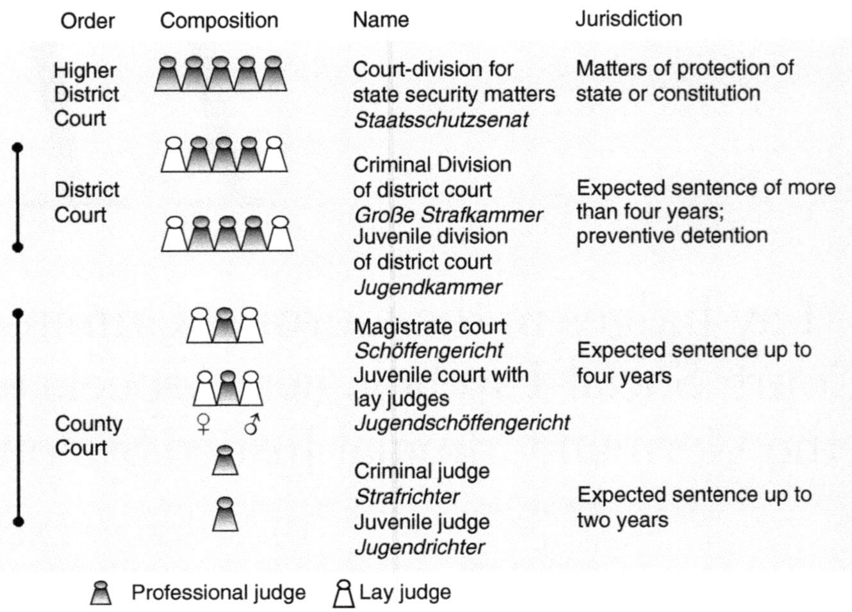

FIGURE 11.1 German criminal court system in the original jurisdiction.

61,000 lay judges are presently active, whereas the number of professional judges was 20,800 in 2000.

Lay judges are called upon to deal with and make decisions about legal disputes. They also carry out their judicial office in full and have the same right to vote on the question of guilt *and* sentencing as the professional judges. However, they are only able to make decisions together with professional judges (mixed tribunals). In contrast to professional judges, lay judges do not have access to the case file to prepare before and during the trial.[1]

According to relevant discussion (Kühne, 1985), lay judges have mainly three functions in the German criminal justice system. The involvement of the ordinary citizen in the judicial system should (1) promote the democratization of justice; (2) achieve an improvement in the quality of the administration of justice; and (3) mediate between the judicial system and the public in order to raise people's trust in the justice system, improve their knowledge of the justice system, and contribute to the internalization of criminal law standards (general prevention; see Brusten & Westmeier, 1992; Kühne, 1989; Villmow, ter Veen, Walkowiak, & Gerken, 1986).

However, the system of lay participation has been criticized. The majority of the 124 professional judges in various district courts who were surveyed by Klausa (1972) voiced more disadvantages than benefits in the participation of lay judges. The following points were mentioned: (1) lack of legal knowledge; (2) loss of time; (3) less contribution; (4) lack of emotional objectivity; (5) high expenses; and (6) inappropriate selection of lay judges (see similar complaints lodged by Polish judges against lay judges in Chapter 10). More than 60 percent of the professional judges and prosecutors who were questioned by Rennig (1993) also complained that lay judges do not contribute their extra-legal expertise. Not surprisingly, 40 percent of the professional judges surveyed by Klausa (1972) voted in favor of eliminating the participation of lay judges. However, there are also some positive aspects. These include (1) beneficial effects in determining penalty; (2) public education and improving people's trust in jurisdiction (Klausa, 1972); as well as (3) better ability to understand main hearings and to prevent professional judges from getting into a rut (Rennig, 1993).

However, the criticisms were mainly based on the individual experience of single persons and possibly affected by stereotypical thinking (see Chapter 10 for detailed discussion of professional judges' stereotypes). Therefore, it is necessary to analyze present data on lay participation in decisions, as well as general models of social psychology and psychology and law, in order to examine whether the goals of the lay participation, intended by the legislature, are achieved. In doing so, it must be taken into account that the structure of mixed juries in German procedural law and its integration into a more inquisitorial procedural system (McEwan, 1995) make it problematic to compare it with the American jury system or magistrates in the English legal system. It is not possible to relate the extensive research and analyses on juries (e.g., Hastie, Penrod, & Pennington, 1983; Kerr & Bray, 1982; for a review see Nietzel, McCarthy, & Kern, 1999) to the German jury system, not only because of the latter's mixed tribunals but also because of procedural differences in determining guilt and punishment.[2]

Therefore, this chapter presents a review of some of the theoretical and empirical work concerning lay judges in Germany pertaining to (1) the recruiting process; (2) the motivation to become a lay judge; (3) the relationship between lay and professional judges; (4) the lay judges' sense of right and wrong; as well as (5) their attitude to offenders, crime, and the justice system. Finally, evidence of whether the legislative goals for appointing lay judges in German criminal proceedings have been achieved will be discussed.

RECRUITMENT OF LAY JUDGES

According to the law regarding the constitution of the courts, the post of a lay judge is an honorary position. All citizens, with few exceptions, are obliged to act as a lay judge. Every German citizen[3] who has been living in a community for more than 1 year and who has not been sentenced to more than 6 months' imprisonment, can act as a lay judge. In the election term 1997–2000, 60,947 lay judges were active in Germany, 19,169 of whom functioned as lay judges in juvenile courts (*Jugendschöffen*; Lieber, 1999). Every 4 years, a municipality committee draws up a list of candidates to recruit lay judges. In accordance with legal requirements, this list should consider all groups of the population according to gender, age, profession, and social status appropriately.[4] With respect to age, legal restrictions stipulate that candidates should be at least 25, but not older than 70, at the beginning of a term. In the case of lay judges in the juvenile court, the law requires also that candidates have qualifications in education and have some experience in juvenile education. Therefore, the applicants are proposed by the youth welfare committee of the youth office.[5] No other qualifications are mentioned in the legal guidelines (see Gerken, 1988). The subsequent selection process is largely regulated by the code on criminal procedures. According to this law, the list should have at least twice as many persons as are needed for selection. The list is to be publicly displayed for 1 week; objections to any nomination can be raised within a second week. Afterwards, the chair sends the list to a judge at county court. A special committee chaired by the judge elects lay judges and alternates for a 4-year term. The number of lay judges is such that every lay judge will probably be called for a maximum of 12 hearings. Because a session may sometimes be extended and the board has to consist of the same individuals from the beginning to the end of a trial, participation over a period of some months may be necessary in extreme cases. With the exception of some professions (e.g., physicians, priests, and midwives), there is generally no reason to refuse to serve as a lay judge. The term of office is 4 years; subsequent reelection is possible but can be refused. Further reelection is possible after an interval of 8 years.

Every year, lay judges are allocated to the individual boards by drawing lots in advance. Matters of the case are not relevant for the allocation to the boards. Only the two lay judges in the juvenile court have to be of different genders.

There have been some studies on the procedure of recruiting lay judges (see Machura, 2001). Brusten and Westmeier (1992), for example, analyzed how communities in a particular district proceed to draw up a list of candidates. Mainly, political parties, welfare institutions, sports clubs, financial and health insurance institutions, trade unions, public authorities, and industrial companies are called to nominate candidates. According to their survey data, only half of the institutions directly approached specific members or employees. In most cases, the letter from the municipality was assigned to another person or simply ignored. The motivations of the institutions to nominate persons are very different. Social responsibility, cultivation of one's image, advertising, participation in the decision on allocating fines, and further education are mentioned in the survey by Brusten and Westmeier (1992). However, a closer look at the criteria used to nominate persons is not possible within these studies. Apart from nominations by institutions, interested citizens can apply to be a lay judge when it is publicly advertised. However, pure volunteers in a sufficient number are rarely found in most communities.

Because the post of a lay judge can be refused for few reasons (e.g., in the case of medical professions or when direct care for a family member is necessary), lay judges who were nominated cannot be considered volunteers. The motives typically associated with volunteerism (Snyder & Omoto, 2001; Snyder, Clary, & Stukas, in press) can rarely be found in lay judges.

WHO GETS TO BE A LAY JUDGE?

One question is: how are the different groups in the population represented by the selection process portrayed above, according to gender, age, profession, and social status? Kronenberger (1989) analyzed the data of 114 lay judges in the

Saarland. In his sample, 61 percent of the lay judges had a moderate or high level of education; 75 percent were employees or officials, half of them worked in public services; only 8 percent were blue-collar workers and 4 percent were classified as self-employed. In comparison to data on the general population, persons with high levels of education, employees, and officials are clearly over represented. As shown in Table 11.1, nearly the same can be seen in data from the federal ministry of justice (Bundesministerium der Justiz, 1997), regarding the professional classification of lay judges.[6]

Again we find a higher number of employees in public services. This composition of lay judges is problematic because it contradicts the intention to select lay judges who do not represent authorities or owe special loyalty to the state (Kühne, 1989). In contrast, the weak representation of pensioners is due to the age restriction in the law regarding the constitution of courts (see also Table 11.2).[7] Greater participation by teachers, social workers, and nursery-school teachers is in accordance with the criteria of educational competence and experience for lay judges in juvenile courts. Another positive development is that the ratio of both genders has been brought into line (Lieber, 2002).

The age distribution of the lay judges in the period 1997–2000 shows a slight increase in the middle age groups at the expense of the younger and older groups (see also Lieber, 2002 for the period 2001–2004 in three selected federal states). Considerable differences in the distribution of certain variables among lay judges and the population were also found in a study by Kronenberger (1989): 92 percent were married and 89 percent had children; 85 percent were members of a

TABLE 11.1 Professional Classification of Lay Judges (Bundesministerium der Justiz, 1997; Completed by Data of Federal Bureau of Statistics)

Professional group	Lay judges (%)	Population (%)
Self-employed	6.1	6.0
Employee	52.7	54.1
In public service	26.7	8.0
In the private sector	26.0	46.0
Housewives	10.0	3.1
Pensioner	7.3	19.5
Others	23.9	17.3

TABLE 11.2 Age of Lay Judges (Bundesministerium der Justiz, 1997)

Age group (years)	Lay judges (%)	Population (%)
25–40	26.1	40.3
40–50	30.9	20.6
50–60	30.3	22.6
60–70	12.7	16.5

political party; and 94 percent were active members of a club or association (sports clubs, welfare institutions, trade unions, etc.) or were holding an office.

Thus, there are some differences between the intended and the actual characteristics of lay judges: the questions that arise are whether these differences influence behavior during trial and deliberation; and whether they affect lay judge information processing, decision-making, and judgment.

LAY STATUS AND EXAMINING THE FILES

Because people with a legal education or some experience in the administration of justice are explicitly excluded, lay judges are not lawyers (Wassermann, 1999). To educate them, a four-page brochure is provided (see Gerstein, 1999; Sens, 1999). In some federal states, there is some additional and more detailed material for new lay judges. Before the main hearing begins, the professional judge, or the rapporteur, gives a short introduction to the case. However, the introduction is often omitted, or if given, is seen as inadequate in some cases. In a survey of lay judges in Brandenburg, more than half of them stated that they had not been introduced to the case at all (Lieber, 1994). Trying to remediate this situation, the Federal Association of Honorary Judges was established in 1993, to compile special information and to organize workshops to support and prepare lay judges.

Permission to examine the case files by the lay judges is not unequivocally addressed by law (Pfeiffer, 2002). Up to now, the jurisdiction has only dealt with the written report of the prosecutor. This practice was declared to be inadmissible. According to the traditional interpretation of law, giving the case files to the lay judges jeopardizes the principle of direct contact and immediacy because the lay judges could confuse impressions from the case file with the hearing. In contrast, it is assumed that professional judges are able to separate these sources of information, owing to their education and professional experience.

Since there is no specific regulation denying lay judges access to the documents, proponents assert a right to examine files under the principle of professional and lay judge equality. Examination is considered particularly essential in certain cases. For example, it is required that the lay judges rely on written documents in cases involving multiple defendants, different offenses, and different participations in the offenses. Therefore, the current predominant opinion is to allow lay judges to examine files, and in certain cases to require such references (Kissel, 2001).

There is no evidence that allowing lay judges to examine files affects their behavior. Haisch (1977, 1979) carried out experiments with lawyers and laymen in simulated juries with and without providing documents for handling criminal information. Results revealed that incriminating information was given greater importance than exculpatory information without access to files. This effect decreased, however, if documents were made available to lawyer mock jurors, but not laypersons. In a field study, Weißmann (1982) interviewed professional judges who were observers but not participants in trials, and who did not have access to documents. In 26.9 percent of the cases, observer and participating judges disagreed in their verdicts. Observers were more influenced by contradictions between defense testimony and other evidence.

In simulation experiments by Schünemann and Bandilla (1989), four groups of professional judges were given access (or not) to documents, with or without actively chairing the trial hearing. Access to the documents affected verdicts only for judges actively chairing hearings. While all active judges with knowledge of the documents voted guilty, the rate of conviction dropped to 27 percent in the group with no access to the documents. Thus, contrary to conventional wisdom, there is strong evidence that professional judges are affected by access to documents (in a pro-prosecution direction), whereas access does not affect (nor confuse) lay judges.

THE PARTICIPATION OF LAY JUDGES IN MAIN HEARINGS AND DELIBERATIONS

In the German criminal justice system, as in most other Western European countries, such as France, Italy, Portugal (see Martín, Kaplan, & Álamo, 2003), lay judges and professional judges have equal rights—with a few exceptions (see also Chapter 10). The German lay judges have the right to question the accused, witnesses, and experts (excluding the questioning of witnesses under 16). They are also, in principle, equally involved in deliberations and decisions in all forms and stages of hearings, e.g., the decision to request evidence or to exclude the public.

While the behavior of judges during main hearings is generally accessible to public scientific study, systematic data on the participation of lay judges are not yet available. According to posttrial surveys of participants, lay judges behave rather passively during main hearings. Despite the fact that most lay judges are aware they have the opportunity to pose questions during trial (Machura, 2001), professional judges chair the hearing (Benz, 1982; Rennig & Machura, 1999). When lay judges ask questions, professional judges consider the questions as rather unimportant or redundant (see Casper & Zeisel, 1979, see also Chapter 10 in this volume).

The fear that some professional judges have of untrained lay judges occasionally leads to attempts to minimize the participation of lay judges by tight scheduling and stressing shortage of time. In addition, their experience in argumentation, and their specific knowledge of the law are used during deliberations in order to minimize the participation and impact of lay judges (Rennig, 1993). However, this trend could be reduced by instructing and permitting lay judges to examine files. In this sense, a Hungarian study shows that, contrary to these fears, the 33 percent of informed lay judges, i.e., those with prior access to files, pose significant questions during the hearings, compared to 12 percent of uninformed lay judges. There were also similar differences in exercising the right to pose questions in the deliberation stage (48 vs. 18 percent; Kulcsár, 1972).[8] So, although access to files has no serious effect on the decisions of lay judges (as is sometimes feared), it does increase their participation, and thus equality, during trial and deliberation.

Unlike main hearings, deliberation is secret. Lay and professional judges may comment on hearings in general terms, but not disclose specifics of the decision process (Rennig, 1991). This makes access for scientific purposes almost impossible, save for subsequent interviews. However, mock juries deliberating fictional cases can be accessed (Brandstätter, Bleckwenn, & Kette, 1984).

The deliberation usually begins with the professional judge summarizing the main hearing from his viewpoint and outlining possible decisions (Casper & Zeisel, 1979; Rennig & Machura, 1999). As Rennig (1993) was able to show in a survey, this practice is expected and welcomed by most lay judges. But Vultejus (1999) also sees a benefit here for the professional judges, since the presence of the lay judges compels them to express their considerations in an orderly way and by so doing, to reconsider matters again. Moreover, if professional judges want lay judges to have real input, they often feel compelled to describe special and legal questions beforehand.

Some available simulation studies also widely confirm the dominant influence of experts in mixed tribunals. Kaplan and Martín (1999) compared mock juries composed of trained and laypersons deciding on guilt and punishment for cases of university code violations. Trained jurors had more impact on consensus verdicts and confidence than laypersons only when the issue was judgmental, and when having to include values in justification. Martín et al. (2003) analyzed pre- and postdiscussion verdict, confidence, discussion content, and subjective reactions to the discussion and outcome of lay and mixed juries in a very similar scenario comparing lay juries (seven undergraduate students) to mixed juries (five undergraduate and two fifth-year law students). Although the two jury types did not differ in their outcomes, within the mixed juries trained jurors influenced outcomes more than did lay jurors when the case involved value-laden issues. In sum, the results led Martín et al. to conclude that lay and mixed juries do not differ in their dynamics, outcomes, and reactions. However, compared to real mixed juries in criminal courts, differences in the degree of experience, status, and expertise in this simulated student judicial system must be quite small. Arce, Fariña, Vila, and Real (1999) studied mixed juries (one professional judge and five laypersons) when making a decision about real trials previously videotaped. By manipulating the judge's predeliberation opinion, they could show that the postdeliberation verdict of the mixed jury tends to follow the judge's opinion. However, questions on generalizability arise as well because the same professional judge was employed in all the mixed juries of this study.

JUDGMENT COMPETENCE

Doubts about the competence of lay judges have been expressed in the literature (see Benz, 1982, for a summary). Lay judges are considered as more error-prone in judging questions of fact, in that they are thought to more easily believe lies, to evaluate expert testimony uncritically, and to insufficiently attend to relevant information (for a litany of complaints about lay juror competence in Poland, see Chapter 10). Furthermore, cognitive capacities of lay judges may be overloaded owing to unfamiliarity with the courtroom situation and trial procedures. With respect to the question of punishment, lay judges are thought to base decisions on irrelevant, purely personal concepts of punishment, being unable to understand the prescribed purposes of punishment: retaliation, deterrence, education, and atonement. Laypersons are not acquainted with the complicated guidelines for determining sentences and the ranges of sentences stipulated in criminal law (Benz, 1982). At the same time, the particular complexity of the information, which is to be handled in the hearings, is frequently emphasized (Heuer & Penrod, 1995).

Survey findings in Germany with respect to the perceived competence of lay judges are inconsistent. Kronenberger (1989) surveyed citizens in the Saarland. The citizens sampled had considerably less confidence in the competence of lay judges to make fair judgments compared to professional judges. At the same time, the sentencing practices of mixed courts were evaluated as predominantly too mild. In a survey of 1100 adults by Kaupen and Rasehorn (1972) only 45 percent preferred the participation of lay judges compared to the jurisdiction of fully trained lawyers. On the other hand, two thirds of those surveyed by Smaus (1985) believed that mixed courts made better judgments. A US study by Shuman and Champagne (1997) was also positive about participation and competence of laypersons. Laypersons who had been jurors gave quite rationally justified criteria concerning the evaluation of expert statements and did not rely on subjective impressions. From the viewpoint of the surveyed experts, laypersons were ranked only slightly less capable than professional judges in understanding expert testimony in the court.

ATTITUDES TO PUNISHMENT AND JUDGMENT PREFERENCES

As mentioned above, according to public opinion, the punishing practice of mixed courts is too mild (Kaupen & Rasehorn, 1972). It is not clear, though, whether the public's preference for stronger punishments is grounded in its general attitude to punishment or in the possibility that the public, basing knowledge on media accounts and not participation in the trial hearing, may be aware of more incriminating than exculpatory evidence (e.g., Zamble & Kalm, 1990). Media representations of criminal offenses focus on the victim, the crime, and the consequences of the crime rather than on the perpetrator and his/her defense (see Oswald, Orth, & Hupfeld, 2003). In Germany, there are presently very few studies on attitudes toward punishment and its aims, and their connection to socio-demographic characteristics.[9] In a survey of over 4300 randomly selected young people and adults, Kury and Ferdinand (1999) found greater punitiveness in male respondents, but no effect for age. In contrast, in a survey of over 15,000 persons over the age of 16, Gabriel and Greve (1996) found a clear age trend in the severity of punishment, and generally higher punitiveness in men than in women. This finding of a gender difference in punitiveness is reflected in international surveys as well (Applegate, Cullen, & Fisher, 2002).

Preferences regarding the aims of punishment are dependent on education. According to Karstedt-Henke (1985), belief systems about the effectiveness of punishment and offender treatment are related to level of education, which in turn moderate attitude to severity of punishment (see Endres & Hommers, 1992; Herbst, Malow, Pfuhlmann, Pfuhlmann, & Pook, 1975; Hough, Lewis, & Walker, 1988).

However, unlike differences owing to gender and education, and despite opinions by professional judges and citizenry, only small differences in severity of punishment can be found between lay and professional judges. Rennig (1991) surveyed 31 boards in Hessian courts and found that lay and professional judges differed neither in their preferred punishment nor in the judged gravity of the crime. However, differences were revealed in the intended aims of punishment: lay judges assigned greater importance to the safety of the general public, whereas professional judges cited the public sense of justice. But lay judges did not form more extreme judgments (i.e., by voting more leniently than the defense counsel or more stringently than the public prosecutor). A recent study by Machura (2001) revealed, surprisingly, preferences for more severe punishment among lay judges compared to lawyers. The great majority of lay judges evaluated the legal standards for punishment as very or quite fair. When lay judges disagreed with standards, they tended to evaluate punishments as too mild. Similarly, almost half of the surveyed lay judges regarded the judgments of the courts as neither too harsh, nor too mild. Of the remainder, about 40 percent evaluated the judgments as too mild, while only about 5 percent considered the punishment as having been too severe.[10] Thus, lay judges believe neither the standards nor the sentences to be too severe, contrary to perceptions of them as being biased toward leniency.

Streng (1979) examined the attitudes of lawyers to criminality and punishment. As in similar surveys of nonlawyers, severity of recommended punishment was primarily determined by perceived threats of criminality and one's own fear of victimization. However, the fear of victimization correlated less with the severity of punishment among experienced lawyers compared with those new to the profession.

Summarizing the available literature on attitudes to punishment and judgment preferences, relatively consistent connections between punitiveness and age or level of education can be found within the population. In contrast, neither are there indications of differences between lay and professional judges, nor is there evidence that lay judges are characteristically lenient, though they do differ from professional judges in their theory about the aim of punishment.

JUDGMENT AND DECISION BEHAVIOR

The law regarding the voting procedure specifies that first the two lay judges vote (the more junior first), and then the judges (in order of length of service). If a judge is designated as a rapporteur, he/she begins, followed by the lay judges and then the remaining judge(s). On matters of procedure, the board decides with a simple majority rule. In decisions on the question of guilt and the legal treatment of the offender (e.g., the imposition of conditions), that is, decisions that are potentially unfavorable for the accused, a two-thirds majority is needed for any one of the several alternative outcomes. In practice, a formal vote is rarely taken following the discussion. Frequently, an agreement is already reached in the course of discussion (Benz, 1982; Lieber & Sens, 2001). Outvoting of the professional judge by lay judges is rare (Klausa, 1972). Casper and Zeisel (1979), examining decision processes, found that half of the professional judges who had a different initial opinion than both lay judges, succeeded in changing the minds of one or both lay judges. Individual lay judges with different opinions, on the other hand, were all convinced or outvoted by the majority. Lay judges succeeded in winning a judgment that was different from that of the professional judges in only 6.2 percent of the observed trials. The resulting judgment was more lenient in 4.8 percent, and more severe in only 1.4 percent of the cases than the initial proposal of the professional judge. However, in 12 percent of the cases, a compromise was reached during discussion. Arce et al. (1996) found similar results in a simulation study with 10 mixed juries consisting of four laypersons and one professional judge. Although the professional judges were always in the minority regarding verdict before deliberation, they succeeded in gaining further support for their position in each case.

Lay judge socialization increases the tendency to vote with professional judges. Machura (2001) found that the tendency to disagree with professional judges decreases with the duration of the lay judge's service.

In the juvenile court, professional judges also hold a dominant position during deliberation. Although lay judges serving in this court have special knowledge and expertise, voting and decision-making processes function similarly to those of other tribunals. The unique contributions of lay judges of the juvenile court are limited to the vote on sanction (Gerken, 1988). The educational qualifications of lay judges are often not known or ignored by both lay and professional judges. Instead, professional judges dominate the deliberation process by purposefully bringing in, or suppressing, additional information, speaking more, and presenting more of their own arguments (Cruz, Henningsen, & Smith, 1999).

Summarizing the literature, it can be stated that lay judges have some influence; however, it rarely results in outvoting professional judges. More frequently, it is expressed in compromises during judgment formation, particularly with respect to punishment (Klausa, 1972).

LAY JUDGES AS SOCIAL MEDIATORS

One desirable function of lay judges is to mediate between the juridical system and the society they represent. This role has not been successfully fulfilled. In a public survey, Villmow et al. (1986) found that scarcely half of those questioned knew someone who had been active as a lay judge in a criminal case. 70 percent of these had been personally informed by someone who had served as a judge. When former judges discussed their experiences with others, they shared their general experiences and problems, information about interesting processes and criminal cases, and the pressure that arises from the role of being a lay judge.

Discussions about particular offenders and sanctions were rare. About 20 percent of lay judges regularly told their family about their lay judge activities, 70 percent often or sometimes, and 10 percent never (Machura, 2001). On the other hand, 9 of 10 lay judges did not report or only sometimes talked to acquaintances and colleagues about their activities, and only a very small number (3 percent) did this regularly. Rennig (1993) obtained similar data in his study. The reticence of lay judges to share their experiences with the public outside of their families may be due, in part, to the requirement of confidentiality with respect to deliberation and voting, even after completing their term in office. However, an investigation in Hungary shows that, even when disclosure is not proscribed, the readiness to divulge information is low. According to Kulcsár (1972), the assessors in Hungary are obliged to report their judicial activity at home and work. However, 40 percent of the assessors questioned had never given a report, and just under a third had done this on two occasions. In view of the often obvious lack of knowledge and the frequently wrong impressions about trials, it is important to know whether the mediator role of lay judges can be used more effectively to provide citizenry with an understanding of the procedures and roles of participants in trials (Köhnken & Dannenberg, 1997).

OPEN QUESTIONS

Both theoretical views and empirical studies on the lay judge system in Germany were presented in this chapter. However, substantial deficits in research on some questions remain. These open research questions refer primarily to the extent the lay judge system can fulfill the intended functions of (1) democratization of the law; (2) increasing the quality of justice; and (3) general prevention.

1. *Democratization of the administration of justice by the participation of the population.* Equal participation in trials (both main hearings and deliberations) is derived from the principle of equality of lay and professional judges. Currently, the type and frequency of lay judge contributions to main hearings and deliberations can only be gathered from a few empirical studies and more or less anecdotal reports, and so the participation and influence of lay judges remains unclear. Existing data tentatively suggest that lay judges do not participate as actively or as effectively as professional judges in either hearings or deliberations. The ability of lay judges to resist the influence of professional judges is questioned, and moreover, the tendency for a lay judge to hold different positions than those of professional judges decreases with the length of the lay judge's service. However, without controlled and systematic research, it is unclear whether factors aside from lay status (e.g., age, gender, level of education, social distance from the judge, and forensic experience) determine these inequalities (Baldwin & McConville, 1979; Casper & Zeisel, 1979). Recognition of the need for information for selecting lay judges is not new (Jescheck, 1977), but only rudimentary

data are currently available. It is particularly unfortunate that no national data on age, occupation, and social standing of lay judges have been compiled since 2000 (Lieber, 2002). This similarly applies to the expenditure of time and the duration of service as a lay judge.

2. *Increasing the quality of justice*. The presence of community representatives on jury panels is intended to improve the administration of justice. There are perceptions, however, that lay judges impede the justice process owing to a variety of alleged shortcomings. The few available empirical studies, however, provide no support for the pessimistic view of lay judge performance. Lay judges, for example, do not confound different sources of information any more than professional judges. Indeed, in the rare instances where lay judges exercise their right to examine case files, and thus become better informed about the case, their performance improves. In the sense of quality management, one must ask (1) whether lay judges possess the necessary competence and qualifications for their judicial activities; (2) whether their judgment processes have sufficient rational criteria; and (3) to what extent lay judges show punitive attitudes and/or tendencies to "short trials." In particular, it is not clear whether the specific qualifications of lay judges in the juvenile court provide an effective contribution to the quality of administration of justice. Furthermore, it is still unknown whether better training and instruction of lay judges can contribute to greater and more effective participation in main hearings and deliberations and in particular which measures are successful in this respect.
3. *General prevention*. Lay judges do not report their activities in the general public to any significant degree. This may be due to the obligation of secrecy. If lay judges do not share with citizenry the legal norms, values, or ideas about crime that emerge during hearings and deliberations, the educational and preventive mission of their service is not fulfilled. How to encourage lay jurors to discuss their experience with fellow citizens without violating the privacy of deliberation and voting needs to be addressed. More broadly, steps need to be taken to raise the status of lay jurors in public consciousness so that they are encouraged to report their experiences to the general population.

PROSPECTS

Empirical data on lay participation in Germany is meager. While Nietzel et al. (1999) could identify more than 250 studies on juries in the USA between 1977 and 1994, there are few systematic studies in Germany (e.g. Crott & Werner, 1994). One possible reason is the fact that Germany employs the mixed jury, with one to three professional judges and two lay judges. It is difficult to recruit professional judges for either simulated trials, or interviews, compared to employing laypersons alone in research on pure juries. It is precisely the imbalance between professional and lay judges in legal expertise and experience, and specific (file) knowledge of the case, which characterizes mixed tribunals. Without the cooperation of real professional judges in simulated studies, the critical feature of mixed juries cannot be studied. It is questionable whether employing trained laypersons to substitute for professional judges in mock trials fully captures all the essential qualities of professional jurors (but see Kaplan & Martín, 1999).

In principle, the public structure of the main hearing makes it possible to analyze many problems, though the private nature of deliberations hinders access to jury deliberation and voting. But as some studies (e.g., Rennig, 1993) have shown, access to even the deliberation and vote does not have to be hermetically closed to researchers. Until means of observing mixed juries in action are devised, we will have to depend on mock jury experiments, posttrial surveys, and anecdotal evidence to understand the dynamics of mixed juries.

NOTES

1. Similar systems of lay participation do exist in many continental European countries, whose legal system is also based on Roman law (e.g., Austria, Croatia, Finland, Hungary, Poland, Sweden; see Ivković, 2000).
2. For some methodological problems in simulation studies in legal psychology see Bierhoff, Buck and Klein (1989); Konečni and Ebbesen (1979, 1992); Shuman and Champagne (1997); and Sporer (1982).
3. Previous efforts to open up the post of a lay judge in Germany for citizens of the European Union have failed.
4. Random selection of lay judges from the local register of residents, as has been done, for example, in France since 1978 (Hoff, 1999) was declared void by the German Federal Supreme Court in 1984.
5. In practice, this educational expertise is limited in many cases: In a sample of 45 lay judges in juvenile courts only one third had a professional qualification in education (Gerken, 1988), and 30 percent reported the upbringing of their own children as experience in education. According to Ostendorf (2003), parenthood is not a sufficient qualification. He demands that only persons who are experienced in (voluntary) youth work should be proposed as lay judges in juvenile courts.
6. More recent lay judge statistics are not available, as a breakdown according to age, gender, and professional group has not been made since 2000.
7. It is proposed, at least in the juvenile courts, that younger persons should become lay judges (Gerstein, 1999; Ostendorf, 2000).
8. The study by Kulcsár, being a survey, cannot tell us whether the more active role of informed lay judges is due to the examination of the file, or whether those who examine files are more motivated, confident, or better educated, and thus more likely to actively participate at trial and in discussion.
9. Gabriel and Greve (1996) consider that descriptive data on punitiveness may not be stable because demands for punishment change over time, in the general population as well as in special subgroups. Indeed, Streng (2000, 2003) found such changes in the attitudes of law students. However, this instability may not be relevant for correlates and mediating variables (Gabriel & Greve, 1996).
10. On the other hand, it is assumed that lay judges in juvenile courts, who are qualified and/or experienced in educational fields, would prefer milder verdicts (Benz, 1982). However, systematic data on this assumption are not available.

REFERENCES

Applegate, B. K., Cullen, F. T., & Fisher, B. S. (2002). Public views toward crime and correctional policies—Is there a gender gap? *Journal of Criminal Justice, 30,* 89–100.

Arce, R., Fariña, F., Vila, C., & Real, S. (1996). Empirical assessment of the escabinato jury system. *Psychology, Crime and Law, 2,* 175–183.

Baldwin, J., & McConville, J. (1979). *Jury trials.* Oxford: Clarendon.

Benz, U. (1982). Probleme der Psychologie des Strafrechtsverfahrens bei Laienrichtern [Psychological problems of juridical procedures in lay judges]. In U. Benz (Ed.), *Zur Rolle der Laienrichter im Strafprozess* (pp. 87–158). Lübeck, Germany: Schmidt Römhild.

Bierhoff, H. W., Buck, E., & Klein, R. (1989). Attractiveness and respectability of the offender as factors in the evaluation of criminal cases. In H. Wegener, F. Lösel, & J. Haisch (Eds.), *Criminal behavior and the justice system—Psychological perspectives* (pp. 193–207). New York: Springer.

Brandstätter, H., Bleckwenn, M., & Kette, G. (1984). Decision-making of industrial tribunals as described by professional and lay judges. *International Review of Applied Psychology, 33,* 137–159.

Brusten, M., & Westmeier, H. (1992). Wie wird man Schöffe? Gesellschaftliche Bedingungen, Auswahlverfahren und Probleme bei der "Schöffenwahl" [How to get a lay judge? Social conditions, selection procedures and problems in jury selection]. In Deutsche Vereinigung der Schöffinen und Schöffen/Stiftung Mitarbeit (Ed.), *Dokumentation/1. Deutscher Schöffentag: Mehr Demokratie am Richtertisch* (pp. 53–79). Bonn: Stiftung Mitarbeit.

Bundesministerium der Justiz (1997). *Geschlechts-, Alters- und Berufsstruktur der Schöffen im Bundesgebiet im Vergleich mit der Bevölkerungsstruktur* [Gender, age, and professional structure of lay judges in comparison to the German population]. Berlin: BMJ.

Casper, G., & Zeisel, H. (1979). Bundesrepublik Deutschland [German Federal Republic]. In G. Casper (Ed.), *Der Laienrichter im Strafprozeß: vier empirische Studien zum Rechtsvergleich* (pp. 21–86). Heidelberg (Germany): C.F. Müller.

Crott, H. W., & Werner, H. (1994). The norm-information-distance model: A stochastic approach to preference change in group interaction. *Journal of Experimental Social Psychology, 30,* 68–95.

Cruz, M. G., Henningsen, D. D., & Smith, B. A. (1999). The impact of directive leadership on group information sampling, decisions, and perceptions of the leader. *Communication Research, 26,* 349–369.

Endres, J., & Hommers, W. (1992). Die Einstellung zu Sanktionszwecken als Moderatorvariable in den Urteilsschemata von Strafe und Ersatz [Attitude to the severity of punishment as a moderator in the judgment on punishment and recompense]. *Zeitschrift für experimentelle und angewandte Psychologie, 39,* 396–418.

Gabriel,U., & Greve, W. (1996). "Strafe muß sein!" Sanktionsbedürfnisse und strafbezogene Einstellungen: Versuch einer systematischen Annäherung ["Discipline is necessary!" Need for sanction and attitudes towards punishment: A first systematic approach]. In C. Pfeiffer & W. Greve (Eds.), *Forschungsthema "Kriminalität": Festschrift für Heinz Barth* (pp. 185–214). Baden-Baden, Germany: Nomos Verlags-Gesellschaft.

Gerken, J. (1988). Bürger als Richter: Über Jugendschöffen und den Erziehungsanspruch des Jugendstrafrechts [Citizens as judges: On lay judges in juvenile trials and the educational claim in juvenile criminal law]. In J. Gerken (Ed.), *Ein trojanisches Pferd im Rechtsstaat: der Erziehungsgedanke in der Jugendpraxis* (pp. 101–125). Pfaffenweiler, Germany: Centaurus Verlags Gesellschaft.

Gerstein, H. (1999). Schöffen im Jugendstrafverfahren [Lay judges in juvenile criminal proceedings]. In H. Lieber & U. Sens (Eds.), *Ehrenamtlicher Richter: Demokratie oder Dekoration am Richtertisch* (pp. 94–98). Wiesbaden, Germany: Kommunal- und Schulverlag.

Haisch, J. (1977). Die Verarbeitung strafrechtlich relevanter Informationen durch Juristen und Laien in simulierten Gerichtsverhandlungen [Processing of relevant information by lawyers and laypersons in simulated trials]. *Archiv für die gesamte Psychologie, 129*, 110–129.

Haisch, J. (1979). Urteilsperseveranz in simulierten Strafverfahren [Preserved judgments in simulated trials]. *Monatsschrift für Kriminologie und Strafrechtsreform, 160*, 157–162.

Hastie, R., Penrod, S. D., & Pennington, N. (1983). *Inside the jury*. Cambridge, MA: Harvard University Press.

Herbst, J., Malow, U., Pfuhlmann, K., Pfuhlmann, R., & Pook, W. (1975). Argumente zu Zielen des Strafvollzuges und zum Modell eines Behandlungsvollzuges [Arguments to purposes of the penal system and to the model of correctional treatment]. *Monatsschrift für Kriminologie und Strafrechtsreform, 58*, 25–40.

Heuer, L., & Penrod, S. D. (1995). Jury decision-making in complex trials. In R. Bull & D. Carson (Eds.), *Handbook of psychology in legal contexts* (pp. 527–541). Chichester: Wiley.

Hoff, M. (1999). Ehrenamtliche Richter in den Staaten der Europäischen Union [Lay judges in the states of the European Union]. In H. Lieber & U. Sens (Eds.), *Ehrenamtliche Richter: Demokratie oder Dekoration am Richtertisch* (pp. 163–167). Wiesbaden: Kommunal- und Schulverlag.

Hough, M., Lewis, H., & Walker, N. (1988). Factors associated with "punitiveness" in England and Wales. In M. Hough & N. Walker (Eds.), *Public attitudes to sentencing—Surveys from five countries* (pp. 203–217). Aldershot: Gower.

Ivković, S. K. (2000). Lawyers about mixed tribunals: do Croatian professional judges, state attorneys, and private attorneys share the same view? *Social Justice Research, 13*, 55–74.

Jescheck, H. H. (1977). Das Laienrichtertum in der Strafrechtspflege der Bundesrepublik Deutschland und der Schweiz [The system of lay judges in criminal law in the Federal Republic of Germany and Switzerland]. In H. U. Walder & K. Trechsler (Eds.), *Lebendiges Strafrecht. Festgabe zum 65. Geburtstag von Hans Schultz* (pp. 229–251) Bern: Lang.

Kaplan, M. F., & Martín, A. (1999). Effects of different status of group members on process outcome of deliberation. *Group Processes and Intergroup Relations, 2*, 347–364.

Kaupen, W., & Rasehorn, T. (1972). Die Einstellung der Bevölkerung der Bundesrepublik zum Strafrecht und Strafvollzug [Attitudes of the German people on criminal law and penal system]. *Zeitschrift für Rechtspolitik, 5*, 21–22.

Karstedt-Henke, S. (1985). Die Einschätzung von Strafen und ihren Wirkungen - ein Beitrag zur Sanktionsforschung [Judgment on punishment and its effects—A contribution to research on sanctions]. *Zeitschrift für Rechtssoziologie, 6*, 70–89.

Kerr, N. L., & Bray, R. M. (Eds.) (1982). *The psychology of the courtroom*. New York: Academic Press.

Kissel, O. R. (2001) *Gerichtsverfassungsgesetz, Kommentar* (3. Aufl.) [Law on the constitution of the courts]. München: Beck.

Klausa, E. (1972). *Ehrenamtliche Richter—Ihre Auswahl und Funktion empirisch untersucht* [Honorary lay judges—an empirical analysis of selection and function]. Frankfurt/Main: Athenäum Verlag.

Köhnken, G., & Dannenberg, U. (1997). Das schleswig-holsteinische Zeugenbegleitprogramm für Kinder [The child witness accompany program in Schleswig-Holstein]. *Praxis der Rechtspsychologie, 7*, 204–212.

Konečni, V. J., & Ebbesen, E. B. (1979). External validity of research in legal psychology. *Law and Human Behavior, 3*, 39–70.

Konečni, V. J., & Ebbesen, E. B. (1992). Methodological issues in research on legal decision-making, with special reference to experimental simulations. In F. Lösel, D. Bender, & T. Bliesener (Eds.), *Psychology and law: International perspectives* (pp. 413–423). Berlin: De Gruyter.

Kronenberger, F. R. (1989). Laien in der Strafrechtspflege? [Laypersons on the criminal law system?]. In H. Jung (Ed.), *Alternativen zur Strafjustiz und die Garantie individueller Rechte der Betroffenen* (pp. 185–191). Bonn: Forum Verlag.

Kühne, H. H. (1985), Laienrichter im Strafprozeß [Lay judges in criminal trials]. *Zeitschrift für Rechtspolitik, 18*, 237–239.

Kühne, H. H. (1989). Laienkompetenz gegen Expertenkompetenz im Strafrecht? [Lay competence versus expert competence in criminal law?]. In H. Jung (Ed.), *Alternativen zur Strafjustiz und die Garantie individueller Rechte der Betroffenen* (pp. 175–183). Bonn: Forum Verlag.

Kulcsár, K. (1972). Sozialer Wandel und die Mitwirkung des Laienelements in der Rechtspflege [Social change and participation of laypersons in the legal system]. In M. Rehbinder & H. Schelsky (Eds.), *Zur Effektivität des Rechts, Jahrbuch der Rechtssoziologie und Rechtstheorie*, Band 3 (pp. 491–508). Düsseldorf (Germany): Bertelsmann.

Kury, H., & Ferdinand, T. (1999). Public opinion and punitivity. *International Journal of Law and Psychiatry, 22*, 373–392.

Lieber, H. (1994). Umfrage zur Arbeit der Schöffen in Brandenburg [A survey on the activity of lay judges in Brandenburg]. *Richter ohne Robe, 6*, 1–13.

Lieber, H. (1999). Die Struktur der Schöffen der Amtsperiode 1997 bis 2000 nach Geschlecht, Alter und Beruf [The structure in gender, age, and profession of lay judges in the term 1997–2000]. *Richter ohne Robe, 11*, 75–81.

Lieber, H. (2002). Schöffenstatistik 2001: Frauen weiter auf dem Vormarsch [Statistics of lay judges 2001: Women on the advance again]. *Richter ohne Robe, 14*, 3–10.

Lieber, H., & Sens, U. (2001). *Leitfaden für Schöffinnen und Schöffen* [Guideline for lay judges]. Wiesbaden (Germany): Kommunal- und Schul-Verlag.

Machura, S. (2001). *Fairneß und Legitimität* [Fairness and legitimacy]. Baden-Baden (Germany): Nomos.

Martín, A. M., Kaplan, M. F., & Álamo, J. M. (2003). Discussion content and perception of deliberation in Western European versus American juries. *Psychology, Crime and Law, 9*, 247–263.

McEwan, J. (1995). Adversarial and inquisitorial proceedings. In R. Bull & D. Carson (Eds.), *Handbook of psychology in legal contexts* (pp. 495–508). Chichester: Wiley.

Nietzel, M. T., McCarthy, D. M., & Kern, M. J. (1999). Juries—The current state of the empirical literature. In R. Roesch, S. D. Hart, & J. R. P. Ogloff (Eds.), *Psychology and Law: The State of the Discipline* (pp. 23–52). New York: Kluwer Academic/Plenum Publishers.

Ostendorf, H. (2000). Jugendgerichtsverfassung und Jugendstrafverfahren [Constitution of juvenile courts and juvenile criminal trials]. In H. Ostendorf (Ed.), *Jugendgerichtsgesetz, 5. Auflage* (pp. 337–783). Cologne: Carl Heymann Verlag.

Ostendorf, H. (2003). *Jugendgerichtsgesetz. Kommentar (6., völlig überarbeitete Aufl.)* [Law on juvenile courts. Comment (6th completely revised edition)]. Cologne: Heymanns.

Oswald, M., & Langer, W. (1989). Versuch eines integrierten Modells zur Strafzumessungsforschung: Richterliche Urteilsprozesse und ihre Kontextbedingungen [Attempt at an integrated model on judgment research: Decision making in layers and its situational influences]. In C. Pfeiffer & M. Oswald (Eds.), *Strafzumessung* (pp. 197–228). Stuttgart, Germany: Enke.

Oswald, M., Orth, U., & Hupfeld, J. (2003). Mikro- versus Makroperspektive der retributiven Gerechtigkeit, Strafziele und die Forderung nach Strafe [Micro versus macro perspectives on retributive justice, punishment goals, and the demand on punishment]. *Zeitschrift für Sozialpsychologie, 34,* 227–241.

Pfeiffer, G. (2002). *Strafprozessordnung, Gerichtverfassungsgesetz.* Kommentar (4. Aufl.) [Code of criminal procedure, law on the constitution of the courts. Comment (4th ed.)]. Munich: C.H. Beck.

Rennig, C. (1991). Zur Analyse von Urteilsberatungen im Schöffengericht: Wahrnehmung und Verarbeitung unterschiedlicher Fallauffassungen [Analysis of deliberations in mixed tribunals. Perception and interpretation of differing case views]. In R. Egg (Ed.), *Brennpunkte der Rechtspsychologie: Polizei, Justiz, Drogen* (pp. 311–328). Bonn: Forum Verlag.

Rennig, C. (1993). *Die Entscheidungsfindung durch Schöffen und Berufsrichter in rechtlicher und psychologischer Sicht* [Decision making in lay and professional judges from a legal and a psychological perspective]. Marburg, Germany: Elwert.

Rennig, C., & Machura, S. (1999). Die Zusammenarbeit zwischen Schöffen und Berufsrichtern [Cooperation of lay and professional judges]. In H. Lieber & U. Sens (Eds.), *Ehrenamtlicher Richter: Demokratie oder Dekoration am Richtertisch* (pp. 65–70). Wiesbaden, Germany: Kommunal- und Schulverlag.

Roxin, C. (1979). Die Besetzung der Strafgerichte [The composition of criminal courts]. In C. Roxin (Ed.), *Strafverfahrensrecht—Ein Studienbuch* (pp. 33–35). Munich: C. H. Beck'sche Verlagsbuchhandlung.

Schünemann, B., & Bandilla, W. (1989). Perseverance in courtroom decisions. In H. Wegener, F. Lösel, & J. Haisch (Eds.), *Criminal Behavior and the Justice System—Psychological Perspectives* (pp. 181–192). New York: Springer.

Sens, U. (1999). Wer soll etwas für uns tun, wenn nicht wir selbst? Aus der praktischen Arbeit für ehrenamtliche Richterinnen und Richter in Nordrhein-Westfalen [Who should help us, if not we ourselves? On the practical work of honorary lay judges in Northrhine-Westfalia]. In H. Lieber & U. Sens (Eds.), *Ehrenamtliche Richter: Demokratie oder Dekoration am Richtertisch* (pp. 26–33). Wiesbaden, Germany: Kommunal- und Schulverlag.

Shuman, D. W., & Champagne, A. (1997). Removing the people from the legal process—The rhetoric and research on judicial selection and juries. *Psychology, Public Policy and Law, 3,* 242–258.

Smaus, G. (1985). *Das Strafrecht und die Kriminalität in der Alltagssprache der deutschen Bevölkerung* [Criminal law and criminal behavior in everyday language of the German population]. Opladen, Germany: Westdeutscher Verlag.

Snyder, M., Clary, E. G., & Stukas, A. A. (in press). The functional approach to volunteerism. In G. R. Maio & J. M. Olson (Eds.), *Why we evaluate: Functions of attitudes.* Mahwah, NJ: Lawrence Erlbaum Associates.

Snyder, M., & Omoto, A. M. (2001). Basis research and practical problems: Volunteerism and the psychology of individual and collective action. In W. Wosinska, R. B. Cialdini, J. Reykowski, & D. W. Barrett (Eds.), *The practice of social influence in multiple cultures* (pp. 287–307). Mahwah, NJ: Lawrence Erlbaum Associates.

Sporer, S. L. (1982). *Reducing disparity in judicial sentencing: A social-psychological approach*. Frankfurt: Lang.

Streng, F. (1979). *Strafmentalität und juristische Ausbildung. Eine Untersuchung der Einstellungen junger Juristen zu Kriminalität und Strafe* [Punishment tendencies and legal education. A study on attitudes of young lawyers on criminal behavior and punishment]. Heidelberg (Germany): Decker.

Streng, F. (2000). Die heranwachsende Juristengeneration und die Aufgabe des Strafrechts [The growing up generation of layers and the responsibility of criminal law]. *Bewährungshilfe, 4,* 422–435.

Streng, F. (2003). Das Legitimations-Dilemma sichernden Freiheitsentzuges—Überlegungen zur neueren Rechtsentwicklung [The dilemma of legitimation in securing imprisonment]. In D. Dölling (Hrsg.), *Jus humanum—Grundlagen des Rechts, des Strafrechts und des Wirtschaftsrechts*. Festschrift für E.-J. Lampe (pp. 611–642). Berlin: Duncker & Humblot.

Villmow, B., ter Veen, H., Walkowiak, A., & Gerken, J. (1986). Die Mitwirkung von Laien in der (Jugend-) Strafgerichtsbarkeit. Rechtsprechung zwischen Professionalität und Bürgernähe [The participation of laypersons in (juvenile) criminal courts. Jurisdiction between professionalism and keeping close to the people]. In H. Ostendorf (Ed.), *Integration von Strafrechts- und Sozialwissenschaften. Festschrift für Liselotte Pongratz* (pp. 306–361). München: J. Schweitzer Verlag.

Vultejus, U. (1999). Schöffen in Hauptverhandlung und Beratung—Ihr Einfluss in Theorie und Praxis [Lay judges in main hearing and deliberation—Their impact in theory and practice]. In H. Lieber, & U. Sens (Eds.), *Ehrenamtlicher Richter: Demokratie oder Dekoration am Richtertisch* (pp. 61–64). Wiesbaden, Germany: Kommunal- und Schulverlag.

Wassermann, R. (1999). Bürgermitwirkung an der Rechtsprechung—Verfassungsrechtliche und rechtspolitische Aspekte [Participation of citizenry in jurisdiction—Aspects of constitutional law and legal politics]. In H. Lieber & U. Sens (Eds.), *Ehrenamtliche Richter: Demokratie oder Dekoration am Richtertisch* (pp. 38–46). Wiesbaden, Germany: Kommunal- und Schulverlag.

Weißmann, U. (1982). *Die Stellung des Vorsitzenden in der Hauptverhandlung* [The position of the chairing judge in main hearing]. Göttingen, Germany: Schwartz.

Zamble, E., & Kalm, K. L. (1990). General and specific measures of public attitudes toward sentencing. *Canadian Journal of Behavioural Science, 22*, 327–337.

12

On Designing a Mixed Jury System in Japan

YOHSUKE OHTSUBO

INTRODUCTION

After about five years of research and discussions by *Shihou Seido Kaikaku Shingikai* (Judicial Reform Council) and *Shihou Seido Kaikaku Suishin Honbu* (Office for Promotion of Justice System Reform), a bill concerning the Japanese mixed jury system (*Saiban'in seido*) cleared the Diet on May 21, 2004. According to the Japanese government's current plan, the mixed jury trials will be instituted in 2009 after a preparation period. Once the trials start, most ordinary Japanese citizens will experience their first participation in the criminal trial process. Japanese citizens have not been allowed to participate in the criminal trial process since the Japanese jury law was suspended in 1943. The jury law was enacted in 1923 and had been in force for 15 years. The Supreme Court of Japan (2004) refers to two major reasons for the introduction of the mixed jury system: (1) it facilitates the general public's understanding of the criminal trial process; and consequently (2) it raises the general public's trust in the judicial system at large.[1]

Currently, the forthcoming mixed jury system can be seen only through the enacted law (i.e., *Saiban'in-ho*). Based on an outline provided by the Supreme Court of Japan (2004) for ordinary citizens, I shall describe five major features of the law:

(1) The law defines types of crimes that require the mixed jury trial. Prime examples of the target cases include murders, robberies involving homicide or injury, killing someone by drink-and-drive, arson to a house, kidnappings for ransom, and custodian's neglect entailing a child's death (Supreme Court of Japan, 2004).[2]
(2) The law defines the standard composition of a mixed jury—three professional judges and six citizens. An exception occurs when a defendant admits the prosecuted fact, no one objects to it, and a court considers that the case

can be appropriately judged by a smaller mixed jury. Then, a mixed jury consisting of one professional judge and four citizens is acceptable.

(3) The law defines what decisions will be made by mixed juries and what decision rule will be used. The Japanese mixed juries will make a wider range of decisions than do the U.S. juries that return a verdict (i.e., guilty or not guilty) but not a sentence, except for capital punishment. The Japanese mixed juries, like juries of some European countries such as Germany, France, and Italy (see chapters on those countries in this volume), will not only decide a verdict but will also decide a sentence, including capital punishment. These decisions must be approved by a majority of the mixed jury members involving at least one professional judge. On the other hand, technical aspects of laws or trials, such as interpretations of an applicable law, can be decided by approval of a majority of three judges.

(4) The law defines eligibility for jurors and sampling procedure. With a few exceptions, all citizens over 20 years old are eligible and sampled from the voters' list.

(5) The law states that citizens can question a defendant and witnesses as do the professional judges.

Although these five issues are set out in an outline, the law itself does not elaborate on the outline. To implement the actual mixed jury trials, many more concrete rules must be made before 2009. In the next few years, the Supreme Court of Japan will conduct a series of mock (but authentic) mixed jury trials in order to determine what rules are still lacking or what procedures can be left as judges' discretion.

The primary purpose of this chapter is to suggest how social psychological research, especially small group research, can contribute to the process of devising the detailed rules for mixed jury trials. However, there are important debates to which psychology, other than the small group research, could make contributions. Thus, I shall first review some debates surrounding the new mixed jury system and discuss possible psychological research concerning those issues. Then, to delineate possible contributions from the small group research, I shall discuss mixed jury decision-making as a special case of group decision-making. The discussion in that section is, in a sense, tentative given the fact that the Japanese mixed jury trials have not yet been enacted and the general rules that have been outlined can be changed or elaborated before 2009. At the same time, because procedural details have not yet been determined, there is ample room for small group researchers to contribute to the system.

DEBATES OVER INTRODUCING THE MIXED JURY SYSTEM

Collectivism and Citizens' Participation

Before the mixed jury law was enacted, there were some legal experts advocating revival of the suspended jury law (e.g., Maruta, 1990). When the Japanese

Cabinet began to consider the judicial reform, the Supreme Court of Japan (1999), however, was not positive about entrusting the legal decision (i.e., the verdict) entirely to lay citizens, while admitting the importance of citizens' participation in the criminal trial process. Consistent with the Supreme Court's opinion, the Judicial Reform Council's report mentioned a mixed jury system but not a pure jury system (*Shihou Seido Kaikaku Shingikai*, 2001). Regardless of whether they endorsed a mixed rather than a pure jury, the government and the legal experts see citizen participation as somewhat desirable. On the other hand, Japanese citizens themselves do not seem to earnestly welcome the system. According to a survey of *Yomiuri Shimbun*, one of the three nationally read newspapers in Japan, a majority of respondents (69.1%) answered negatively to a question asking whether they wish to participate in a trial as a juror, although a majority of respondents (50.4%) approved the introduction of the mixed jury system (e.g., "Citizens' Opinion," 2004).

Some critics consider the survey results to favor their opposition to citizen participation in the trial process. It has sometimes been pointed out that Japanese authoritative/collectivistic values would not go well with participation in the trial process: "Authoritative" ordinary Japanese citizens prefer being judged by professional judges. Citizen juries would not have the same validity as bench trials. Also, it is often said that ordinary Japanese citizens are not able to speak out in front of professional judges (i.e., authority figures), even when their opinions are different from the judges' (see Kiss, 2000, for these debates). Fujita (2004) examined the validity of these arguments by administering a series of questionnaires to participants in a mock mixed jury experiment. He assessed participants' collectivistic attitude and their expectation of how much ordinary citizens can speak out in mixed jury deliberation. Responses to these two items were not correlated with each other (i.e., the collectivistic individuals were not necessarily pessimistic about the citizens' participation). He also assessed participants' attitude toward the mixed jury system and its change due to the experience of the mock mixed jury trial by asking the following question twice (i.e., before and after deliberation): "How easy is it to speak out during deliberation?" Once they experienced the mock mixed jury deliberation, participants found it easier to voice their opinions in mixed jury deliberation. Accordingly, Fujita argues that the collectivist culture is not necessarily an obstacle to the mixed jury system, and that once Japanese citizens are more adequately informed of the system, the negative attitudes toward their own participation might be substantially reduced. The same issue has been addressed in the context of the US and Spanish juries by Martín, Kaplan, and Álamo (2003). More studies on this issue are needed to facilitate Japanese citizens' willingness to participate in mixed jury trials.

Trial Period and the Mixed Jury System

An opinion often cited in favor of introducing the mixed jury system is about its effect on the trial period. Under the current trial system, trials proceed in a series of hearings and examinations of witnesses scheduled at intervals of a month or longer. Accordingly, the current Japanese trial process is notoriously lengthy. The

Supreme Court of Japan (2004) calculated the average trial length for cases that would be the subject of the mixed jury trial. There were 3089 such cases in 2003. On average, it took 8.0 months to return a verdict to each of these cases. For cases where the defendant confessed before the trial, the average length was 6.2 months, whereas for cases where the defendant denied his or her commitment to the suspected crime, the average length was 12.4 months. Obviously, ordinary citizens would not like to serve as a juror for such long periods of time. Therefore, some argued that citizen participation would force the procedure to be changed. The Supreme Court of Japan (2004) currently estimates that most of those cases could be completed within a few days, if trials are conducted on consecutive days.

The Japanese trial process will probably be changed to some kind of condensed procedure because of the above concern. The envisaged effect of this change is thus to make citizens' participation easier. Other possible psychological effects of the trial length, however, have been little discussed so far. The trial length should have effects related to the human memory and information processing research. For example, if examinations of witnesses are held over long intervals, even when witnesses are associated with different levels of credibility, all testimonies might be taken into account with equal weight because source credibility is more likely to be ignored than the information contents (i.e., the sleeper effect; Hovland, Lumsdaine, & Sheffield, 1949). In this sense, one might consider that short trials are less likely to produce the sleeper effect and thus more likely to lead to decisions informed by source credibility. However, it is worth noting that lay jurors could erroneously assess credibility with heuristic cues, such as witnesses' social status (e.g., Chaiken, 1980). Psychological effects of the trial length should be carefully examined before changing the trial procedures related to the trial length.

Lay Citizens' Legal Judgments

It is sometimes argued that highly publicized cases, where innocent defendants were erroneously convicted and given lengthy sentences, have fueled the criticisms of trial by judge in Japan (Kiss, 2000). One reason that these cases trigger doubt about trial by judge is related to Japanese judges' customary reliance on dossiers (Maruta, 1990). In the current Japanese judicial practice, defendants' confessions are submitted to judges in a summary form, or as "dossiers." In the dossier, segmented confessions are integrated as a coherent story excluding police's questions, interruptions, or threats to confess (if they existed). Consequently, the reliance on a dossier has made judges easily accept confessions as valid evidence (Kiss, 2000; Maruta, 1990), ignoring context. Some advocates of a mixed jury system claim that the presence of citizens as members of mixed juries obliges prosecutors to be more accountable for their accusation (Hirano, 2000; Kikuchi, 2000). Accordingly, it is expected that the introduction of a mixed jury system will reduce the false conviction rate due to the over-reliance on the dossier. The Supreme Court of Japan (1999), however, was skeptical about this effect from the outset of the judicial reform discussion, and it does not include this argument in the list of reasons for the introduction of the mixed jury system (see Supreme Court of Japan, 2004).

Whether the citizens' participation reduces the false conviction rate might be related to not only the issue of dossier use but also several other issues that could be psychologically investigated. First, it is related to the jury's leniency bias, which refers to a tendency for juries to be less likely to convict a defendant than judges or a tendency for the faction endorsing a not guilty verdict to have greater influence than the faction endorsing a guilty verdict (Kalven & Zeisel, 1966; MacCoun & Kerr, 1988; Nemeth, 1977). This tendency might be (or at least was) present in Japan: The conviction rate of the Japanese jury trials during 1928–1943 was lower than the conviction rate of trials by judge in the same period (93.73% conviction rate in trials by jury vs. 99.93% in trials by judge; Maruta, 1990). Whether the leniency bias is present in Japan today merits study. If it is present, there is then the broader empirical issue of how likely the citizen faction's opinions are reflected in the final verdict of mixed jury.

The problem of the false conviction rate is also related to jurors' fact-finding ability or jury competence. It is arguable that the leniency bias (i.e., low conviction rate) lowers the false conviction rate. At the same time, it could heighten the false acquittal rate. The problem here is whether the jurors are more lenient only to innocent defendants or to any defendants. The problem of jury/juror competence has been intensively studied in the United States (see *Law and Contemporary Problems*, Vol. 52, No. 4, 1989, for a special issue on the jury competence). However, the North American studies, which are mostly concerned with the jurors' absolute ability, might not be directly relevant to problems of the Japanese mixed jury, to which the jurors' ability relative to the professional judges' ability might be more important. The Japanese scholars working on the jury competence problem should address the questions of what are the characteristics of lay citizens' legal judgments, what are the characteristics of professional judges' legal judgments, whether citizens tend to make different judgments than judges do, and what are the differences, if any, between them. Finally, whether the leavening influence of citizens on the mixed jury is desirable is a philosophical question for legal jurisprudence. That is, it is a question of whether false convictions or false acquittals are more damaging to the social fabric.

A relevant experiment was conducted by Hatano, Takahashi, and Takeda (1998). Employing civil case scenarios, Hatano et al. compared lay students' patterns of legal judgments and legal experts' patterns of legal judgments. The primary difference between lay students and legal experts was their use of judicial precedents in their judgments. As one might expect, the legal experts were more likely to refer to judicial precedents than the lay students. Hatano et al. point out that by using the judicial precedents, the experts viewed the legal problems, which would be cognitively demanding for lay people, as more or less patterned, familiar problems. Accordingly, the legal experts were able to use many constraints in a coherent manner. Hatano et al.'s results imply that legal experts' judgments are more or less similar to each other (i.e., interjudge reliability is high) because of their use of legal precedents. Therefore, one might consider that Hatano et al.'s results support legal experts' superiority to lay citizens. On the other hand, one could argue that the citizens' participation is necessary rather because the similarity (or reliability) exists in the judges' judgments. Lempert (1992) points out that "given the likely homogenizing of the way judges are selected and trained, there may well be points relevant to fact-finding that Japanese judges as a group would be prone to miss although ordinary Japanese citizens, sitting on a jury, would not" (p. 49; see Fujikura, 2001, for a similar point). In other words, citizens may be better able to recognize and apply individualizing rather than categorical information. It is clear that we need more careful examinations of the differences in legal judgments made by professional judges and lay citizens.

GROUP PROCESSES IN MIXED JURY TRIALS

Jury decision-making has been an area of important application of the small group decision-making research. Therefore, a substantial amount of findings have been accumulated regarding jury decision-making (see Devine, Clayton, Dunford, Seying, & Pryce, 2001 for a review). In this section, I shall discuss three issues: (1) aggregation rules in mixed jury decision-making; (2) social influence processes in mixed jury decision-making; and (3) deliberation style in mixed jury decision-making. I do not intend to argue that these three are the only important issues for the mixed jury decision-making. Rather, mixed jury studies conducted so far are related to these three issues. Since empirical data are not available for the other important issues, I shall only briefly address them in the concluding section.

Aggregation Rules in Mixed Jury Decision-Making

Davis (1973) developed a mathematical model to analyze group decision processes: the social decision scheme (SDS) model. The SDS model is a tool to analyze aggregation rules of group decision-making (i.e., what kind of individual preference distributions results in what kind of group decisions).[3] Accordingly, this model is useful to assess effects of various factors that influence the group decision outcome. For example, employing the SDS model, Laughlin and Ellis (1986) noted that appropriate aggregation rules hinge on task type (i.e., intellective vs. judgmental): When a task is an intellective task with a demonstrably correct answer, the truth-wins model is an accurate descriptive model of the aggregation process (i.e., groups return a correct answer when at least one member can individually find it), whereas when a task is a judgmental task, in which individual values and subjective judgments matter and no objective criteria to evaluate group decisions are available, the majority-wins process is an accurate descriptive model (i.e., groups choose an alternative endorsed by the majority of group members).

The SDS model has revealed that the jury decision-making process is well captured by the majority-wins model (Stasser, Kerr, & Bray, 1982).[4] One might suppose that the SDS model is also applicable to the analysis of mixed jury decision processes. As Kirchler and Davis (1986) point out, however, the SDS model in its original form assumes that group members are indistinguishable (i.e., all group members have equal power). The assumption does not hold in mixed jury decision-making, in which the professional judges obviously have greater power (but see an exception in Kaplan and Martín, 1999, and in the chapter on Spanish juries in this volume, where in certain issues, lay jurors had more power). Therefore, the SDS model needs to be somewhat modified to apply to the mixed jury research, and there is a huge gap between research on groups consisting of equal status members and research on groups consisting of unequal status members (e.g., mixed juries).

In an attempt to fill the gap, Kirchler and Davis (1986) modified the model for groups of unequal status members, and conducted an experiment to test the modified model. In their experiment, the member status was manipulated by the following procedure. Members of three-person groups first took an aptitude test. Then, they received some bogus feedback concerning their relative ability assessed by the test. One third of groups were assigned to the outstanding power condition, in which one randomly chosen member received a test score much higher than the other two members' test scores. Another one third of groups were assigned to the equal power condition, in which it was told that all three members' test scores were equal. Notice that the former groups assigned to the outstanding power condition relatively resemble mixed juries, whereas the latter groups assigned to the equal power condition relatively resemble pure juries. Kirchler and Davis had these three-person groups engage in three group decision-making tasks (i.e., one intellective and two judgmental tasks). Kirchler and Davis found an interaction between the task type and the predictive model. Regardless of whether the status difference was present among group members, the group decision pattern was best predicted by the truth-wins model for the intellective task. On the other hand, for the judgmental tasks, the group decision pattern was best predicted by the majority-wins model in the equal power condition but by the power-wins model in the outstanding power condition. The power-wins model assumes that groups choose an option that is initially endorsed by the high status member regardless of whatever options the other two low status members prefer. Although the power-wins model fits the judgmental task data best in the outstanding power condition, the results should not be overstated. The majority-wins model also fits the same data modestly well. It was only slightly inferior to the power-wins model in terms of fit to the observed data. Thus, a more accurate model for groups of unequal status members might be a hybrid of these two.

Ohtsubo and Masuchi (2004) attempted to develop such a hybrid model. They called their model the weighted majority-wins model, in which a high status member is counted as more than one person. For example, suppose that there is a four-person group consisting of one high-status member and three low-status members, and their preferences for two options, A and B, are as follows: The high-status member and one low-status member prefer option A to option B, while the other two low-status members prefer option B to option A. If there is no status difference among the four members, both options A and B are preferred by two members, respectively. Thus, the majority-wins model is not applicable. At best, it predicts that either option is equally likely to be chosen. Now, assume that the high status member is counted as two persons. With this assumption, option A is preferred by three members while option B is preferred by two members. Accordingly, the weighted majority-wins model predicts the choice of option A. This model incorporates both the majority-wins process and the greater influence of the high-status member (i.e., a hybrid model of the majority-wins and power-wins models). However, Ohtsubo and Masuchi found only modest support for the weighted majority-wins model. Note that both the power-wins model and the weighted majority-wins model are deterministic. Recall that, in the above example, the weighted majority-wins model predicted that the group always chooses option A (i.e., the probability of A choice is 1.0). Ohtsubo and Masuchi suggested that the real group processes, especially when status differences exist among members, might be best depicted by some stochastic model. For example, a model assuming that the probability of A choice is 0.7 might fit the data better than the deterministic weighted majority-wins model.

Although a model of the mixed jury decision-making (or more generally, a model for groups of unequal status members) needs further research, it is worth considering its utility at this point. The SDS model was useful to determine how various factors affect the aggregation process. Thus, the model for groups of unequal status members should be useful to analyze effects of various factors that can be manipulated in the mixed jury system. How the Japanese mixed jury deliberations will be conducted is not yet concretely determined. Therefore, effects of various factors unique to the mixed jury system need to be examined. For instance, whether jurors express their personal opinions before (or after) listening to judges' opinions might result in different group decision processes, and consequently in different verdict patterns.[5] By treating the different initial preference configurations separately, the SDS-like model will allow us to conduct more sensitive assessment of group process than typical statistical analyses, such as ANOVA. There is little doubt that many mock mixed jury experiments will be conducted in Japan in years to come. With the support of the SDS-like model, we will be able to extract more information from those experiments.

Social Influence Processes in Mixed Jury Decision-Making

As we have just seen, high status members tend to exercise greater influence over low status members in the group decision-making process, especially when a group discusses judgmental issues (Kaplan & Martín, 1999; Kirchler & Davis, 1986). Thus, it is expected that professional judges tend to have greater influence on the final verdict in mixed juries than lay citizens. Whether the greater influence of professional judges is desirable may depend on one's attitudes or beliefs. For those who worry that citizens' participations would undermine the reliability of legal judgments (e.g., Nishino, 2000), the greater influence of experts is desirable. For those who believe that professional judges' judgments are somewhat biased (e.g., Fujikura, 2001; Lempert, 1992; see the second section of this chapter), the greater influence of experts is not desirable. Either position, in its extreme, might be too simplistic. There are other factors that affect desirability of the judges' greater influence, for example, the source of social influence. The greater influence could be based on either informational influence or normative influence (Deutsch & Gerard, 1955; or expert power vs. legitimate power in French & Raven's, 1959, terminology). It would be reasonable if judges were influential because of their knowledge of legal issues (i.e., informational influence), but it would be problematic if they wielded greater social pressure because of the mere fact that they are the legal experts (i.e., normative influence).

Kaplan and Martín (1999) examined types of social influence that are practiced by experts and lay people in a mock mixed jury experiment, in which three ordinary undergraduates deliberated with two trained graduate students who had attended training sessions given by a university's Student Judicial Office. Each five-person mock mixed jury judged two cases, one of which was presented as an intellective task and the other as a judgmental task. Kaplan and Martín coded utterances that participants had made during deliberation. The utterances were divided into two broad categories: informational influence and normative influence. Utterances of facts or inferences from those facts were coded as informational influence. Utterances of their personal verdict preferences or pressures to conform to other members' expectations were coded as normative influence. The results showed that both trained faction and lay faction were more likely to employ informational influence in the intellective case than in the judgmental case. More importantly, the trained faction was more likely to use normative influence than was the lay faction. Thus, in a case presenting primarily judgmental issues, the trained jurors were both more active and more influential than the lay jurors, whereas the latter were more active and influential in intellective cases.

Based on Kaplan and Martín's result, one might infer that the professional judges would tend to exercise normative influence in some real mixed jury trials. Brandstätter, Bleckwenn, and Kette's (1984) interview study, however, showed the reverse. Brandstätter et al. interviewed judges and lay jurors who had actually experienced mixed jury trials in Austria. Both judges and jurors ascribed the judges' larger influence to their expert power: Judges were more influential because they were perceived more knowledgeable about legal issues than were lay jurors. Thus, in the real Austrian mixed juries, the professional judges seemed to have more informational influence than normative influence. Martín et al.'s (2003) mock mixed jury experiment in Spain converges on this point. Lay faction participants in their experiment reported that the trained faction had more informational influence, although the content analyses revealed that the trained factions were more active in terms of both types of social influence (i.e., informational and normative). Martín et al. along with Kaplan and Martín showed that task type (i.e., judgmental vs. intellective) mediates which social influence is exercised and to what extent. Also, these studies were conducted in different countries. Therefore, various differences among these studies prevent us from singling out a responsible factor causing some contradictory results. It is possible that various factors interact with each other to lead to different social influence patterns. In the next section, I shall treat an issue of deliberation styles. Although I shall argue the issue from a different perspective, the deliberation style might be one factor causing the different social influence patterns. It is important to investigate what factors other than task type affect each faction's appeal to informational and normative influence.

Deliberation Styles in Mixed Juries

Hastie, Penrod, and Pennington (1983) found two typical deliberation styles in their mock jury experiment: the "verdict-driven" style and the "evidence-driven" style. The verdict-driven style is characterized by public polling of the jurors at the outset, citing evidence in support of a specific verdict position, saying verdict preferences frequently, and polling the jury frequently. The evidence-driven style, on the other hand, is characterized by reviewing evidence without referring to verdict categories, engaging in story construction, and public polling only in a relatively later stage of deliberation. Note that the mixed juries might have a different repertoire of deliberation styles. For example, for the mixed jury, verdict-driven style could be divided into subtypes: Whether lay jurors' verdict preferences are stated before (or after) judges' preferences might make at least two subtypes of the verdict-driven style. However, at this point, there is no study that directly examined the deliberation style in mixed jury decision-making. Research in "pure" mock juries finds no effect of early vs. late ballot on normative vs. informational influence, but does find that an orientation toward centering discussion on resolving voting discrepancies vs. focusing on understanding case facts affects ballot timing (Kaplan, 1999).

To think about deliberation style in mixed juries, it is useful to refer to a mixed jury experiment conducted in Japan by Ode and his students (Ode, 2003). Two groups represented two compositions in the experiment, one consisting of three legal experts (e.g., lawyer, retired judge) and four lay citizens, and the other consisting of three legal experts and 10 lay citizens. Their result was cited in a newspaper article in support of an argument that the citizens' participation becomes increasingly more active as the number of lay jurors increases (The More Jurors, 2003). The article reports that 69% (i.e., 6.9 × 10) of utterances in the large group's deliberation were made by lay citizens, while only 34% (i.e., 8.6 × 4) of utterances in the small group's deliberation were made by lay citizens. Given only these numbers, one might be tempted to conclude that the larger the faction size is, the more powerful the faction members are. However, a closer scrutiny of these two groups' deliberations reveals a slightly different picture.

Admittedly, because they had only one group per condition, any argument based on the experiment is tentative. However, the difference between the two groups is so large that comparison can be interesting. Looking at the complete deliberation transcripts found in the book, I have noticed contrasting practices of the legal experts in the two groups. In the large group in which 10 lay jurors were involved, the legal experts refrained from expressing their own opinions or providing explanations about technical aspects, especially at the early stage of their deliberation. Instead, the legal experts facilitated lay citizens to publicly express their opinions (but not verdict preferences). In the large group, for example, once all 10 jurors expressed their initial opinions, one expert attempted to explain the term "complicity" to lay jurors, but another expert stopped him and commented that "it would be better to explain [it] a little later" (p. 120). One expert also stated that "[experts] are better not to tell our opinions [at this point]" (p. 121). Once this statement was confirmed by another expert, he asked lay jurors if their opinions had changed by hearing other lay jurors' opinions. On the other hand, in the small group involving only four lay jurors, one legal expert expressed his or her personal verdict preference for not guilty as soon as the four lay jurors expressed their verdict preferences (p. 145). Also, from the relatively early stage of their deliberation, the experts in the small group actively engaged in discussions, providing explanations of technical aspects.

To examine whether the aforementioned difference in the two groups' deliberation style is reflected on their discussion contents, I reanalyzed the transcripts. First, I counted the number of questions and prompts that could be answered by anyone in the group. Examples of such questions/prompts are "Please say whatever [you think]" (p. 117) and "Is there anyone who has a different opinion?" (p. 126). Questions and prompts directed to a specific member, such as "Go ahead, Mr./Ms. A" (p. 159) were not included. The result was clear: Twenty eight percent of judges' utterances (18 of 57) were coded as such questions/prompts in the large group, while only four percent of judges' utterances (4 of 103) were such questions/prompts in the small group. None of lay citizens' utterances fell in this category. This difference in the experts' style was also reflected in patterns of participation hierarchy in the two groups. The notion of participation hierarchy was proposed by Bales, Strodtbeck, Mills, and Roseborough (1951). According to Bales et al., when group members are ordered in terms of their participation rates, the difference between an adjacent pair of members decreases as the member rank goes down. For example, the difference between the first-ranked member and the second-ranked member is greater than the difference between the second-ranked member and the third-ranked member. I counted the number of turns taken by each lay juror and plotted the data in Figure 12.1. (Notice that the figure only plots the participation hierarchy of lay jurors.) One remarkable difference between the two lines is that the small group's line is steeper than the large group's line. That is, inequality of participation rate is greater in the small group, in which the experts did not prompt unspecified members to speak out. Within-group standard deviations of the participation rates are 8.90 for the large group and 18.83 for the small group.

At first glance, it might appear that the large group's deliberation style was more desirable than the small group's deliberation style: The large group's experts seem more active in inducing lay jurors' opinions (and thus more democratic). The matter, however, is not as simple as it might first appear. Ode (2003) also presents data from the postdeliberation questionnaire, which included an item that asks

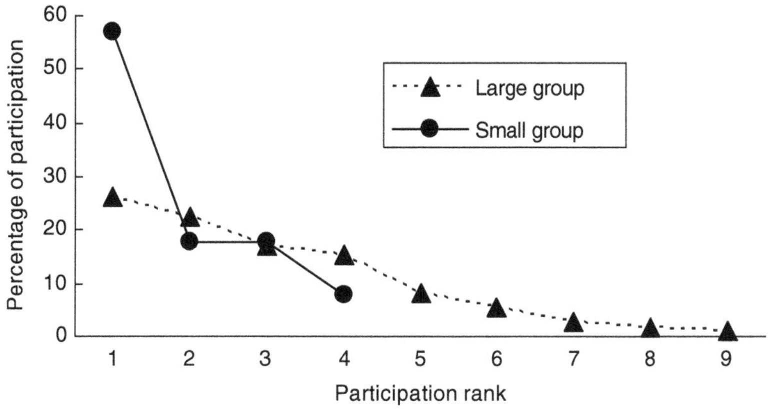

FIGURE 12.1 Participation hierarchy patterns of Ode's (2003) experimental groups.

participants whether they think they sufficiently participated in the deliberation. All four lay jurors in the small group answered "yes" to this item, while 3 of 10 lay jurors in the large group answered "no." The negative answers in the large group could be due to its large group size (i.e., large groups are more likely to have members who take very few turns) or some other factors, and thus should not be attributed only to the deliberation style. The important point here is that all four members in the small group answered the item positively despite their unequal participation rates. Another item asked lay jurors about their impression of the legal experts in their group. Two of the four lay jurors in the small groups spontaneously mentioned something related to the experts' intelligence or knowledge. Two of ten lay jurors in the large group (i.e., 20% of lay jurors) did so. One lay juror in the large group mentioned the difficulty of judicial terminology, while none of the lay jurors in the small group did so. These data suggest that although the style and attitude of the large group's experts appeared more desirable than those of the small group's experts, there is evidence implying that the small group members perceived their deliberation as more desirable than the large group members, and as equally informed.

To speculate about the apparently paradoxical pattern, note first that in both groups, after the lay jurors expressed their initial verdict preference, the judges did not probe lay jurors' verdict preferences until the final stage of the deliberation. Thus, neither group's deliberation style could be categorized as verdict-driven. Rather, the judges repeatedly set small sub-fact-finding goals (e.g., whether the defendant indeed had the motive proposed by the prosecutors) and attempted to assess related evidence. If we take these processes as story constructions, both groups' deliberation styles may be characterized as evidence-driven. The difference between the two groups was whether judges collaboratively participated in the evidence assessment activities. In the small group, the experts and lay jurors engaged in the deliberation more collaboratively. The experts, for example, tended to give feedback to lay jurors' statements immediately. On the other hand, the legal experts in the large group tried to let lay jurors freely discuss each issue, refraining from interrupting lay jurors' discussion with legally complicated matters. Accordingly, in the large group, the legal experts' explanations and comments tended to be concentrated in a relatively later stage of the deliberation. The presence of the collaboration might have resulted in more positive impressions of the small group jurors. The collaboration might also have influenced the legal experts' impressions. In the postdeliberation questionnaire, all three experts in the small group described the lay jurors positively (e.g., their statements were based on rational thoughts, their way of asking questions was appropriate), while two of the three experts in the large group found at least some aspects of lay jurors' participation problematic (e.g., appropriate except their evaluation of "complicity").

Based on the above speculation, it is possible that what differentiates the two groups' deliberation styles is the presence of collaboration. At the same time, the questions/prompts might also differentiate the two groups' deliberation styles. These differences in deliberation style must have some effect on verdict quality or jurors' satisfaction. Thus, more research on deliberation style seems in urgent need. First of all, we should conduct an experiment including a larger sample, otherwise we are not assured of what kind of categorization scheme well describes the variation of mixed jury deliberation styles. Also, given the fact that the standard composition of the Japanese mixed jury (i.e., three judges and six citizens) was set after Ode's experiment, we should focus on that composition. Including different compositions will increase confounding factors and lower the experimental reality, which is essential for the purpose of determining the categorization scheme appropriate for the Japanese mixed jury. After determining it, we then should attempt to determine pros and cons of each deliberation style. For example, it could be possible that citizens' trust in the judicial system would be heightened by collaboration with judges. At the same time, as the collaboration, which necessarily entails judges' active participation, increases, citizens' opinions might become less likely to be expressed. It is possible for social psychologists to experimentally show which way of conducting mixed jury trials will lead to what consequences.

CONCLUSION

In this chapter, I have explored some issues related to the introduction of the mixed jury system in Japan. I briefly reviewed Japanese debates surrounding the mixed jury system: (1) citizens' participation might not fit well into collectivist societies such as Japan; (2) citizens' participation makes the trial process shorter; and (3) lay citizens and professional judges see cases and evidence from different perspectives than professional judges do, and thus trials by mixed jury are associated with better fact-finding ability than trials by judges only. I suggested that psychological studies could make contributions to resolve these debates, or at least give some empirical basis for the arguments. Then, the focus was shifted to group processes in the mixed jury and examined three issues in particular: (1) aggregation rules in mixed jury decision-making; (2) social influence processes between the judge faction and the lay juror faction; and (3) deliberation style of mixed jury decision-making.

Besides the issues discussed in this chapter, there seem to be important issues to which sufficient attention has not yet been paid. According to the mixed jury law, for example, the decision rule is basically a simple majority rule, although the majority faction needs to include at least one judge. Therefore, in an extreme case, three judges and two citizens could decide a verdict leaving the other four citizens unconvinced. In mock jury experiments, it has been found that holdout jurors tend to be dissatisfied with the verdict (e.g., Hastie et al., 1983). If there are many dissatisfied jurors, one goal of the mixed jury system (i.e., raising the general public's trust in the judicial system) might not be achieved. The other issue that is not discussed in this chapter is how judges should handle jurors' questioning. The US jurors are not allowed to question a defendant or witnesses. Thus, this problem has been little studied. This problem is, however, not negligible because this is related to how much legal explanation should be given to jurors early in the trial (in this case, even before starting deliberation). Also, it certainly mediates jurors' information processing and impression formation.

The Supreme Court of Japan and other related organizations, such as the Japan Federation of Bar Associations, have begun research, including mock mixed jury experiments. The first experiment was conducted on 22–23 July 2004 (Supreme

Court of Japan, 2004). It is very likely that, as more mock mixed jury experiments are conducted, we will find many other issues that should be addressed. For one thing, the mixed jury law at this point leaves many aspects of mixed jury trials undetermined. Therefore, neither the general public nor professional judges know how the mixed jury trials will (or should) be conducted. In interviews after a meeting at the Supreme Court of the Presidents of the eight High Courts and chief judges of district courts and family courts, some chief judges of district courts expressed their uncertainty about how they should conduct or prepare for mixed jury trials (Can't have a concrete image, 2004). Accordingly, Chief Justice Machida stated that "I wish that during the five years to the enforcement, there will be many motivated judges who actively participate in discussions over the system design and the operation in order to construct its concrete image" (Participate in discussions, 2004). Many motivated psychologists, too, should participate in the discussions and make contributions by providing empirical grounds to the discussions.

NOTES

1. The government has not considered and is not planning to introduce a civil jury system.
2. These crimes are more precisely defined by the following two criteria: (1) crimes that are called for capital punishment or life imprisonment (*muki-choeki*) and (2) intentionally committed crimes in which someone has been killed. Even though one of these criteria is met, the mixed jury trial might not be held for some cases if it is likely that lay citizens' engagement in a trial process of certain cases causes risk of themselves or their family members being harmed.
3. Note that the SDS model is concerned with implicit aggregation rules that are inferred from the distribution of observed group decisions, but not with explicit assigned decision rules, such as two-thirds majority rule or unanimity rule. For example, it is known that even when a unanimity rule is officially assigned, actual juries' decisions are well predicted by a majority-wins model, which assumes that groups choose an alternative initially endorsed by a majority of group members (see Miller, 1989, for a review).
4. More precisely, the jury decision-making process is captured by a slightly modified version of majority-wins process. It is known that jurors endorsing a not guilty verdict tend to be more influential than are jurors endorsing a guilty verdict. For example, when 5 of 12 jurors prefer a not guilty verdict and the remaining seven jurors prefer a guilty verdict, the minority of five jurors sometimes overwhelms the initial majority's judgment. On the other hand, when five jurors prefer a guilty verdict, the comparable minority influence process rarely occurs (Stasser et al., 1982).
5. Davis, Stasson, Ono, and Zimmerman (1988) addressed the issue of speaking order in the pure jury context and found that the speaking order had little effect on the final verdict. However, when there is status difference among group members, it is plausible that different results will be obtained. This issue has not yet been addressed in the mixed jury context.

REFERENCES

Bales, R. F., Strodtbeck, F. L., Mills, T. M., & Roseborough, M. E. (1951). Channels of communication in small groups. *American Sociological Review*, *16*, 461–468.

Brandstätter, H., Bleckwenn, M., & Kette, G. (1984). Decision-making of industrial tribunals as described by professional and lay judges. *International Review of Applied Psychology*, *33*, 137–159.

Can't have a concrete image of the mixed jury trials: Expressed uneasiness of judges in local courts. (2004, June 18). *Asahi Shimbun*.

Chaiken, S. (1980). Heuristic versus systematic information processing and the use of source versus message cues in persuasion. *Journal of Personality and Social Psychology*, *39*, 752–766.

Citizens' opinion about the *Saiban'in seido*. (2004, May 27). *Yomiuri Shimbun*.

Davis, J. H. (1973). Group decision and social interaction: A theory of social decision scheme. *Psychological Review*, *80*, 87–125.

Davis, J. H., Stasson, M., Ono, K., & Zimmerman, S. (1988). Effects of straw polls on group decision making: Sequential voting pattern, timing, and local majorities. *Journal of Personality and Social Psychology*, *55*, 918–926.

Deutsch, M., & Gerard, H. B. (1955). A study of normative and informational social influences upon individual judgment. *Journal of Abnormal and Social Psychology*, *51*, 629–636.

Devine, D. J., Clayton, L. D., Dunford, B. B., Seying, R., & Pryce, J. (2001). Jury decision making: 45 years of empirical research on deliberating groups. *Psychology, Public Policy, and Law*, *7*, 622–727.

French, J. P. R. Jr., & Raven, B. H. (1959). The bases of social power. In D. Cartwright (Ed.), *Studies in social power* (pp. 150–167). Ann Arbor, MI: Institute for Social Research.

Fujikura, K. (2001). *Shimin niyoru shimin no tameno sihou* [The law by the citizens, for the citizens]. *Hōritsujihō*, *73*(7), 16–19.

Fujita, M. (2004). Effects of the mock jury deliberation experience on the evaluation of the *Saiban'in seido*: In relation to the collectivism and perceived social power. *Japanese Journal of Law and Psychology*, *3*, 68–80.

Hastie, R., Penrod, S. D., & Pennington, N. (1983). *Inside the jury*. Cambridge, MA: Harvard University Press.

Hatano, G., Takahashi, K., & Takeda, S. (1998). Knowledge and reasoning for estimating damages in traffic accidents: Expert-novice comparison. *Japanese Cognitive Science Society Technical Report* (No. 27).

Hirano, R. (2000). *Sanshin seido saiyo no teisho* [Proposal for adopting a mixed-jury system]. *Jurist*, *1189*, 50–57.

Hovland, C. I., Lumsdaine, A. A., & Sheffield, F. D. (1949). *Experiments on mass communication*. Princeton, NJ: Princeton University Press.

Kalven, H. Jr., & Zeisel, H. (1966). *The American jury*. Boston: Little, Brown.

Kaplan, M. F. (1999). Verdict-driven and evidence-driven juries. In W. F. Abbott & J. Batt (Eds.), *A handbook of jury research* (Chapter 22). Philadelphia: American Law Institute-American Bar Association.

Kaplan, M. F., & Martín, A. M. (1999). Effects of differential status of group members on process and outcome of deliberation. *Group Processes and Intergroup Relations*, *2*, 347–364.

Kikuchi, H. (2000). *Baishin seido yorimo sanshin seido wo* [A mixed jury system rather than a pure jury system]. *Hanrei Jiho*, *1723*, 21–22.

Kirchler, E., & Davis, J. H. (1986). The influence of member status differences and task type on group consensus and member position change. *Journal of Personality and Social Psychology*, *51*, 83–91.

Kiss, L. W. (2000). Reviving the criminal jury in Japan. In N. J. Vidmar (Ed.), *World jury systems* (pp. 353–379). Oxford, UK: Oxford University Press.

Laughlin, P. R., & Ellis, A. L. (1986). Demonstrability and social combination processes on mathematical intellective tasks. *Journal of Experimental Social Psychology*, *22*, 177–189.

Lempert, R. (1992). A jury for Japan? *American Journal of Comparative Law*, *40*, 37–71.

MacCoun, R. J., & Kerr, N. L. (1988). Asymmetric influence in mock jury deliberation: Jurors' bias for leniency. *Journal of Personality and Social Psychology*, *54*, 21–33.

Martín, A. M., Kaplan, M. F., & Álamo, J. M. (2003). Discussion content and perception of deliberation in Western European juries versus American juries. *Psychology, Crime, and Law*, 9, 247–263.

Maruta, T. (1990). Baishin saiban wo kangaeru [*Considering the trial by jury*]. Tokyo, Japan: Chuo-Koron-Sha.

Participate in Discussions (2004, June 18). *Mainichi Shimbun*.

Miller, C. E. (1989). The social psychological effects of group decision rules. In P. Paulus (Ed.), *Psychology of group influence* (2nd ed., pp. 327–355). Hillsdale, NJ: Lawrence Erlbaum Associates, Inc.

Nemeth, C. (1977). Interactions between jurors as a function of majority vs. unanimity decision rules. *Journal of Applied Social Psychology*, 7, 38–56.

Nishino, K. (2000). *Baishin shinri no sho-mondai* (1)–(3) [Problems of the trial by jury (1)–(3)]. *Hanrei Jiho*, *1714*, 3–16, *1716*, 8–16, *1717*, 3–10.

Ode, Y. (Ed.). (2003). Saiban'in ga yuzai, muzai wo kimeru: Saiban'in saiban no jikken to seika [*Jurors decide guilty or not guilty: A mixed jury experiment and its results*]. Tokyo: Gendai-Jimbun-Sha.

Ohtsubo, Y., & Masuchi, A. (2004). Effects of status difference and group size in group decision making. *Group Processes and Intergroup Relations*, 7, 161–172.

Shihou Seido Kaikaku Shingikai (2001, June 12). *Shihou seido kaikaku shingikai ikensho* [Opinions of the Judicial Reform Council].

Stasser, G., Kerr, N. L., & Bray, R. M. (1982). The social psychology of jury deliberations: Structure, process, and product. In N. L. Kerr & R. M. Bray (Eds.), *The psychology of the courtroom* (pp. 221–256). New York: Academic Press.

Supreme Court of Japan (1999). *Thinking of the 21st century judicial system*. Supreme Court of Japan. Online. Available at http://courtdomino.courts.go.jp/topics.nsf/ea145664a647510e492564680058cccc/a9a398bd0296abd74925684d00144b76?OpenDocument (accessed August 9, 2004)

Supreme Court of Japan (2004). *About the mixed jury system*. The Supreme Court of Japan. Online. Available at: http://courtdomino2.courts.go.jp/saibanin.nsf (accessed August 9, 2004)

The more jurors, the greater participation: Mock trials by Kyushu University (2003, September 8). *Asahi Shimbun*.

Author Index

Subject Index

For Product Safety Concerns and Information please contact our EU representative GPSR@taylorandfrancis.com
Taylor & Francis Verlag GmbH, Kaufingerstraße 24, 80331 München, Germany

www.ingramcontent.com/pod-product-compliance
Ingram Content Group UK Ltd.
Pitfield, Milton Keynes, MK11 3LW, UK
UKHW021719240926
475702UK00029BA/1510
9780415652971